A GUIDE TO THE ZOROASTRIAN RELIGION

HARVARD UNIVERSITY
CENTER FOR THE STUDY OF WORLD RELIGIONS

Studies in World Religions

edited by
Jane I. Smith

Studies in World Religions publishes monographs, translations, and collections of essays on the comparative study of religion, on religious traditions, and on methodological issues in the study of the world's religions, as well as proceedings of conferences and colloquia sponsored by Harvard's Center for the Study of World Religions.

Number 3

A GUIDE TO THE ZOROASTRIAN RELIGION
A Nineteenth Century Catechism with Modern Commentary

Edited and Translated by
Firoze M. Kotwal and James W. Boyd

A GUIDE TO THE ZOROASTRIAN RELIGION

A Nineteenth Century Catechism with Modern Commentary

Edited and Translated by
Firoze M. Kotwal
and
James W. Boyd

Scholars Press
Chico, California

A GUIDE TO THE ZOROASTRIAN RELIGION
A Nineteenth Century Catechism with Modern Commentary

Translated and edited by
Firoze M. Kotwal and James W. Boyd

Library of Congress Cataloging in Publication Data

Meherjirana, Erachji, Sohrabji, Dastur, 1826–1900.
A guide to the Zoroastrian religion.

(Studies in world religions ; 3)
Includes index.
1. Zoroastrianism—Catechisms and creeds.
I. Kotwal, Firoze M. P. II. Boyd, James W. III. Title.
IV. Series: Harvard studies in world religions ; 3.
BL1571.M4313 295 82–3236
ISBN 0–89130–573–4 AACR2
ISBN 0–89130–574–2 (pbk.)

Printed in the United States of America

Dedicated
to the pious memory of
Dastur Erachji Sohrabji Dastur Meherjirana
(1826–1900 A.C.)

CONTENTS

FOREWORD

I am pleased to have been asked to write an introductory word to this interesting and unusual book. This work arises out of several different conversations and thus exists at several interstices. As such it is both difficult to characterize, and has a complexity that enhances its inherent interest. On the face of it, the book is a translation of a nineteenth century Zoroastrian catechism written by a conversative priest of the Parsee community in India. But it also contains comments by a contemporary Parsee priest, Dastur Dr. Kotwal, that arose in the translation process. His remarks often go beyond a simple exegesis of the original text to form a kind of conversation between these two conservative Parsee leaders, separated by a century, each seeking to serve his community by providing instruction in matters of faith. This interchange is the heart of the book.

Areas of disagreement revealed between the two priests are useful indices of some of the changes that have taken place in the Parsee community in the past century. One finds, for example, that Dastur Kotwal's acceptance of some of the criteria of Western scholarship has led him to disagree with his predecessor on the authority of certain texts. The conversation of Parsee scholars such as Dastur Kotwal with the tradition of Western scholarship has lead to a restructuring of scriptural authority within the tradition.

Most of the areas of disagreement, though, have to do with changes in ritual practices and social values among the Parsees. Dastur Kotwal's comments on these issues arise out of his participation in discussion among contemporary Parsees. His is but one voice, though an authoritative one. It should be clear from a reading of the text that much has remained unchanged in the faith and practice of the Zoroastrian community in the past century (and, in fact, for the past millenia). The Zoroastrian tradition has been remarkably conservative. One agency in this is the priestly tradition, the means by which the present has been in conversation with and learned from the past. This translation-commentary well exemplifies that process.

This work also arises out of a continuing conversation between Dastur Kotwal and Professor James Boyd, an "insider" and an "outsider" working together to illumine for both the "insider's" religious tradition. This conversation is reflected both in the translation process and in Professor Boyd's useful introduction. Dastur Kotwal was invited to come to Harvard in 1979 as a Visiting Scholar at the Center for the Study of World Religions. Professor Boyd arranged to come in the same capacity during that academic year so that he could continue his collaboration with Dastur Kotwal. In the spring term the Dastur and I worked together in a general comparative course on religious ritual, with special emphasis on Zoroastrian ritual. Professor Boyd also joined us for this course and we were able later to document on videotape the central Zoroastrian ritual, the *yasna*. I therefore have been a close listener in one phase of the continuing interchange between Dastur Kotwal and Professor Boyd.

The Center for the Study of World Religions has long encouraged attention to the lived religious traditions of today, with the premise that the study of a given tradition should involve insider and outsider in continual conversation. This work is thus particularly appropriate for the Center's publication series both as a collaborative effort and for the attention it directs to recent Parsee intellectual history. With a few important exceptions students of Zoroastrianism have focused on the religion attested in pre-Islamic periods. I hope that this work will stimulate further research in the religious history of Zoroastrianism in the present and the recent past.

William Darrow
Williams College

INTRODUCTION

This book is twofold in nature. First, it is a translation from Gujarati of a Zoroastrian catechism written in 1869 A.C. by a learned Zoroastrian priest, Dastur Erachji Sohrabji Meherjirana.[1] As such it documents the articles of faith held by a much respected priest of the Parsi (Zoroastrian) community of India over a 100 years ago. Secondly, the book contains a commentary on the catechism written by a contemporary Zoroastrian high priest, Dastur Dr. Firoze M. Kotwal.[2] Dastur Kotwal, who has been trained in modern philological methods, provides us with a contemporary statement of orthodox Zoroastrian beliefs. This is an especially valuable addition in light of the great impact modern linguistic and historical studies have brought to this ancient, long-lived faith.

The purpose of this introduction is to provide some background in the Zoroastrian tradition for readers unfamiliar with the particulars of the faith in the nineteenth and twentieth centuries. First certain basic features of the Zoroastrian faith as set forth in Dastur Erachji's text and Dastur Kotwal's commentary will be discussed. This will be followed by a resume of some of the religious issues being debated by Zoroastrians at the time each of the Dasturs wrote. This section will also include a sketch of the personal background of each Dastur. The concluding portion will highlight a few contemporary orthodox concerns which Dastur Kotwal addresses at several points in his commentary.

I. TEXT AND COMMENTARY: Fundamentals of the Zoroastrian faith

A. *Ohrmazd, the Lord of Wisdom*

The central Zoroastrian teaching according to Dasturs Erachji and Kotwal is the religious primacy of the one true God, the Lord of Wisdom. In His own nature, Ohrmazd is "the invisible among invisibles", the "unseen among the unseen", He who "has no shape" (3-4).[3] God is holy, beyond human conceptual reach, incapable of being defined as He is in and of Himself.

But God is not total mystery, for man as creature can relate to God the Creator. Through a revelatory vision that permeated "the totality of his consciousness" (19) Zoroaster came to know the "qualities" of God. Through the power of the Good Mind (*Vohuman*) Zoroaster saw (18) the Lord of Wisdom as "full of radiance and glory", "self-created," "omnipresent" and "omniscient", the Creator of both the "spiritual and material worlds" (3-4). These are a few of the "honorific terms" (4) applied to God by the prophet, characteristics by which man can remember God day and night in worshipful attitude.

Among the chief characteristics of God is His power to create. Erachji asserts with uncompromising clarity that "God Himself is Creator; no one except Him"; God alone "cares for and nourishes all" (3). No suggestion is given anywhere in this Zoroastrian catechism of a cosmogonic dualism, that is, of a primeval principle of evil, coeternal with the Good, which miscreates spiritually demonic and materially degenerate forms of existence. Although dualism is a prominent theme in some of the ninth century Pahlavi books, Dasturs Erachji and Kotwal speak only of the supremacy of the one true God basing their claim on Avestan passages with this emphasis. Ohrmazd alone is Creator. He created the two worlds, "the one which cannot be seen" (the spiritual world) and "that which can be seen or which is liable to death" (the material world) (4). Through God's revelation to Zoroaster we know that God first created Wisdom [Good Mind: *Vohuman*] in the spiritual world, and then created the material world in the following order: sky, water, earth, vegetation, animals and man (5).

B. *The Spiritual and Material Worlds*

Many of the secrets and mysteries of the two worlds were revealed to Zoroaster. Such revelations included the purpose of creation, what constitutes the good life, the realities of life after death, and the identities of the spiritual powers that dwell in the "unseen world" above and around us. During Zoroaster's revelatory vision, six "Bountiful Immortals" (*amahraspands*) were also present with God: Good Mind (*Vohu Manah*), Best Righteousness (*Asha Vahishta*), Dominion (*Khshathra*), Bountiful Devotion (*Spenta Armaiti*), Health (*Haurvatat*), and Life (*Ameretat*) (20-21, 176). Dastur Erachji clearly understands these Bountiful Immortals to be spiritual realities distinct from Ohrmazd and created by Him, sometimes referring to them as *fireshtes* (a Persian term for all good spiritual powers or "angels"). They are not in the same category as the "qualities" or "honorific terms" applied to God Himself. Nor does Erachji speak of them as emanations from God, for the unity of God is in no way compromised. As created spiritual entities distinct from God, the Bountiful Immortals are of the highest order of spiritual power next to Ohrmazd Himself.

Each of the Bountiful Immortals is intimately associated with an aspect of the material creation. Dastur Erachji speaks of the Bountiful Immortal "Good Mind" presiding over animals, "Righteousness" over fire, "Dominion" over metals, "Bountiful Devotion" over earth, "Health" over the waters, and "Life" over vegetation (21). Each of these representative aspects of the material creation is thus in the "custody" (21) of a *fireshte* (angel, Bountiful Immortal). The whole of the material world, in other words, has protective guardian angels in charge of it, a view of the world very reminiscent of the Talmudic assertion: "There is not a stalk on earth that has not its angel in heaven."[4] All phenomena point toward that which transcends them, and these transcending spiritual powers in turn protect and bless the material world.

Every Zoroastrian has several duties he or she should perform each year which are directly related to this view of the interrelationship of the two worlds. A Zoroastrian should participate in the six festivals of creation (*gahambars*) (75, 148-150) which commemorate Ohrmazd's creation of the sky, water, earth, vegetation, animals and man. These festivals of creation celebrate not only the origin of the physical world as we know it, but are also held in honor of their presiding *fireshtes*. Every Zoroastrian adult also should recite three times every day a litany to the sun (*Khorshed*), and three times every month a litany to the moon (*Mah*) (75). Both the sun and moon are called visible spiritual powers (*yazads*)[5] by Erachji (147). In addition, litanies are to be said at designated times to three invisible spiritual powers: *Srosh*, *Rapithwin* and *Mihr*. *Mihr* is the name of a *yazad* who is the spiritual power of loyalty, friendship and love accompanying the light of the sun as it spreads across creation (88). *Rapithwin* is the spirit of noon, that time of the day when the sun is in ascendancy, its purifying rays (151) bestowing their life-giving light and warmth to creation. *Srosh* is the guardian spirit of the prayerful litanies themselves, and is Ohrmazd's vice-regent on earth, the *yazad* in charge of protecting the entire material creation (177). By reciting these litanies and participating in these festivals, the pious Zoroastrian celebrates the full protective and health-giving presence of these visible and invisible powers which embrace the whole world.

Frequently no distinction is made between a particular phenomenon in this world and its spiritual custodian. For example, the names of the days and months in the Zoroastrian calendar refer both to a time period (a day or month) and to the spiritual powers which bear these same names. Hence to refer to the day *Ohrmazd* of the month *Mihr* is to refer, simultaneously, to a particular time period and to the spiritual powers presiding over that calendar date (156, 177 ff). And when the day name, e.g., *Mihr*, and the month name coincide, then that is an especially auspicious day and a *jashan*, an assembly of rejoicing, is in order (157) (See Appendix II, The Zoroastrian Calendar).

Zoroaster asked God: "Who is the best man?" An important part of the answer was, he "who loves fire, water, and animals is the best man" (19). A fundamental purpose in the lives of all human beings is to establish and maintain the purity and well-being of the created order in which they live. By loving fire, water and animals, man is not only acting responsibly, but he is also establishing a proper relationship with the spiritual powers of Righteousness, Health and Good Mind, the three Bountiful Immortals who preside over these three aspects of creation.

C. *Fire*

The Zoroastrian view that all phenomena point to spiritual powers which transcend them, however, does not fully explain the unique relationship of fire to its Bountiful Immortal Righteousness (*Asha*). Dastur Erachji reflects on the theological question, "Since we cannot see God, how should we do our *bandagi* (our prayers to God)?" His answer is: "We must do our *bandagi* facing all shining things because the sun, moon, stars and fire are the natural lights out of the original light of God" (54). Dastur Erachji is affirming here the Zoroastrian practice of facing a shining thing (a *qibla*) while praying, as it enables the worshipper to focus his attention and concentrate deeply. But on a more fundamental level, Dastur Erachji is talking about the central role of fire in his religious tradition. The sun and the moon, we have already noted, are visible spirit powers (*yazads*), and like the stars, shine with radiant glory. As such they are similar to the consecrated fires within the inner precincts of the Zoroastrian fire temples (*Atash Bahrams*). Such fires are 'sparks' of the infinite light of Ohrmazd Himself and are replete with divine presence.

Dastur Kotwal notes that "it is difficult for non-Zoroastrians to understand the function of fire" (55). Perhaps one of the reasons for this is that the language Zoroastrians use to describe fire is so rich in connotations that non-Zoroastrians are likely to understand far less than what is being said. To Dasturs Erachji and Kotwal, the light of a fire, like that of the sun, connotes purity, healing warmth, and the plentitude of health and life, as opposed to the coldness of darkness and the decrepitude of disease and decay. Radiant light also connotes wisdom. It is the light of wisdom, the infinite glory of the Lord of Wisdom, Ohrmazd, that dispels the darkness of ignorance and displaces unrighteousness.

Fire also epitomizes for Zoroastrians the proper relation between God and man, between the Creator and his creation. The term for this proper relation is "Righteousness" (*Asha*). "Righteousness" is both the name of a Bountiful Immortal of the highest spiritual order and an aspect of human experience. As a spiritual principle, Righteousness is the basis for the fundamental 'rightness' of the created universe, the basis of the life-giving process by which day follows night, spring follows winter, and persons find meaning and order in their lives. Righteousness thus refers to universal cosmic order (like the Vedic *Ṛta*). But it also refers to a person's proper relation to God as part of that order. This fundamental relation to God makes all life meaningful and true knowledge of God possible. In this respect Righteousness is the foundational concept in Zoroastrian theology.

But Righteousness, *Asha*, is more than just a theological concept or experiential stance. Righteousness is concretely embodied in a visible, glowing, physical fire, called the "son of God" (55). Each consecrated fire in the heart of a Zoroastrian fire temple is, like the sun, moon and stars, the actual presence of the cosmic life-animating principle of "Righteousness", replete with wisdom, health and holiness. There is a deeper metaphysical correspondence between the material fire and its spiritual power than between other physical phenomena and their spiritual guardians (*fireshtes*). A consecrated fire is a physical epiphany of the spiritual realm of Ohrmazd Himself. As such, fires are the most appropriate *qibla* (objects of attention) to face in one's devotions to God. Dastur Erachji speaks of the temple fire as one who "watches the hand of all comers" to see what gifts they bring (57). An offering of sandalwood to the "son of God" brings blessings to the worshipper who approaches Him with good thoughts, words and deeds. Conversely, if anyone were to put out a consecrated temple fire, says Erachji, he is a *margarzan* sinner, one deserving death (113).

D. *Ritual*

It is the close interrelation between material phenomena and their spiritual guardians, and the special confluence of spirit and matter in sacred fires, that makes the liturgies of the Zoroastrian tradition so meaningful to Dasturs Erachji and Kotwal. Throughout the catechism Dastur Erachji refers to a great variety of rituals observed by Zoroastrians, and a discussion of the significance of each cannot be adequately summarized in an introduction of this nature.

There are three basic types of Zoroastrian ceremonies: 1) high liturgies, 2) individual observances, and 3) common ceremonies. In an attempt to convey a sense of the intricacy and richness of a high liturgical service, one liturgy, the *Yasna*, will be described in some detail in the following pages. Mention will then be made of shorter rituals observed by individuals, followed by a brief description of some common ceremonies.

High Liturgies

High liturgies are called *paw mahal* (pure place) ceremonies. They are always performed in the ritual area of the fire temple by priests who have undergone prior purification rites. The laity have no participating role in these services other than sponsorship and providing the unleavened bread cakes (*dron*) used in the ceremonies. The names of the high liturgies are the *Yasna, Dron, Visperad, Vendidad* and *Nirangdin* (See Glossary).

The high liturgy performed most frequently within the precincts of a Zoroastrian fire temple is the *Yasna* ('act of worship') (92). It is conducted within a fixed enclosure, called a place of purity (*pawi*). Within this designated area the priest purifies a number of ritual items which taken together constitute a microcosm of the good creation. Besides metal implements and vessels, the priest assembles a freshly cut date-palm leaf, twigs from a pomegranate tree, sacramental bread, properly purified *hom* twigs (twigs of an *ephedra* plant imported from Iran), hairs from a living consecrated white bull, and pure water from a temple well. A ritual fire is ignited, kindled with frankincense and sandalwood, and afterwards fed **babul** logs.

Each ritual item, once consecrated and made pure, invites the full presence of its corresponding Bountiful Immortal. The ritual area of purified earth and stone manifests the spirit of Devotion. The consecrated water and plants and wheat cake (*dron*) bestow the presence of Health and Life. The hairs from a living white bull manifest the holy power of Good Mind. The consecrated fire, with His radiant glow and divine glory, is the physical embodiment of the principle of Cosmic Order (*Asha*), and the metal implements, like the crystal sky, embody the power of Dominion. The priest who is the liturgist is the representative of Ohrmazd Himself.

The officiating priest, who is called a purifier (*yozdathregar*) of creation, must establish himself in the right relation with the representative aspects of the created order about him. He must seek to inculcate the desire for righteousness and be responsive to the spiritual dimension of creation. He must be in good health, his thoughts concentrated, and he must have completed several preliminary purification procedures before he is qualified to be a high liturgist. For example, he must have performed a cleansing ritual (*padyab-kusti*) of washing his hands, face and feet three times while saying prayers. He must also know with utmost accuracy both the holy *manthras*[6] (Avestan prayers) and the appropriate ritual gestures.

Manthras, or holy Avestan utterances, are regarded as the very soul of Ohrmazd in Zoroastrian liturgical thought. When spoken properly by a righteous person in a purified place, *manthras* become "glorious, powerful and health-giving" (*Yasht* 1.1-3; 2.6) sacred sounds. *Manthric* speech, unlike ordinary conventional speech, is believed to possess an inseparable link or connection (a metaphysical correspondence) between the sound uttered and the reality signified by that sound. This means, for example, that when a priest intones an Avestan *manthric* reference to a particular Bountiful Immortal, he thereby invokes the presence of that spiritual reality in that very place where he has uttered the sound. *Manthric* speech thus has power, for the utterance itself participates in the spiritual reality.

The appropriate ritual gestures the priest must know and properly perform are also believed to be an effective means of actualizing the spiritual powers in the ritual area. The fundamental purpose of all ritual gestures in the *Yasna* service is to establish and maintain the purity of the ritual area. All implements must be purified three times with water and *manthric* consecration. In addition, the priest must crush the *hom* twigs with a pestle in a mortar in a specific way, and while so doing recite *manthric* formulas which speak of 'smiting the wicked Angra Mainyu' [the Evil One] and all of his monstrous, wicked, lustful, life-denying demons (*daevas*). While thus smiting Angra Mainyu, the priest crushes the *hom* twigs and thereby releases the life-giving essence of this juice of immortality. The priest also ties knots in a sacred cord, and while so doing chants *manthras* with the intention of binding the Evil One and his hordes of robbers and thieves. Through the physical act of tying knots the Evil One and his *daevas* are bound.

This ritual thus becomes a power center of all that is good and beneficial in creation. The *manthras* uttered by the righteous priest invoke the named spirit realities, the ritual gestures establish purity (holiness) and bind and smash the power of evil, and the material objects themselves, once purified, manifest the Bountiful Immortals. Their holy presence bestows protection and blessings on the participants and observers of the ritual. Likewise, and of major importance, the presence of the sacred *hom* drink and the consecrated bread (*dron*) serve as tangible material offerings to the spirit powers. The spirit powers now being more fully manifest in the material realm derive sustenance and pleasure from these offerings. So strengthened (as is the priest by partaking of the sacred drink and bread), the spirit powers are further sustained in their efforts to bring health and life and bounty to the whole of the good creation. The priest, through this *Yasna* offering, is thereby contributing to the salvation of the world and bringing closer to fruition the end days when all the righteous will attain heaven.

Individual Observances

There are many examples of individual observances throughout the catechism. The principal ones performed daily by Zoroastrians are *padyab-kusti*, mentioned previously, and *bandagi*. Every Zoroastrian act of worship, whether lay or priestly, begins with the short ceremony of *padyab-kusti*. It is a cleansing ritual (*padyab*) involving the washing of one's hands, face and feet three times, actions which are preceded and followed by Avestan recitation. This is followed by the untying and retying of the *kusti* (a sacred belt) which is tied over a white cotton shirt called *sudre*. The *sudre* and *kusti* serve as protective shields around the body, guarding against evil pollution, and at the same time helping to contain the goodness within man.

Having performed *kusti* the worshipper then begins his *bandagi* for the day. *Bandagi* means "service to God" (52) and refers to the ritually prescribed prayers suitable for the period (*gah*) of the day (called *gah* prayers), and other fixed litanies and hymns dedicated to specific spirit powers (*yazads*). After saying the prescribed *bandagi* of the day, a Zoroastrian contemplates upon personal matters in his or her own native language. The purpose of *bandagi* is to invoke God and his spiritual workers, seek their blessings and thereby bring down the bounty of all that is good.

Common Ceremonies

The names of the principal common ceremonies are: *Stum* (praise), *Afrinagan* (blessings) and *Farokhski* (all souls). These ceremonies can be performed in the home or in the ritual hall (*Dar-e Mihr*: gateway of *Mihr*) of the fire temple. The liturgical requirements for these ceremonies are far less exacting than those of the high liturgies. Each can be performed, for example, at anytime during the five watches of the day, the liturgist can face any direction but north during its performance, and the service can be celebrated by knowledgeable lay persons or priests--three allowances not applicable to high liturgies. All common ceremonies are performed principally for the sake of the souls of the departed and invoke the names of various spirit powers (*yazads*) and Bountiful Immortals.

In the *Stum* ceremony (92), the names of the departed are remembered and the ceremony is conducted on the anniversary day of their demise. A fire is lit in a fire vase, usually placed on a white cloth on the floor, and fed frankincense and sandalwood. Cooked foods, milk, water and fresh fruits (apples, bananas, oranges) are placed on a tray near the fire vase so as to feed, satisfy, and please the souls of the departed. The departed souls (*rawans*), who are in a delicate condition as sojourners in the other world, descend to the ritual offering, and are pleased and strengthened by the sweet savors and odors.

Their well being in the afterlife is thereby sustained and they continue to advance in stages toward their heavenly goal (*behesht*). There are in all seven stages of heaven, the first located among the stars, moon and sun, the last stage being the realm of "endless lights" (144).

The *Afrinagan* ceremony (92) also consists of offerings to souls of the departed and to various *yazads* and is the most frequently performed ritual of all the common ceremonies. *Farokhski* is a Parsi term which refers collectively to all holy souls and guardian spirits (*fravashi*). The distinguishing feature of this ceremony is the recital of the *Frawardin Yasht* (Hymn to All-Souls, i.e., *Yasht* 13) and its dedication to all departed souls.

E. *Evil, Impurity, Unrighteousness*

Zoroastrian liturgies are performed not only to praise Ohrmazd, the Creator of all goodness, and to help bring about goodness in the two worlds; the rituals also effectively counter those forces in the world which seek to destroy this health-giving goodness, namely, the evil powers of decay, destruction and death. The power of Bad Thought (*Akoman*) opposes the Good Mind; Disorder (*Spozgar*) opposes Righteousness; Sloth (*Bushasp*) is the antagonist of Dominion: Death (*Astwihad*) opposes Devotion; Greed (*Az*) opposes Health; and Thirst (*Tishn*) opposes Life. Also Anger (*Kheshm*) opposes the *yazad Srosh* (145-146).

Although Dastur Erachji clearly believes that spiritual powers of evil exist and are led by the Hostile Spirit named Angra Mainyu (21), nonetheless, in his catechism it is the activities of human 'evil-doers' that most concern him. The sins of mankind range from extinguishing a consecrated fire (*Atash Bahram*) and polluting water and earth to giving false evidence against an innocent person or striking another with the intention of wounding him (123 ff.). The greatest enemies man encounters, in fact, are the "vices in us which cause pain and damage" (122). There is a tendency in the catechism to demythologize many references to evil spirits. For example, in the chapter which deals with Good and Evil Spirits (147 ff.), Dastur Erachji poses the question "who is an evil spirit (*daeva*)?" His answer is: "A person who does bad deeds is himself an evil spirit."

Closely linked with these internal evil traits are the external evils of pollution and contamination. It is the Zoroastrian belief that in general anything that flows out from the interior of the body is polluting, as well as any dead matter which is full of decay and can bring disease and loss of well-being to God's healthful creation. A woman in menses is polluted and must be kept separate from all that is health-giving. She should sit apart from everyone in her periods of menses, and should endeavor not to touch anything at all, especially not pure water or priestly ritual implements, nor approach a fire. Likewise, during maternity, a woman should stay in a separate place in the house. Not until 40 days after giving birth does her condition of pollution cease. At this time the new mother must ceremonially purify herself with *gomez* (bull's urine) and water before she returns to an active role in the household (129 ff.).

The greatest danger of contamination, however, comes from the impurity of a dead body with its demons of pollution, such as the foul odor of the corpse. Extensive ritual precautions, therefore, are taken to guard the living from the contamination of the dead, and the proper disposal of a corpse is of major concern for the Zoroastrian. The corpse must be taken to a *dakhma* or tower of silence, and there, far removed from human habitation, exposed to the birds of prey that God created to remove the dead matter quickly and efficiently (76 ff.). Clothing that has come in contact with dead matter, or anything useful to man that has been polluted, must be purified through special procedures before it can be used again by the living.

For Dastur Erachji, then, the power and reality of evil, which is expressed in the Pahlavi books as the primordial spiritual principle of evil in cosmic warfare against

Ohrmazd and his good creation, finds its principal expression in unrighteous persons and polluting conditions which man encounters in everyday life. Victory over evil is very much an immediate, daily, practical and ritual concern in the religious life of the individual. This emphasis reflects Dastur Erachji's dominant pastoral concern which motivated the writing of this catechism, but it also reflects the principal orientation of his theology which is to give full expression to the glory of God and the bounty of His creation.

F. *The Righteous Life, now and hereafter*

The reward for a life of good deeds in this world is the attainment of paradise (*behesht*), a place of lofty mansions full of light and happiness (144). A life of bad deeds in this world, on the other hand, leads to hell (*dozakh*). This is a dwelling place full of pain and difficulties, and is the consequence of the sinful life (144-145). Since the soul of man is given a reward or retribution according to his deeds in this world, the soul's passage from this world to the next is of major religious concern. Therefore the ceremonies for the deceased are of crucial importance.

According to Zoroastrian belief, the soul of the deceased stays in this world for three days at the place where ceremonies for it are performed. During this time the soul is almost like a new-born infant in that it is newly separated from the body and subject to negative demonic influence as well as aided by the positive spiritual powers. Ceremonies with *manthric* invocations for the benefit of the deceased must be said during these three days to bring solace and strength to the soul. On the morning of the fourth day the soul leaves the area, follows the light of the rising sun, and proceeds toward the Chinwad bridge which connects this world with the next. Here judgment is made before *Mihr yazad*. The good soul advances across the bridge and proceeds toward heaven, the Abode of Songs (144); and the bad soul goes to hell, there to await the final judgment day when all souls will be joined to their resurrected bodies and restored to a state of purity.

Since it is one's thoughts, words and deeds that determine the destiny of the soul after life in this world, to live a righteous life is of fundamental importance. As we have discussed, righteousness means properly relating through correct ritual and ethical behavior to God and his spiritual order, including all spirit powers (*fireshtes*) in creation. For Dastur Erachji, to be morally righteous especially means being truthful, charitable, industrious, keeping promises and respecting elders; it also means avoiding greed, arrogance and vengeance. Such a life not only earns merit which leads to heaven but also earns happiness in this world. A pious Zoroastrian should enjoy wealth and/or authority that he has earned through his own honest endeavors. To earn "fame in this world" is praiseworthy, for "God gives . . . greatness" (99). An important aspect of obtaining this bountiful happiness which is the rightful part of God's creation is to seek learning and wisdom. As Dastur Erachji states, "Everyone should yearn for knowledge because through learning the advantage of both worlds is gained" (106).

II. ISSUES AND AUTHORS

A. *Western influence on Zoroastrianism in the nineteenth century*[7]

In 19th century British India, scholars and missionaries from the West had considerable impact on the religious thought of the Parsis. In 1829 for example, the Parsis of Bombay were confronted by the forceful Scottish missionary, John Wilson, who sought to bring them into the Christian fold. Wilson attacked the Zoroastrian notion of dualism, i.e., their belief in two primordial principles, one good, the other evil, and their preoccupation with purity laws. In 1843 in Bombay he published *The Parsi Religion . . . unfolded, refuted and contrasted with Christianity*, in which he mocked a spokesman for the orthodox interpretation of the Zoroastrian tradition (Dastur Edalji Sanjana) as being entirely out-of-touch with the scientific studies of his own tradition.[8]

The Parsis also were feeling the impact of Western education. Bombay's Elphinstone College was founded in 1827 to teach 'the languages, literatures, sciences and moral philosophy of Europe.'[9] Since most of the pupils in this college throughout the nineteenth century were Parsis, reform movements within the Zoroastrian community naturally began to develop. Early Parsi reformists, basing their arguments on seventeenth and eighteenth century European studies of Zoroastrianism (e.g., the works of Thomas Hyde and Anquetil du Perron) argued that Zoroaster preached a simple monotheism void of rituals and that Parsis should return to the 'original' faith.

This general movement was given even greater credibility when Martin Haug, the famous German philologist, discovered that the *Gathas* (17 Avestan hymns) were a more ancient dialect than the rest of the Avestan writings (the *Yashts* and the *Vendidad*). During the 1860's Haug was in India teaching Sanskrit at Poona University. While there, he taught many Parsis about his discovery. But his claims went far beyond the linguistic evidence. He argued that because the *Gathas* were linguistically older, they alone could be regarded as the authentic utterances of Zoroaster. He also asserted that the *Gathas* taught a simple, pure monotheism, and since they were silent on matters of ritual observance, Zoroaster must not have considered ritual an important aspect of the religion. The reform movement among the Parsis readily embraced Haug's interpretation of the essentials of the Zoroastrian faith, for he appeared to provide them with a scholarly backing for their own reforming attitudes.

But the influence of Western scholars on Parsi beliefs in the 1860's did not end with Haug. E. W. West, an Englishman serving as chief engineer in the Indian railways system, was also in India at this time; in fact he both collaborated with Haug and differed with him. West was a scholar of the Pahlavi literature of the late medieval period of the Zoroastrian tradition (third through the ninth century A.C.). West believed that the Pahlavi texts he was editing and translating were important for a proper understanding of the Zoroastrian religion. In light of the religious issues of the day, this was an important stand, for much of the Pahlavi literature cannot be interpreted as teaching simple monotheism, nor is it uninterested in ritual. Quite the contrary, it presents a preoccupation with ritual matters and affirms a dualism: evil in combat with a superior God of Wisdom, Ohrmazd.

B. Nineteenth century orthodox response: Dastur Erachji Meherjirana (1826-1900 A.C.)

It was in this context that Dastur Erachji Meherjirana published in 1869 his Gujarati book *Rehbar-e Din-e Jarthushti* (*A Guide to the Zoroastrian Religion*). Although Dastur Erachji was aware of the issues being debated by his contemporaries, the purpose of his catechism was not directly to refute the reformists through argumentation. Rather Dastur Erachji sought to reaffirm the essentials of the Zoroastrian faith as it had been understood through the centuries, on the authority of the scriptural and commentarial texts of the tradition. At the same time he maintained a stance of intellectual openness to new methods of historical and philological research as taught by Western scholars.

Dastur Erachji assumed from the outset the continuity of the basic teachings of the Zoroastrian religion throughout its history. All aspects of the Avestan writings, the *Gathas*, *Yashts* and *Vendidad*, were sacred scripture and foundational to the Zoroastrian faith. His catechism was an effort to bring together all the important teachings which were then largely inaccessible to the ordinary layman. They were inaccessible principally for two reasons: most texts were still in manuscript form (there was little printing of Zoroastrian texts until the late 19th century), and the literature was written in a variety of languages (Avestan, Pahlavi, Persian and Arabic).

The catechism has had wide use among the orthodox since its publication. The Zoroastrian community sees in it the summation of the best work of an outstanding scholar and continues to hold the memory of Dastur Erachji in highest esteem.

Dastur Erachji was trained in his native town of Navsari, Gujarat, in the traditional languages of Avestan, Pahlavi and Persian, as well as in the system of writing called Pazand. His studies were guided by Ervad Kavasji Darabji Dastur Meherjirana. It is said of Ervad Kavasji that his command of the Avestan language was so remarkable that he was able to cite from memory all the verses in which any single word appeared in the holy Avestan scriptures.

Erachji was worthy of such a teacher. The catechism is evidence of his wide learning, for he quotes verses from manuscript texts in four different languages. He not only wrote in his native Gujarati tongue but composed verses in Persian and wrote a book (similar to the *Guide*) in Persian, titled "*Furugh-e Din*" (A Catechism on Zoroastrianism) for Irani Zoroastrians. In 1869 he published a Pahlavi dictionary titled *Hujvaras Ane Pehelavi Farhang* (Ideograms and the Pahlavi Dictionary) in which he arranged in alphabetical order the ideograms found in the Pahlavi language and gave their Iranian equivalents with Gujarati transliteration and meanings. During the period in his life when he was librarian of the Mulla Firuz Library in Bombay (1862-1887) he also did significant work as a scribe, copying with beautiful calligraphy many Persian, Avestan and Pahlavi manuscripts in duplicate, one for his own work and another for the library. When in old age Dastur Erachji donated his personal library to the First Dastur Meherjirana Library in Navsari, his collection contained hundreds of manuscripts and other printed books and pamphlets.

Although Dastur Erachji was trained in the traditional way in these various languages he also investigated what European philological research could add to his understanding of the most ancient of them, the Avestan language.

When the Parsi scholar K. R. Cama offered to teach the new scientific approach to Avestan studies, Dastur Erachji took advantage of the opportunity. Cama was a graduate of Elphinstone Institute (called Elphinstone College prior to 1840) and had spent the year 1859 in Europe studying with Avestan scholars. Because Erachji's knowledge of the tradition was so thorough, K. R. Cama often asked him to compare traditional renderings with the new philological meanings given the text. Dastur Erachji's contributions were especially helpful in passages where it was difficult to understand the meanings of terms in light of philology alone. In this way Dastur Erachji, like K. R. Cama himself, served as a bridge between the old and new systems of Avestan and Pahlavi studies. Together with his friend Ervad Mancherji Shapurji Vatcha, he published in 1872 a modern translation of ten of the Avestan *Yashts* according to this new method. Erachji's scholarship also influenced the Gujarati translations of such learned men as Ervad K. E. Kanga, another Avestan scholar who made use of the work of European philologists.

In addition to his knowledge of the scriptural and commentarial languages, Dastur Erachji was well-informed about the great legends and history of the Zoroastrian tradition. According to Dr. J. J. Modi, the noted scholar of the customs, history, and beliefs of the Parsis, Erachji was known for his recitations of the *Shahnama* (*Book of Kings*, a verse epic about the ancient kings and heroes of Persia). He recited from memory portions of this epic at festive occasions of well-to-do Parsis.[10]

Erachji also was known within the community for his honesty. Evidence of this can be found in the present book. Following the traditional style of writing, namely stating brief questions followed by direct answers, Erachji occasionally poses questions for which he can find no authoritative answer. When such an instance occurs, Erachji simply writes straightforwardly that he does not know the answer. If there are differences of opinion in the tradition concerning any particular issue, Erachji cites all the opinions he knows and then offers his own conclusion.

Whenever religious controversies or problems pertaining to the Zoroastrian community arose, Dastur Erachji frequently served as an arbiter. He was able to present from memory evidence from a variety of sources which pertained directly to the issue at hand. Likewise his knowledge of the intricacies of the high liturgical ceremonies conducted by priests in the sacred precincts of the fire temples was considerable. Other priests (*mobeds*), when performing the high liturgies, often would be somewhat uncomfortable when conducting ceremonies in his presence, for his knowledge of their proper performance was unquestioned. When in 1862, Dr. Martin Haug requested to see a demonstration of the central Zoroastrian high liturgy called the *Yasna*, Dastur Erachji was the chief officiating priest (*zot*).

There is a well-known story in Navsari about Erachji's commitment to the proper performance of Zoroastrian high liturgies. It happened one day, while Dastur Erachji was performing the *Yasna* ceremony in Navsari's *Vadi Dar-e Mihr*, that the great Dastur Kekobadji Rustamji Dastur Meherjirana presented himself. Being the high priest of the Navsari orthodox community, proper respect was due Dastur Kekobadji. The other priests in the ritual area greeted Dastur Kekobadji, but Dastur Erachji did not salute him. Nor did Erachji even look at him. Afterwards the other priests asked Dastur Erachji why he had behaved in such a manner. Erachji's reply clearly reveals his understanding of the ceremonies and his disciplined behavior during their enactment. Erachji said: The priests who perform ceremonies in the ritual area are in an exalted position. Once they enter the ritual area they come in contact with Ohrmazd, His Bountiful Immortals (*amahraspands*) and other spirit powers (*yazads*). At such a time they cannot and should not greet any person who stands outside the ritual area. If they do so, their ceremonies are vitiated and there is doubt as to their *barashnom* (the name of a purification rite which qualifies priests to perform high liturgies).

Dastur Erachji then went on to compare this episode with a similar one associated with the legend of the Iranian King Noshirwan the Just. He related the story of King Noshirwan's visit to a fire temple with his Prime Minister Buzorg-Mihr. The king and his minister saluted the priests performing the high liturgies in the ritual area. Not one priest returned the salute to the king. The prime minister then explained to the king that priests performing ceremonies in the ritual area were of an even higher status than that of a king. Since the priests were in contact with spiritual beings they could not salute any person outside the ritual precinct. To do so would be to lower their position and render their ceremonies null and void.[11]

Erachji related this story in order to instruct other priests as to the nature of their high position and also to demonstrate the applicability of history to the ongoing ritual tradition in Navsari. Unlike the reformist view which dismissed much of the later Zoroastrian tradition as a falsification of the original teachings of Zoroaster, Dastur Erachji was able to mold much of his life's values and disciplines from the historical materials left him by his tradition.

Erachji also differed from the reformists in his theology. Although he shared their monotheistic emphasis (the catechism begins with and continually reaffirms the proclamation of the one true God, Ohrmazd the Lord of Wisdom), the reality of evil remained a prominent feature of his religious outlook. Unlike the reformists, Erachji defined evil in the ritual context as all that can be associated with decay, disease and death. In the ethical context, it is unrighteous human behavior and all that that entails. As for the ontological status of evil, however, Erachji never makes the assertion that evil is co-eternal with God. He understands the supremacy of Ohrmazd to be the central teaching of Zoroastrianism. It may be that this monotheistic emphasis reflects what has always been the heart of the living Zoroastrian concern. If so, the dualism of the Pahlavi texts appears as an attempt to reconcile logical tensions in the relationship of evil to good. The monotheistic tone, however, may be a reaction to the influence of Christian missions among the Parsis. Perhaps both explanations have a degree of validity.

In summary, the key features of Dastur Erachji's catechism in light of nineteenth century issues are his belief in the fundamental integrity of the ancient Avestan scriptures, his unwavering faith in the efficacy of Zoroastrian rituals, and his commitment to the righteous life as informed by the rich history of his tradition. Spiritually undergirding all this is Erachji's sincere devotion to the Lord God, Ohrmazd, who is bountiful in His righteousness. Perhaps Dastur Erachji's basic convictions become most transparent in the following prayer which he composed in Persian:

> O God, whatever you have given me in the past, and whatever you will do for me in the future, I am content with it. I am pleased for all that you have done, and remain patient. I am deeply grateful.

C. *The intervening century*

The more than 100 years that have elapsed since Dastur Erachji wrote the *Guide* have seen even more religious diversity in the Parsi community. In 1885 Henry S. Olcott, founder of the Theosophical Society in New York, arrived in Bombay. In his approach to the Parsis he emphasized the "sublime" and "occult mysteries" discovered by the ancient Zoroastrian Magi, mysteries which were safely embodied and preserved in the rituals of the tradition. Rituals were important, he claimed, if understood in mystical terms. The Parsis now were listening to a Westerner who spoke not only in praise of rituals, but also asserted that "Dualism. . .the personification of opposing powers" as taught by Zoroaster was both a "scientific and philosophical statement of a profound truth." Olcott added that Parsi graduates from Elphinstone College had "no cause to blush" for being Zoroastrian.[12] Some Parsis began to give theosophical interpretations to Zoroastrianism.

In addition to theosophy, the Zoroastrians had their own indigenous occult movement. Founded by Behramshah Shroff, the Ilm-e Khshnum (Science of [Spiritual] Satisfaction) movement began in the early 1900's. Shroff's movement emphasized belief in one God, reincarnation, multiple planes of being and strict observance of purity laws and their attendant rituals. Adherents of this group differed from the Parsi theosophists largely on the degree of strictness in observing the rituals. Also they did not allow the creation of new rites as some theosophists did. But in matters of doctrinal interpretation, they shared some of the views of the theosophists.

Some Parsis today, though not formally members of any of these sects, venerate contemporary 'gurus' of the Hindu tradition while maintaining their traditional practices and attendance in the fire temples. In fact, the Parsi Association in Calcutta recently published (1967) a translation of the *Gathas* by a Hindu scholar who has identified the Avesta as the missing 'fifth Veda.'[13]

Besides the debates over ritual and theological matters, divisive positions have been taken on the issue of calendar reform. The importance of the calendar for the proper celebration of festivals and commemorative rituals is fundamental to Zoroastrianism. Commemorative rituals, for example, are prescribed on a daily and monthly basis by the tradition, and the continuity of these observances through time is highly valued by Zoroastrians. Consequently, when it was discovered in the 18th century that the Parsi religious calendar was one month behind that of the Irani Zoroastrians, considerable debate over a proper solution ensued. As early as 1780 a movement was founded in Bombay called the Qadimi sect, which adheres to the 'ancient' (*qadimi*) calendar of Iran for determining festival and ritual dates.

Parsis who rejected this move and sought to retain their own traditional calendar called themselves Shahanshahis or 'monarchists' maintaining that theirs was the calendar of the ancient Persian kings. Both Dasturs Erachji and Kotwal follow the Shahanshahi calendar. The Qadimi and Shahanshahi calendars are based on traditional 360-day calendars (12 months of 30 days each), plus 5 supplementary days added at the end of each year, do not stay in sequence with the seasons, and require the intercalation of a month every 120 years.

Another movement known in India as the Fasli or 'seasonal' movement, began in the present century. This small group among the Parsis argues that the original Zoroastrian calendar must have remained in harmony with the seasons and therefore should be fixed, like the Gregorian calendar, to the seasons. Calendrical arguments have been more divisive among the Parsis than any of the previously mentioned theological issues because changes in calendar alter the specific times when commemorative services for the departed souls are held and also effect each Parsi's immediate sense of what is appropriate behavior for those who seek to live a righteous life.

D. *A twentieth century orthodox response: Dastur Dr. Firoze M. Kotwal (1935-   ).*

In the midst of this wide range of controversy Dastur Firoze Kotwal has written his commentary to Dastur Erachji's catechism. Dastur Kotwal, like other orthodox Parsis, continues to affirm and be nurtured by his ancient religious heritage, and agrees with Dastur Erachji on all the fundamentals of the faith. His commentary is not intended to be a detailed exegesis of the catechism nor a correction of it. Rather the commentary is basically a further elucidation of the essentials of the Zoroastrian faith presented in the same spirit as Erachji's catechism.

Like Dastur Erachji, Dastur Kotwal is a native of Navsari and is an accomplished scholar in Zoroastrian scriptural and commentarial languages. His childhood studies began at a madressa in Navsari, followed by priestly studies at the M. F. Cama Athornan Institute in Bombay. He received an M.A. from Bombay's St. Xavier's College and completed research at Bombay University leading to the Ph.D. degree in 1966 in Avestan and Pahlavi studies. His doctoral work was guided by Dastur Dr. H. K. Mirza. In 1966-67 he went to London to study under the directorship of Dr. Mary Boyce, Professor of Iranian Studies at the University of London. There he studied Middle Iranian materials including Inscriptional Pahlavi, Manichaean Middle Persian, Parthian, and Middle Iranian grammar and sound laws. He also completed his research on *The Supplementary Texts to the Shayest Ne-Shayest*,[14] and subsequently has published numerous articles on subjects related to the Zoroastrian religion. He returned to England in the summer of 1973 to lecture on Zoroastrian ritual at the School of Oriental and African Studies, University of London.

On May 1, 1977, Dr. Kotwal was installed as Dastur of the Wadiaji *Atash Bahram* in Bombay, one of the eight major fire temples in India. In the installation service Dr. Kotwal was cited as one worthy to be invested with the *dasturi* shawl (the official sign of *dastur*ship) because of his extensive academic learning and his comprehensive knowledge of Zoroastrian liturgies. Over 100 priests from all over India participated in the service. The occasion was truly a *jashan*, i.e., a festival of rejoicing, with the priests and hundreds of lay people reciting the benediction which confers health and blessings upon the new *dastur*.

What Dastur Erachji had begun to explore toward the end of his career--Western scholarship on the Zoroastrian tradition--Dastur Kotwal has continued to pursue. Kotwal brings to the present translation of Erachji's book a more thorough knowledge of comparative linguistics, but at the same time shares with Erachji an intimate knowledge of the tradition as it can be known only by one schooled in it. It is Dastur Kotwal's awareness of modern scholarship as it relates to his tradition that accounts for a number of the differences between the two Dasturs on certain points of historical and textual interpretation.

In his commentary Dastur Kotwal frequently disagrees with Dastur Erachji on matters of philology, though these disagreements seldom have any serious doctrinal implications (e.g., 10). A far more important difference between the Dasturs concerns the authority of certain Zoroastrian texts. Dastur Kotwal does not accept, as Erachji does, the authenticity of texts like the *Vaetha Nask*, the *Dabestan* and the *Dasatir* (see Appendix I for descriptions). He is aware, e.g., that portions of the *Dasatir* (*Ordinances*) are in an artificial language (elements from Indian and Iranian dialects) and that the text is generally regarded as a literary forgery (6, 193). The significant extent of this difference can be seen by looking at Dastur Kotwal's descriptions of the more than 40 texts that Erachji refers to in his catechism (Appendix I).

Kotwal is also more critically aware that an historical literalism cannot be applied to the whole of the Avesta (5) and that original stories can undergo considerable elaboration and modification in the course of their preservation by the tradition (32-33, 161-162). This does not mean that later texts have to be discounted, for they can still preserve a core of authentic tradition. But in matters of clear conflict between the Pahlavi and Avestan texts, he asserts that the Avestan writings should have the decided preference (162).

When Dastur Kotwal refers to the Avesta he, like Erachji, means the total corpus of books extant in the Avestan language. Unlike the reformists and many Western scholars, Kotwal does not accept the view that the *Gathas* are the only genuine record of Zoroaster's teachings. He is cognizant of the fact that the *Gathic* dialect differs from that of other Avestan texts (i.e., the 'Younger Avesta'), but he questions whether that fact warrants the wider claim that the *Gathas* are the only true source of

Zoroastrian teaching. This is not to suggest that all of the Avesta was spoken by Zoroaster himself. Rather Kotwal's position is that the 'Younger Avesta' is an accurate record of the teachings of the early disciples of Zoroaster. He notes that the Pahlavi tradition itself maintains that "for 300 years the religion was in purity and men were free from doubt" (50). Kotwal as yet has found no compelling reason to doubt the integrity of the early tradition and argues that the burden of proof rests on those who wish to make the claim of a fundamental disparity among Avestan writings.

Dastur Kotwal realizes that some of his counter-arguments to reformist and Western claims about the relation of the *Gathas* to the rest of the Avesta may not be totally convincing to all, and he is open to further discussion on these matters. However, what is of greater import is the basic perspective he brings to the discussion of the nature and meaning of the sacred texts of his own tradition. While agreeing that philological discussions of the Avestan texts are essential in understanding the scriptures (6), he also maintains that there are interpretive issues that go beyond questions of philology (11). There are some scholars, Dastur Kotwal suggests, who have a skeptical or secular attitude built into their approach to Zoroastrian textual studies (49). His basic dispute is with those scholars who discount claims about normative truth, prophetic insight or spiritual meanings. They do not wish to entertain the possibility that the texts convey a perspective informed by insights rooted in realities beyond man's ordinary vision.

Dastur Kotwal asks: "Is there not a place in modern discussions about the Avesta for what the priest can bring to the study of these texts?" (50) A priest trained in the tradition brings a different attitude to the Avesta, a viewpoint which intuitively finds beauty and grace, meaning and power in these scriptures. Kotwal's concern is that this perspective is missing in the philological studies of these sacred books. In other words, modern studies too often miss what is the basis of the whole Zoroastrian tradition, that quality in the writings which elevates the human spirit and enables man to live on a higher plane of existence (22, 50, 53).

As for the reformist claim that ritual prescriptions and laws of purification do not appear in the *Gathas* and therefore should no longer be followed, Kotwal replies that this view not only rejects much of the Avesta as inauthentic but fails to understand the very nature of the *Gathas* themselves. The *Gathas*, he argues, are a collection of hymns; they are poetry, not prose. "You don't look for geometry in a poetry book. The *Gathas*, as hymns, have a different purpose . . ." from the other Avestan writings which deal with laws of purification (50). Dastur Kotwal believes that the reformists' dismissal of ritual stems less from scholarly linguistic arguments and more from a deeper questioning of the whole matter of the efficacy of religious ritual itself. Kotwal again feels he is confronting a basic secularized viewpoint which refuses to hear the tradition's age-old claims. His basic response is to assert counter-claims: he points out all the good that comes through ceremonial observances and reasserts the religious purpose of all Zoroastrian ritual, namely, the purification of the physical world resulting in blessings from the spiritual world (155). Kotwal has no need for the mystical and symbolic interpretations that Zoroastrian theosophists and occultists give to ritual because the rituals are efficacious in and of themselves (165-166). As for the divisive nature of calendrical arguments within his community, Dastur Kotwal makes a profound personal appeal, provided the integrity of the tradition is preserved, for all Zoroastrians to unite as a real community (158-159).

In these various ways Dastur Kotwal speaks to the issues that have been debated by Zoroastrians and Western scholars over the past two centuries. His commentary brings a contemporary orthodox perspective to Dastur Erachji's catechism which both illuminates specific matters in the text and brings counterclaims to bear on important issues which have challenged the orthodox community.

III. CONTEMPORARY ORTHODOX CONCERNS

Many contemporary Zoroastrians seem to have taken to heart the teaching that one's "first duty is to acquire knowledge" (107). Parsis have learned well a variety of business, professional and technical fields and are engaged in all types of vocations. Having thus successfully sought secular knowledge, the question is raised, should orthodox Zoroastrians also seek religious knowledge from other faith-traditions? Dastur Kotwal addresses this matter when discussing Dastur Erachji's attitude to other world religions. In the catechism Erachji suggests that the most desirable goal for all good people of the world is to believe in the Zoroastrian religion (25). Even at the time of Zoroaster, learned persons from other parts of the world (India and Greece) (32) realized the universal validity of Zoroaster's teachings. It follows then, for Erachji, that if a man is converted to another religion he has left the true faith (104), his name must be deleted from the ceremonies (96), and after a year his wife becomes eligible for remarriage (129).

Speaking from a different time than Erachji's, Kotwal is more aware of the dilemmas of Erachji's position on this question. On the one hand, it is axiomatic that the truth claims Zoroastrians make about the nature of God and the world are universal claims (25, 183). Likewise, the blessings brought to this world through their ceremonies are efficacious beyond the confines of the small community and have power positively to effect the entire world (183). On the other hand, Kotwal is also aware that other world religions have merit and through their own ceremonies have been vehicles of spiritual uplift and progress for countless peoples outside the Zoroastrian community. How then does one admit the truth and efficacy of other religions while maintaining the universal validity of one's own?

The way Kotwal resolves this problem is to distinguish between the truths taught by various religions and the ceremonial practices of those separate faiths. The truths proclaimed by Zoroaster are universal truths; goodness and benefit to mankind is a universal goal. In this sense he wishes the good Mazdaean religion to spread over the seven regions of the earth (183). But it is not necessary that Zoroastrian ceremonies should become universally practiced (183). Other religions have ceremonies of their own that bring benefit to men's souls (167). Therefore one can appreciate and have respect for other religions (123), but --and here is the important point--not at the expense of one's own religion. While respect is due other religions, one can worship only in one's own religious tradition (167). Zoroastrian ceremonies are a fundamental part of the very identity of the Zoroastrian community (25) and of the individuals that make it up. If a Parsi is to be pious, know righteousness (*Asha*) and be a disciplined individual he must live the faith of his birth and be a devout Zoroastrian (183).

That Parsis should totally embrace their faith, making it the foundation of their lives, is a deep conviction of both Dasturs. Persons born of Parsi parents will not only find life's fulfillment in their own faith but also keep alive the primeval faith of mankind (188) and of the ancient Iranian peoples themselves. Dastur Kotwal defines the contemporary Zoroastrian community that exists today as "the sum and substance of ancient Iran" (183). Contemporary reformists, who see the numbers of their co-religionists dwindling at an alarming rate (there are about 129,000 Zoroastrians in the world today)[15] argue vigorously that mixed marriages and conversion should not only be allowed but encouraged. The orthodox who are opposed argue that purity of lineage and tradition must be maintained. Dastur Kotwal asserts that as descendants of the Persian Zoroastrians who emigrated to India centuries ago, Parsis have the right and responsibility to preserve their heritage. In his words: "We are preserving a nation, and like every nation, we have the right to exist" (183).

This ethnic, national and religious identification of Zoroastrianism with the ancient Iranian peoples clarifies why lineage is of such paramount importance in Zoroastrian observances. Preserving one's lineage in the religious terms of this catechism specifically means dedicating ceremonies to one's ancestors by name, thereby nourishing their souls through offerings of consecrated foods and remembering the names and deeds of the great personalities of the Iranian nation. In the high liturgies performed daily in Zoroastrian fire temples, the names and deeds of the great saintly leaders of ancient Iran are always remembered and in this way remain historical examples for the living. Erachji's discussion of the personalities in the history of Iran (chapter 31) are not mere references for the sake of historical information but are the names of great figures who continue to serve as norms for conduct of pious Zoroastrians today. Kotwal also sees the continued preservation of the Iranian nation as a duty incumbent upon all Parsis.

These, then, are a few of the concerns contemporary Parsis have regarding their religious heritage. Their identity as a people and as a religious community is in great jeopardy; hence there is increasing need for scholar-Dasturs like Erachji and Kotwal to explain and interpret the faith. It is hoped that this translation and commentary will contribute to this goal.

James W. Boyd

NOTES TO INTRODUCTION

1. Rehbar-e Din-e Jarthushti (Bombay: Apakhtyar Press, A.Y. 1238).

2. The procedure for translating the text and writing the commentary was as follows. Dastur Kotwal orally translated Erachji's catechism to me. While doing so he frequently commented on the text, often in response to my questions. Typed notes of these conversations then served as the basis for further discussion and finalization of the translated text and commentary.

3. Page numbers in parenthesis refer to passages in the translation and commentary.

4. Cited in Gustav Davidson, A Dictionary of Angels (New York: Free Press, 1967), p. xv.

5. *Yazad* is a Pahlavi term for created spiritual beings worthy of worship and is used interchangeably with the modern Persian term *fireshte* by both Dasturs Erachji and Kotwal.

6. Sanskrit: *mantra*

7. The following discussion is deeply indebted to Dr. Mary Boyce's succinct presentation of Parsi history in her book Zoroastrians: Their Religious Beliefs and Practices (London: Routledge and Kegan Paul, 1979).

8. Ibid., p. 198.

9. Ibid., p. 196.

10. Cf. Ervard Rustamji Dinshahji Meherjirana's Forward to Erachji's Pursesh-Pasokh (Questions and Answers) (Bombay: H. T. Anklesaria, 1941), p. 21.

11. Ibid., p. 22.

12. Cf. Henry S. Olcott, Theosophy, Religion and Occult Science (London: George Redway, 1885) pp. 303, 314-315; and Boyce, p. 204.

13. Boyce, p. 224.

14. Copenhagen: The Royal Danish Academy of Sciences and Letters, 1969.

15. Figures from 1976. Cf. Boyce, p. 226.

TRANSLATORS' NOTE

The translators have endeavored to convey as accurately as possible the content and structure of Dastur Erachji's text. It follows a question and answer format, in the style of ninth century Pahlavi books. Dastur Kotwal's commentary on Erachji's text is printed in italic type. Words and phrases set off in brackets are editorial insertions. Verse numbers for Avestan references are also inserted in brackets. Specific chapters and passages of the Pahlavi, Persian and Gujarati materials are not provided, however, nor are words supplied with diacritics. In Dastur Erachji's text the Avestan references are cited in Avestan first, followed by a Gujarati translation. The present work translates the Gujarati. Spellings most familiar to the Zoroastrian community are used, and a glossary of special Zoroastrian terms defined according to contemporary orthodox understanding is included at the end of the Book. In addition, there are two appendices, the first describing the various texts Dastur Erachji refers to in the *Guide*, and the second explaining the Zoroastrian calendar.

The completion of this work was possible because of the generous assistance of many persons and institutions. Of special importance was a grant from the American Institute of Indian Studies which enabled the two translators to work together in Bombay, India, during the academic year 1975-76. Harvard University's Center for the Study of World Religions provided the translators with the opportunity during the academic year 1979-80 to complete the work. We are also thankful to our families for their underlying support of the whole project, and to all those who have given encouragement and guidance in the preparation of this work.

James W. Boyd
Colorado State University
Fort Collins, Colorado
U.S.A.

Firoze M. Kotwal
H.B. Wadia Atash Bahram
Bombay
India

TRANSLATION OF REHBAR-E DIN-E JARTHUSHTI

With a Modern Commentary
by Dastur Firoze M. Kotwal

PREFACE

With the help of Ahura Mazda

The holy Zoroastrian religion is a bounteous source of goodness. In it are found commandments of all sorts, and from each of these commandments flow great benefits. Those Zoroastrians who know all or many of these commandments and follow them in this world will go before the Holy Creator in the next world with a joyful face. The commandments will open the way to the enjoyment of eternal bliss.

The commandments of our religion are not known to all because they are written in a variety of books many of which are in different languages. For this reason many of us do not know exactly what is proper or improper in regard to our holy religion. Zoroastrians often go astray because of their ignorance and continue to do so for years and years without knowing their mistakes. That must stop. There must be a way to correct these mistakes. All Zoroastrians will agree that there is a great need for a book that contains a collection of the important religious teachings. In view of that need, it seemed both appropriate and my duty to write such a work. I have prepared it to the best of my ability. In its preparation and in the process of collecting quotations I have had to refer, in all, to 36 books in different languages, such as Avestan, Pahlavi, Persian, etc. The names of these books are listed below:

<u>Ardag Wiraz Namag</u>	<u>Dasatir</u>
<u>Bundahishn</u>	<u>Denkard</u>
<u>Burhan-e Qate</u>	<u>Farhang-e Jahangiri</u>
<u>Dabestan</u>	<u>Farziyat Nama-e Darab Pahlan</u>
<u>Dadestan i Denig</u>	<u>Gulshan-e Farhang</u>

Hadokht Nask
Khorda Avesta
Khwestab
Menog i Khrad
Mojezat-e Zartoshti
Nirangestan
Pahlavi Rivayat
Pand Namag i Adurbad
Pand Namag i Buzorg-Mihr
Persian Rivayats
Persian Vajarkard Dini
Qissa-e Sanjan
Qissa-e Zartoshtian-e Hindustan
Saddar Nasr
Saddar Nazm
Shahnama
Shamsu- 'l Lughat
Sharestan
Shkand Gumanig Wizar
Siruza
Vaetha Nask
Yasna
Vendidad
Vishtasp Yasht
Visperad
Zardusht Namag

The Avestan passages selected from these books have been rendered into Gujarati based on their Pahlavi translation. Some of them are translated verbatim; others are paraphrased. In addition, I have taken explanations from other books and stated them here in condensed form. I trust that this book will be very useful to Zoroastrians for I have prepared it with great labor. My reward will be if those Zoroastrians who read it will follow its advice. A few copies of this book have been financed by Sheth Bahramji Noshirwanji Seervai, Sheth Pestanji Hormasji Cama, Sheth Dosabhai Hormasji Cama and Sheth Sharshedji Rustamji Cama. With their assistance I have been able to publish this work. For that I would like to thank them here.

Erachji Dastur Sohrabji Meherjirana

CHAPTER ONE

The potency and power of God

Question: Who is the Creator of all things in both the spiritual and material worlds?

Answer: God Himself is Creator; no one except Him. Yasna 16[.1] states that Almighty Ohrmazd is "the worshipful one, giving goodness; the well-wisher and promoter of the world and creator of the good creation."

Q. Who cares for all and nourishes all?

A. God Himself. In the Ohrmazd Yasht [Yt.1.12] Ohrmazd says: "I am the protector, creator and nourisher."

Q. Where is God?

A. He is omnipresent; he sees everything and knows everything. In the Ohrmazd Yasht [Yt.1.12,8] Ohrmazd says: "I am far-seeing by name"; "My 17th name is all-seeing." Yasna 51[.22] states: "Ohrmazd is aware of what has happened and what is to happen."

Q. Since God is not visible to us, where is He?

A. He is the invisible among the invisibles. That is, there are some splendorous creations which we cannot see with our own eyes. In the same way God cannot be seen by the radiant creation. Yasna 4[.7] states: "Ohrmazd is glorious, shining, and unseen among the unseen."

Q. Since we cannot see God, how can we know Him?

A. We see and we know that the whole universe exists through Him and that He has created everything. Yasna 24[.3] states: "All creations are manifest as being created by Ohrmazd through righteousness."

Q. What is the shape of God?

A. He has no shape, face or form. Yasna 4[.3] states: "The creator Ohrmazd is full of radiance (raevato) and glory (khvarenanghato)."

Q. What is the meaning of the word khuda?

A. It is a Persian word for God, and it means self-created i.e., one who has no creator. The Avestan word is Ahura Mazda.

Q. What is the meaning of Ahura Mazda?

A. Omniscient, Master of Masters.

The Avestan Ahura literally means 'existing one'; Mazda means 'great knowing one, omniscient'.

Q. Was there anything before God?

A. No. We should have no doubt about that, because He was there always, existing forever and He will be forever. The Pazand prayer Nam Stayishn states: "Ohrmazd always was, always is, and always will be."

Q. How many names are there for Ormazd?

A. There is only one personal name: Ohrmazd. Other terms applied to Him in the Ohrmazd Yasht and other Avestan references and also the 101 names in Pazand are appellations, i.e., adjectives denoting characteristics or honorific terms.

Q. What is meant by 'honorific terms' applied to God?

A. Terms derived from His works and His qualities which indicate His omnipotence. For example, in the Ohrmazd Yasht [Yt.1.7] Ohrmazd says: "My second name is protector of cattle, third, omnipresent."

Q. When do we use terms denoting His qualities?

A. Priests remember the 101 names in Pazand when they perform the Yasna and Vendidad ceremonies. Every day and every night we must remember these names of God, for it is stated in the Ohrmazd Yasht [Yt.1.16]: "Recite my names day and night with a loud voice."

Q. What are the Avestan terms for the spiritual world and for this material world?

A. Mainyava, that which cannot be seen, and gaethya, that which can be seen or which is liable to death.

The Pahlavi terms are menog (spiritual) and getig (material).

CHAPTER TWO

Creation of the two worlds and the beneficent reigns of kings prior to Zoroaster and their miracles

Q. What did God create first in the creation of the spiritual world?

A. The Denkard, Book 7, states that He first created the angel Bahman [i.e., Wisdom].

A fundamental tenet in Zoroastrian theology is that there are two realms, this physical (getig) world and a spiritual (menog) world. The good spiritual realm is comprised of the holy reality of Ohrmazd, His Bountiful Immortals (amahraspands), one of which is Bahman, and other spiritual beings.

Q. What did God create first in this world?

A. First the sky, then water, the earth, vegetation, animals and man. Cf. Yasna 19[.2,4] and the Afrin i Gahambar.

Q. Who was the first man created in this world?

A. We cannot give a definite answer to this question. It is stated in the Denkard and the Bundahishn that Gayomard was the first man.

The reason for this qualified answer is that there are conflicting statements in the various Zoroastrian texts, some referring to Gayomard and others referring to Mashye and Mashyane. One type of resolution to this apparent conflict is to say that Gayomard was the first man and from his seed the parents of all mankind, Mashye and Mashyane, were brought forth. But there is a deeper issue here. Are we to treat these references as literal history or as mythical? Neither extreme is satisfactory. Such references to the first man or first human couple obviously cannot be historically verified, but our inability to verify them should not force us to dismiss such ancient references as 'invented' or 'imaginary'. Some kind of authentic truth is being preserved here: that man was created by God, that the first man was created mortal (Av. gayo-maretan, 'mortal life'), and that man's origins lie beyond the reach of literal, historical knowlege.

Q. Was there any man in this world before Gayomard?

A. The Persian books Dasatir, Sharestan, and the Dabestan state that there was prosperity in the world for thousands of years before Gayomard.

The Persian books here cited have less authority for orthodox Parsis than do such works as the Dadestan i Denig and the Denkard, which were written and compiled by learned dasturs in the ninth and tenth centuries A.C. The Dabestan is an anonymous mystical writing from the 17th century, and the Dasatir has been shown to be a mixture of Hindu, Buddhist and Platonic philosophies. The science of philology has helped us determine which texts are artificial ones and which are not, and it is my conviction that philology, when combined with a thorough knowledge of the Zoroastrian tradition, will help us understand better the greatness and richness of our religion. In fact, philology seems to have changed the whole fibre of traditional Zoroastrianism. Books like the Dabestan were looked upon by some with great respect during the last century and used as an indispensable guide to the Zoroastrian religion.

Q. When did the world begin?

A. From the three mentioned books and other historical texts we learn that we are not able to fix a time when the world began.

Q. What is the Avestan word for Gayomard and what is its meaning?

A. The Avestan word is gayehe-marethna (i.e., 'life-mortal'). The Persian term is gilshah: 'first king created from dust'. Cf. the Burhan-e Qate.

Q. What was Gayomard's religion?

A. The religion of Gayomard was more or less related to the Zoroastrian religion. Cf. the 8th Book of the Denkard.

There were many aspects of the religion of Gayomard that are more or less like the good religion as defined by Zoroaster. In the Frawardin Yasht (Yt. 13.87) it is said that Gayomard was the first man who listened to the voice of God.

Q. Before Zoroaster what religion did the kings of Iran follow?

A. They were believers in one God (yazdan parast) and they followed more or less the same religion as Zoroaster. The holy fravashis of them all are remembered in Yasht 13 and other Avestan prayers.

Although the Pahlavi term yazdan (spirit beings) is grammatically plural in this phrase, it is customarily translated by Parsis as 'God' as any reference to yazdan is always in the context of their being instruments or ministers of the one, true creator God who alone is worthy of worship. Fravashis are the spirit guardians of the souls of the living and the dead. They protect and guide us; remembrance is due them.

Q. In what language did the kings prior to Zoroaster say their prayers?

A. They said their prayers in the common man's language and also in the celestial language which they received from God. According to the Persian Rivayat of Kaus Kamdin some Avestan prayers did exist from the time of Gayomard.

Since Gayomard was fit to hear the voice of God, the holy language was known to man from the beginning.

Q. Who were the benefactors who flourished before Zoroaster?

A. According to the 3rd book of the Denkard, the Dasatir and Sharestan, the kings and prophets who flourished before Zoroaster were: Gayomard, Syamak, Hooshang, Tahmurasp, Jamshed, Faridoon, Minocheher, and Kay Khosraw.

Q. What miracles did they perform?

A. A summary, according to the Sharestan, is as follows:

Gayomard: He understood the language of all animals and could talk to them;

Syamak: In the presence of people he put this question to a stone: "Which is the best saying and which is the best command." The stone replied: "That which orders the worship of God is the best saying and the best command.

Hooshang: Once he went into the jungle and saw a serpent. He hurled a stone at it, but instead of hitting the serpent, the stone dashed against another stone, and produced fire. He brought the fire to the city and told the people to make it their qibla. The people asked, "What is your proof?" "Ask the fire", Hooshang replied. So the people asked the fire, "Are you worthy of the qibla?" The reply from the fire was: "I am the nur (light), a portion of the light emanated from the original light of God, so follow what Hooshang says."

A qibla is any light which people face when saying their prayers. For the story about Hooshang, see also Firdausi's Shahnama.

Tahmurasp: People wanted Tahmurasp to perform some miracles. So Tahmurasp lit a fire and took a man with him and passed through the fire. Neither of them was hurt.

Jamshed: People said to Jamshed: "You claim to be a prophet, so perform the miracle of preventing our death." Jamshed invoked God's help, and for some time in that period there was no pestilence and people lived a long, healthy life.

'Preventing death' refers here to premature death.

Faridoon: He knew all sorts of incantations (nirangs)

and with the aid of them he could change his form and appear as any type of animal he wished.

Faridoon was the first spiritual healer in the world and many incantations in the Pahlavi language are ***ascribed to him.***

Minocheher: A maid servant in his house was totally blind. He touched her eyes with his hands and made her see. He also cautioned King Nozar that his death would be at the hand of Afrasiyab, a Turanian king hostile to the Iranians. He also predicted the birth of Rustam and his bravery.

Kay Khosraw: He walked through the great ocean called Jehun [Oxus] without a ship, and because of his blessings, his mother **Ferangiz** and a warrior named Gev also were able to walk through it.

Q. What are the Avestan names for the prophets cited above?

A. The Avestan name for Gayomard is Gayehe-marethna; Syamak is Syamaka; Hooshang is Haoshyangha; Tahmurasp is Takhma-urupa; Jamshed is Yima; Faridoon is Thraetaona; Minocheher **is Manush-chithra**; Kay Khosraw is Kavi-husrava.

Q. What did the kings and prophets of Iran before Zoroaster use for qibla at prayer time?

A. It is stated in the Aban Yasht [Yt.5], the Dasatir, the Sharestan and Shahnama that they faced the sun, moon, stars, fire and water while in prayer.

The first four, the sun, moon, stars and fire, have nur or light, real reminders of the glory of God. Water is also an important qibla since water has a natural luster in the presence of the sun. Prayers are to be said before water only during the daylight hours (gahs).

Q. Why are we called the Parsis?

A. Originally our ancestors were living in a place called

Pars in the country of Iran. Originally also, the whole country was called Pars. Hence we are called Parsis. It is written in the Sharestan.

Q. Why did our ancestors come to India from Iran?

A. Our ancestors were ruling over Iran and our kingdom was conquered by Caliph Omar. Some of our ancestors, in order to preserve our religion, came here.

Q. Did our ancestors come to Iran after the downfall of the Iranian empire, or did they start before that?

A. Our ancestors saw the weak condition of our kingdom. Therefore, they decided to go to the mountains and take the religious books with them. Later they came to know of the Muslim conquest of Iran, and after some time, started for India. Cf. the Burhan-e Qate and **Shamsu- 'l** Lughat.

Q. Who was our last king?

A. Yazdegird Shahriyar.

Our Parsi calendar begins with the coronation date of Yazdegird Shahriyar, the last Sasanian king. This catechism, for example, was written by Erachji in 1238 A.Y. (Anno Yazdegird). The date of Yazdegird's coronation was 632 A.C.

CHAPTER THREE

Life of Zoroaster, his prophethood and miracles

Q. What is meant by prophet?

A. The Arabic word for prophet is payghambar; Pahlavi, paygambar; Persian wakhshur. The term means 'one who carries the message' and refers to one who brings a message from God for the people of the world.

Erachji takes payghambar to be an Arabic word, but it is Persian. The Arabic **is rasūl.** *The Persian word wakhshur is derived from the Pahlavi word wakhshwar which means 'one who carries the word (of God)'.*

Q. What is the name of our prophet and what does the term

mean?

A. Zoroaster. The name means 'divine light,' 'God's mercy,' 'truth speaker,' according to the Sharestan. *Erachji is speaking here of the religious significance of Zoroaster and not of the philological meaning of the word. In our rituals, Zoroaster is the only human being who has a dedicatory formula (khshnuman) spoken in his honor; all other dedications honor spirit beings (yazads), the Bountiful Immortals (amahraspands), or Ohrmazd. Hence the Avesta calls Zoroaster "the yazata (Phl. yazad) of the renowned name" (Yasna 3.21). Zoroaster is a yazad incarnate in that he brought a divine message to humanity. In this religious context, other meanings have also been given the term Zoroaster. For example, the Avestan Zarathushtra (Zoroaster) was understood to mean 'the golden star'.*

The actual philological meaning of the Av. Zarathushtra is still being debated among scholars. Probably the most accepted meanings are 'he who can manage camels' or 'one possessing yellow (golden) camels'. Many ancient Iranian names are compound words involving the names of animals. For example, in Avestan the word for 'horse' is aspa; Zoroaster's father's name was Paorushaspa; the patron king of Zoroaster was Vishtaspa.

Q. What is the Avestan word for 'prophet'?

A. Manthrano, which means 'one with the tongue of the manthras', i.e., one who has brought the Avesta.

Q. What are the names of Zoroaster's father and mother?

A. His father's name is Pourushasp , his mother's Dogdo. It is so written in the Denkard and the Zardusht Namag.

Q. Is there any reference to Zoroaster's father in the Avesta?

A. Yes. There is reference in the 19th chapter of the Vendidad and also other Avestan texts. Vendidad 19 [.6] states: "O Zoroaster, you are the son of Pourushasp ."

A. If his father's name was Pourushasp , why do we remember Zoroaster in our ceremonies by the name Spitama and not as Pourushasp ?

A. Because Spitama was an illustrious ancestor of Zoroaster, and the term also means 'very holy'.

Q. What are the names of Zoroaster's ancestors?

A. According to the Denkard [Book 7] they are:

Zarthosht	Hardar	Manushkhurnak
Pourushasp	Spitaman	Neryosang
Peterasp	Vaedisht	Varzidden
Urvatasp	Niyazem	Vizak
Hechatasp	Erach	Eryak
Chakhshnush	Durasrob	Izam
Peterasp	Manushcheher	Erach
Hardarashn	Manushkhurnar	Faridoon

Q. Who is the greatest prophet among all?

A. The greatest prophet is Wisdom (Khrad). Wisdom gives divine knowledge to the people of the world, acts as a mediator between God and the world and shows the right path. Another prophet is the one in the shape of a man. God has sent him to explain the religion to the people of the world. It is so stated in the Dasatir.

A prophet is always guided by the spiritual powers.

God sent Zoroaster to explain religion to the world.

Q. Why should we have a prophet in this world?

A. The people of the world are actively dependent on each other as they conduct the worldly duties of their lives. Hence they need some established canons which will prevent them from being cruel to each other. If certain rules are given by a prophet from God, and explained, then the people will have a proper fear of God and will act according to his commandments. It is so stated in the Dasatir.

People will obey God's rules, as they are the will of God and not just man's will.

Q. How can we know whether one is a genuine, honest prophet?

A. The prophet will know subjects which others do not know; he will be able to say what is on our minds; whatever we ask of him he will reply to in such a way as to satisfy us; he can work miracles which no other person can work. Cf. the Dasatir.

Q. Was there anyone who predicted the birth of Zoroaster long before it took place?

A. Yes, Jamshed, Faridoon, Minocheher, Kay Khosraw and many other sages predicted that Zoroaster would be born in the future. Cf. the 7th Book of Denkard; also the Dasatir and Sharestan.

Q. How was Zoroaster conceived?

A. The leaves of a good tree were eaten by a cow which was in the garden of Zoroaster's father (Pourushaspa). This produced milk in the cow. Pourushaspa drank that milk, his body produced semen from it, and from that semen Zoroaster was conceived. Cf. the 7th Book of the Denkard and the Sharestan.

The cow (gaw) is the embodiment of the good, beneficent animal creation of Ohrmazd, and the tree is a part of earth itself. Zoroaster is thus a natural product of God's good creation. One should also remember that each aspect of Ohrmazd's creation participates in the protective power of one of the seven Bountiful Immortals, the chief spiritual instruments of Ohrmazd's will. The cow manifests Good Mind (Vohuman); earth (trees), through its sustenance, invokes Immortality (Amurdad).

Q. Where was Zoroaster born?

A. He was born in the city of Ragha which in Pahlavi is called Ray. Cf. Yasna 19[.18].

Pahlavi commentaries say that Ray was a city in the area known today as Azerbaijan. Many contemporary scholars would argue, based on linguistic evidence, that north-eastern Iran is a more probable location. The Yasna passage alluded to mentions Zoroaster as being both the temporal and spiritual leader of Ray. If Zoroaster was born in Ray, then the Kayanian King Vishtasp, to whom Zoroaster preached, may have given the prophet rulership of that city.

Q. On what day was Zoroaster born?

A. Zoroaster was born on the day Khordad of the month Frawardin.

Q. Who was the governor of the city of Ray at the time?

A. Durasrun was governor. It is so stated in the Zardusht Namag.

Q. What was the religion and behavior of Durasrun?

A. He was a cheat and idol worshipper. He knew beforehand that Zoroaster would be born and would show the good path to people. He was very worried about that and contemplated destroying him as soon as he was born. Cf. the 7th Book of the Denkard.

Q. Who was the King of Iran at the time of Zoroaster's birth?

A. Lohrasp, son of Arwand.

Q. What dream did the mother of Zoroaster have?

A. When she was five months and 20 days pregnant she had a dream at night. There was a cloud around her house, and from that cloud some ferocious animals such as tigers and wolves came out. Then one tiger pierced the stomach of Dogdo, and took out Zoroaster. At the time she wanted to cry out, being afraid of them, but Zoroaster asked her not to and told her not to worry at all about him. Thereafter a burning mountain fell down from the sky in front of her house and a man came out of that mountain. In one hand he held a staff, in the other a book. He passed the book over the animals and they sped away. That man then returned Zoroaster to his mother's womb. Then Dogdo awoke, frightened. Early in the morning she went to a nearby soothsayer and told him the dream. The soothsayer told her to return in four days and he would explain its meaning. On the fourth day the soothsayer said: "The dream was very good. You have been pregnant now for five months and 23 days. You will give birth to a son whose name shall be Zoroaster. He will become a prophet and destroy evil in the world." Cf. the Zardusht Namag.

Q. What was Zoroaster's first miracle?

A. When he was born he laughed. There were other women seated there at the time. They heard it and saw it. Cf. the Denkard and Zardusht Namag.

Q. Why do you call a laugh a miracle?

A. All children cry when they are born. Here is the opposite case, and quite wonderful.

Q. What was the second miracle?

A. When Durasrun learned of Zoroaster's birth, he knew that Zoroaster would destroy evildoers. Durasrun went straight to Zoroaster's home in order to kill him. As he lifted the weapon, his hand became twisted and he could not kill him. Frustrated in his effort, he left. Cf. the Zardusht Namag.

Q. What was the third miracle?

A. Since Durasrun could not kill Zoraster he believed that anyone who tried to kill him would get his hand twisted. Therefore he thought of another plan. He ordered his men to collect lots of wood from the forest and to put sulphur and inflammable oil on it. Then he told them to throw Zoroaster in it so that he would burn in the fire. Because of this order some evil persons secretly took Zoroaster to the forest and put him on firewood. But by the grace of God, that fire could not be ignited and could not harm Zoroaster. Soon Zoroaster's mother came searching for him and took him away. Cf. the Denkard.

Q. What was the fourth miracle?

A. When Durasrun learned that Zoroaster could not be killed by this method either, he ordered that Zoroaster be taken from his home, laid on the ground in a narrow street through which herds of cows pass, and thus be crushed under their feet. The evil demons did as they were ordered. The cows approached. A very big cow came forward and stood over Zoroaster, surrounding him with her four legs, and allowed the other cows to pass by. After all the cows had passed by, she also went away. Zoroaster was saved and his mother came and took him home. Cf. the Denkard and Zardusht Namag.

Q. What was the fifth miracle?

A. When Durasrun learned that Zoroaster could not be killed in that way, he ordered him put in a lane where horses passed. (The same thing occurred as in the previous miracle.) Cf. the Denkard and Zardusht Namag.

Q. What was the sixth miracle?

A. When Durasrun learned that Zoroaster could not be killed that way, he became very angry and ordered his men to put Zoroaster in a den where ferocious wolves were living. He ordered them to kill the wolf cubs and place Zoroaster where the wolves could see both the dead cubs and Zoroaster. The men did as directed. The wolves returned, saw the dead cubs and rushed towards Zoroaster. But God was kind to Zoroaster. The wolves were unable to open their mouths and harm him. His mother came searching and took him home. Cf. the Denkard and Zardusht Namag.

Q. What was the seventh miracle?

A. When Zoraster was seven years old, two evildoers, Durasrun and Bradrosh, went to Zoroaster's house and showed him some terrible images, but did not succeed in harming Zoroaster's heart. They left ashamed. Cf. the Denkard and Zardusht Namag.

These evil-doers were idol worshippers, persons who practiced black magic with bones, skulls and the like. But Zoroaster was not harmed by them and he remained stout-hearted.

Q. What was the eighth miracle?

A. At one time in his childhood Zoroaster was a bit sick. The evil doer Bradrosh gave him poisonous medicine to drink, but Zoroaster easily recognized it and spilled it on the ground.

Q. What heated discussion did Zoroaster have with those

deceivers?

A. Once in his childhood Bradrosh and his accomplices were praising falsehood in the presence of Pourushasp in Zoroaster's home. Zoroaster put them to great shame by exposing their lies and threadbare arguments.

Q. What did Zoroaster do after he was 15 years old?

A. Day and night he conscientiously remembered God and was charitable and good to everyone. He continued in this manner until he attained the age of 30. Cf. the Denkard and Zardusht Namag.

Q. What did he do when he reached the age of 30?

A. He decided to go to Iran with his family. On the way he came upon a big river which he crossed with his family without having a ship, just as a man would walk on a bridge. Cf. the Zardusht Namag.

Zoroaster lived the first part of his life in Ray (south of Tehran) according to this account. Then he journeyed to Balkh (Bactria) in eastern Iran, to the court of Vishtasp, to preach his religion.

Q. What was the name of the river?

A. The river was called Veh Rud ['Good River']. Cf. the Zardusht Namag.

Q. On what day did Zoroaster reach Iran?

A. On the 30th day Aneran of the 12th month Asfandarmad he entered Iran. There was a big festival at that time, but as it was night Zoroaster could not take part.

Zoroastrian jashans or festivals are not held at night, as the powers of darkness and the demons of night are too prevalent.

Q. What dream did Zoroaster have in Iran?

A. In a dream he saw a big army rushing toward him from the north and blocking the road. Then another army came from the south and routed the army from the north. Cf. the Zardusht Namag.

Q. What is the meaning of that dream?

A. Zoroaster will come into the presence of God and proclaim the religion to the world and destroy evil in the world.

The southern army represents people of the good religion defeating the followers of evil.

Q. On what day did Zoroaster approach God and what was his age?

A. On the 15th day Day-pad-Mihr in the second month Ardibehesht he approached God. He was 30 years old. Cf. the Denkard Book 7 and Dadestan i Denig.

Q. How did Zoroaster enter into the presence of God?

A. On the day when he crossed the Veh Daiti river into Iran he stood on the other side and took a bath and prayed to God. While doing this the Bountiful Immortal Good Mind (Vohuman) approached him. This is stated in the Denkard Book 7, and the Zardusht Namag. Yasna 43[.7] says: "O Beneficent Ohrmazd. When I was remembering you, I received Vohuman."

Like most yazads, Vohuman is conceived as both a personified spiritual reality, in this instance the wisdom of God (Good Mind or Good Intention), and as an experienced quality of human life. Zoroaster received knowledge from God and was gifted with the power of the Good Mind (Vohuman).

Q. What did Vohuman do when he approached Zoroaster?

A. Approaching Zoroaster, he asked, "What boon do you wish?" Zoroaster replied: "I do not wish anything but to please God." Vohuman said: "Close your eyes for a brief time. I will take you near God." Zoroaster closed his eyes and when he opened them he had reached God. Cf. the 7th Book of the Denkard and the Zardusht Namag.

Q. Did Zoroaster desire to approach God?

A. Yes, he had wished, in the presence of the Good Mind, that he could approach God for spiritual conversation. It is recorded in Yasna 31[.12] that Zoroaster said he would go through Good Mind (Vohuman) for spiritual discussion and would reside there.

Zoroaster expressed his readiness to establish spiritual contact with God through Vohuman and make Good Mind his own for life.

Q. What was the first question Zoroaster asked God?

A. "Who is the best man among all the people in the world?"

Q. What reply did Zoroaster receive?

A. He who goes on the right path, who gives charity, who sees with both eyes in a just manner, who loves fire, water and animals, is the best man. Cf. the Zardusht Namag.

Q. What was the second question Zoroaster asked God?

A. "Whom do you approve of most, even more than the yazads?"

Q. What was God's reply?

A. "I approve of doing goodness and am displeased by those who do evil deeds. One who does good deeds has a very high position."

Q. What did God explain to Zoroaster?

A. God acquainted him with all mysteries and secrets of both worlds. In Yasna 45[.3] Zoroaster says: "Ohrmazd has given me inspiration, He has explained to me all secrets."

Secrets such as the purpose of creation, life after death, etc.

Q. Did Zoroaster see God?

A. Yes, he saw him with both his eyes. In Yasna 31[.8] Zoroaster says: "With both eyes I seized Thee (i.e., beheld Thee)."

For Zoroaster it was a total experience; the vision permeated the totality of his consciousness.

Q. Did Zoroaster hold discussions with God?

A. Yes. Various places in the Avesta refer to that; e.g., Yasna 12 [.5]. "In all questions and in all visits discussion was held between Ohrmazd and Zoroaster."

Q. Did God bestow wisdom upon Zoroaster?

A. Yes, he conferred on him innate wisdom. This is stated in Yasna 45[.6]. Zoroaster says to God: "You taught me very great wisdom."

The Pahlavi term for innate wisdom is asn khrad, 'inborn wisdom' or natural wisdom, that which nature bestows. The correlate to it is 'acquired wisdom' goshosrud khrad, 'ears-heard-wisdom.' Innate wisdom enabled Zoroaster to speak not only logically and clearly, but also convincingly; hence it was useful in his future prophetic career. All men are born with the potential of innate wisdom, but not all men cultivate or realize this potential.

Q. What did Zoroaster ask God about qibla?

A. "What direction should one face while saying prayers?"

Q. What reply was given to the above question?

A. God said that all things that shine are from His own shining splendor, and commanded that those things that have shining glory (nur) should be faced when one prays. In that way the prayer becomes more efficacious. Cf. the Zardusht Namag.

Q. Why did he not ask God for immortality?

A. Zoroaster wished to be immortal so that he could show the true path to people by living forever. But he was told that if he was made immortal then there would not be a day of resurrection. Cf. the 6th Book of the Denkard.

Zoroaster longed for immortality, but Ohrmazd told Zoroaster that he should die at the hand of his murderer who in turn would die because of the spiritual power of Zoroaster. But if Zoroaster were made immortal, his murderer Bradrosh would also be made immortal. Then there could be no resurrection and renovation, for evil would not be totally conquered.

Q. Then did he agree to die?

A. Yes, he did desire to leave this world and enter into the presence of God. In Yasna 28[.0] Zoroaster says: "Oh Ohrmazd, I shall certainly come near you."

A. Were there others present when Zoroaster was in the presence of God, and did they ask Zoroaster to do anything?

A. Yes, the six Bountiful Immortals (amahraspands) spoke on their own behalf to Zoroaster, asking him to explain to the people of the world that Good Mind (Vohuman) presides over cattle, Best Righteousness (Asha Vahishta) over fire, Desirable Kingdom (Khshathra Vairya) over metals, Bountiful Devotion (Spenta Armaiti) over earth, Health (Haurvatat) over the waters, Life (Ameretat) over plants and vegetation.

Q. Why did these fireshtes [spirit beings] say these things?

A. They said so because God has vested into the custody of fireshtes certain things of this world. These things are in their custody, and thus they said so.

Q. What proof is there that this religion was given to Zoroaster by God?

A. The Bahram Yasht [Yt. 14.52] states: "This religion pertains to Ahura and Zoroaster." This means that God has given this religion to Zoroaster.

Q. Why did Ahura send this religion to us?

A. God sent this religion to us so that we can follow the principles of the religion and walk on the right path. In Yasna 31[.11] it says: "O Ohrmazd, you first created religion [daena] in this world for us."

Q. On what day did Zoroaster receive the religion from God and what was his age at the time?

A. On the day Khordad of the month Frawardin Zoroaster received this religion. At that time he was 40.

Zoroaster held spiritual conference with Ohrmazd and received the revelation from Him over a 10 year period. The Pahlavi text The Selections of Zadspram (Wizidagiha i Zadspram) states that Zoroaster passed 10 years in conference with the seven Holy Immortals including Ohrmazd.

Q. When Zoroaster returned from God, did he experience any difficulty?

A. Yes. The evildoers wanted to harm him in any way possible. At that time Zoroaster said the Ahunwar prayer [yatha ahu vairyo] and the evildoers were unsuccessful and were warded off. Vendidad 19 [.1-2] states: "Angra Mainyu said: 'O druj, rush and kill

Zoroaster.'" The evildoers rushed toward Zoroaster with the intention of harming him. Thereupon Zoroaster said the Ahunwar prayer and because of that prayer, the evildoers who intended to inflict harm ran away from Zoroaster terrified.

The Ahunwar prayer, which begins with the Avestan phrase yatha ahu vairyo, is the most sacred, powerful and health-bestowing manthra in our tradition. It is the chief among the great prayers of Zoroastrianism.

Q. Is there any efficacy in the prayer yatha ahu vairyo?

A. Yes, it protects our body. In the Srosh Baj we say "Ahunwar protects our body".

A baj is a spoken Avestan formula (manthra) which precedes, accompanies or follows an action. By uttering the sacred formulas the act is encircled with the power of holy speech.

Q. After Zoroaster received the religion were the evil doers destroyed?

A. Yes, Zoroaster banished the evildoers from earth. Yasna 9[.15] states: "Oh Zoroaster, you made all evildoers hide underground."

Q. What did he (Zoroaster) bring from God?

A. He brought 21 Nasks of the Avesta, the fire named Adar Burzin ('exalted fire') and a cypress tree. Cf. the Sharestan and the Shahnama.

Q. Did God teach the Avesta to Zoroaster?

A. Yes, he explained the 21 Nasks to Zoroaster. Yasna 28[.7] quotes Zoroaster as saying: "Oh Ohrmazd, you have shown to Zoroaster your true words".

"True words" refer to the Avesta.

Q. Was the Avesta created by God?

A. Yes. Zoroaster himself says in Yasna 29[.7]: "Ohrmazd himself created the beneficent manthras through righteousness."

Q. Did Zoroaster agree to bring the Avesta?

A. Yes, he agreed before God. In Yasna 50[.7] Zoroaster says: "Oh Ohrmazd, I shall take with me the Avestan prayers."

Q. What benefit is there in Avestan prayers?

A. There are many benefits in reciting the manthras. Cf. the Srosh Yasht Hadokht [Yt. 11.3]: "The grand Avestan prayers keep away the sly evil-doer;" the Ardibehesht Yasht [Yt.3.5]: "The Avesta prayers are the most victorious;" and the Ohrmazd Yasht [Yt.1.3]: "They give us much courage."

Sly evildoers are those who practice secret, invisible black magic and seek evil revenge on other persons. The Avestan prayers are victorious in that they are like shields against evil.

Q. How can it be proven that Zoroaster brought a fire from that world?

A. In Yasna 31[.3] Ohrmazd says to Zoroaster: "You have been given fire from the spiritual world."

Q. Why did God give that fire to Zoroaster?

A. In order to prove his prophethood, for the miraculous aspect of this fire was that when one held it he would not be burned. Cf. the Sharestan.

Q. Was that fire miraculous in any other way?

A. Yes, it burned without fuel nor did any smoke come from it. Cf. the Shahnama.

Q. Why did God give the cypress tree to Zoroaster and in what way was it miraculous?

A. It was given so that Zoroaster could perform another miracle. When Zoroaster planted the tree, every leaf had written on it "Vishtasp, accept the Good Religion." Cf. the Shahnama.

Q. Who was the king of Iran when Zoroaster brought the religion?

A. Vishtasp was the king of Iran. His father's name was Lohrasp, his mother's Azadeh. His wife's name was Ketayun, and his sons were named Aspandyar and Peshotan. The time was the 30th year of Vishtasp's reign. Cf. the Persian Vajarkard Dini.

Erachji, later in the text (p. 33), takes the date of Zoroaster to be sixth century B.C., the Achaemenian period of Persian history. But we now know that Pahlavi writers and chroniclers of the Sasanian and post-Sasanian times erred in identifying the Achaemenian Vishtasp, the father of Darius the Great, with the Kayanian Vishtasp, the patron of Zoroaster. The oral tradition of the Parsis points to an ancient date for Zoroaster, some would say even anterior to the Rig Veda.

Q. Where did Zoroaster go first with his religion?

A. To the court of Vishtasp.

Q. Why did he go to the court of King Vishtasp first?

A. At the court of kings there were always many learned persons. If Zoroaster could first convince the learned persons at the court through miracles, the people of the world would automatically accept the religion. It was also the command of God that he should first ask Vishtasp to accept the religion. For that purpose God had given Zoroaster a book called the Vishtasp Nask. In that Nask the acceptance of the religion by Vishtasp as well as other matters was stated. At present we have eight chapters of that Nask preserved.

Q. Did Zoroaster want Vishtasp to accept his religion?

A. Yes. Zoroaster had wished before God that Vishtasp would become his disciple, i.e., accept his religion. In Yasna 28[.8] Zoroaster says: "O Ohrmazd, give me the discipleship of Vishtasp who desires perfect mindedness."

Q. Did God tell Zoroaster that Vishtasp would accept the religion?

A. Yes. In Yasna 46[.14] it says "Courageous Kay Vishtasp is himself a praiser of your religion."

Q. Did Zoroaster bring the religion only for those who lived in Iran?

A. It is stated in the 5th Book of the Denkard that God had sent this religion for all the people of the world. *The lofty teachings of Zoroaster are universal. His teachings will remain forever and are a benefit to the whole of humanity. Parsi and Irani Zoroastrians, however, are the only followers of Zoroaster who have continuously maintained the traditions taught by Zoroaster in the form of daily practices and ritual observances. Insofar as Zoroastrian practices are concerned, therefore, it is the Parsi and Irani people who possess the indigenous tradition. Hence, although everyone can advantageously follow the ethical principles, not everyone can become a part and parcel of this ethnic group.*

Q. How did Zoroaster approach the court of Vishtasp?

A. He took the 21 Nasks, the fire Adar Burzin and the cypress tree and placed these before the learned persons seated there, after first blessing Vishtasp and announcing "I am the prophet of God". Vishtasp had him seated with respect. Cf. the Zardusht Namag.

Q. In what language did he bless Vishtasp?

A. In the Avestan language. In Yasht 23[.1] it is stated: "Then Zoroaster spoke to the Kayanian Vishtasp: I bless you, O brave man, the lord of the country." *Formerly the Vishtasp Nask, known as Yasht 24, had 60 chapters, of which eight survive. A small Avestan text known as Afrin i Paygambar Zardusht ('Blessings of the prophet Zoroaster') is derived from this once extant Vishtasp Nask and is called Yasht 23.*

Q. Then what did he do at the court of Vishtasp?

A. He told him [Vishtasp] to accept the religion. He said: "If you, Vishtasp, will accept the religion, your sons will do the same." Cf. the Vishtasp Nask.

Q. Did Vishtasp accept the religion?

A. No, not immediately. In his court there were many learned people, so Vishtasp asked him to converse with them. Zoroaster did that for three days. He defeated them in debate. Observing this, Vishtasp was very happy and paid great respect to Zoroaster. Cf. the Zardusht Namag.

Q. What miracles did Zoroaster perform for Vishtasp?

A. Zoroaster recited the Avesta and said to Vishtasp: "I will show you miracles as you wish." Thus saying he handed Vishtasp that fire, and then he handed it to all those present at the court. No one was burned and everyone was astonished. On each leaf of the cypress tree was written: "Vishtasp, accept the religion." All wondered at it. Cf. the Sharestan.

Q. Did Jamasp also test Zoroaster?

A. Yes, when the fire did not burn anyone, Jamasp thought to himself: If he is a true prophet, molten bronze poured on his body should not hurt him. So thinking, he poured molten bronze on his [Zoroaster's] chest four times. Seeing it did not harm him, Jamasp was astonished and accepted his prophethood. Cf. the Sharestan. *Jamasp was Vishtasp's minister of state and a faithful follower of Zoroaster. He married Zoroaster's youngest daughter Porochist.*

Q. Why did Vishtasp send Zoroaster to prison?

A. Zoroaster had defeated all the learned persons at the court of Vishtasp in debate. They sought vengeance. One day they bribed the door-keeper at Zoroaster's home, entered his house and scattered hair, nails and other unclean things all around. Later they told Vishtasp that Zoroaster was a magician and asked him to go to his house and see. Vishtasp ordered an inquiry and was informed that such was the case. Vishtasp became angry and sent Zoroaster to prison. Cf. the Zardusht Namag.

Q. How was he released from prison?

A. Vishtasp owned a special horse named asp-e siyah ['black horse']. All four of his legs were folded under his stomach. The king had consulted many doctors, but none could cure the horse and the king was greatly grieved. Zoroaster learned about it, so he sent a message to the King saying he would cure the horse. The king summoned him. Cf. the Zardusht Namag.

Q. How did he cure the four legs of Vishtasp's horse?

A. Zoroaster asked Vishtasp to first promise four things. After that he would straighten the legs of the horse. Cf. the Zardusht Namag.

Q. What were the four things Vishtasp had to accept?

A. Zoroaster said: first, accept my religion in good faith after witnessing this miracle; second, let your son Aspandyar accept it and explain it to the people of the world so that they will accept it; third, let your wife Katayun [Hutos] accept the religion and explain it to other women; fourth, make an inquiry about the unclean things which were scattered in my house. These conditions Vishtasp, Aspandyar and Hutos accepted. They called for the keeper of the house, who told the truth and gave the names of the learned persons who had scattered those dirty things throughout the house. So the king punished them. Zoroaster then prayed to God and touched each of the horse's four legs and pulled them out from under his stomach. Seeing that, all [present] accepted the religion. Cf. the Zardusht Namag.

The name Katayun is given for Vishtasp's wife in the Shahnama. Her Avestan name is Hutaosa, Hutos being the Pahlavi form.

Q. Did Zoroaster cure some diseases?

A. Yes. Once the father of Vishtasp, named Lohrasp, and his brother named Zarir, became ill. They consulted many doctors but could not be cured. Through the blessings of Zoroaster their health was restored. Cf. the Sharestan.

Q. Is it true that we can obtain health through recitation of the Avesta?

A. Yes. Avestan prayers are health-giving. Vendidad 7 [.44] states: "O Zoroaster, there are many doctors.

Some give health through instruments, some through medicine, and some give health through recitation of manthras. Among these three the best and the greatest health is given by the reciter of the Avesta."

The reciter of the Avesta heals through the innermost power, the purity of the priests. A surgeon gives health through instruments.

Q. What wishes did Vishtasp ask Zoroaster to fulfill?

A. First Vishtasp asked if he could, in his own lifetime, see his future destiny in the next world. Secondly, he wished to live forever. Third, he sought to be invincible from any weapon that could inflict harm on his body. Fourth, he sought foreknowledge of events that were to occur. Cf. the Zardusht Namag.

Q. Was he granted all four wishes?

A. No. Zoroaster said he would grant one out of the four, since all four could not be given to one man. Thus he granted one wish to Vishtasp, another to his son Aspandyar, a third to Peshotan and the fourth to Jamasp.

Q. Who was Jamasp?

A. Jamasp belonged to the house or family of Hvogva and was Vishtasp's minister of state. Yasna 51[.18] mentions "That wise dastur Jamasp, the lover of glory (nur), the son of Hvogva."

Q. What did these persons receive from Zoroaster?

A. Vishtasp saw his destiny in the future world; Peshotan was made immortal; Aspandyar became bronze-bodied; Jamasp could foretell coming events. It is so stated in the Zardusht Namag.

Q. How did these persons obtain these four things?

A. One day Zoroaster consecrated dron. Beside that dron he placed wine, milk, flowers, and pomegranate. After consecrating them, he gave the wine to Vishtasp to drink. Vishtasp then fell asleep and his soul traveled to the other world and he saw his place in it. He gave the milk to Peshotan to drink, who thereby became immortal. He gave the flowers to Jamasp to smell, after which he **could** foretell future events. He gave the pomegranate to Aspandyar to eat, and his body became as hard as bronze. Cf. the Zardusht Namag and the Sharestan.

Dron is the name of sacred bread prepared from wheat flour.

Q. Is Peshotan alive?

A. It is written in the Zardusht Namag that he was given milk to drink; thus he is immortal. It is also stated in the Vishtasp Nask [Yt. 24.4], in which Zoroaster blessed Vishtasp, that Peshotan is immortal: "Be without disease and death like Peshotan."

Peshotan is one of the immortals, like Kay Khosraw, to whom the epithet ayaska amahrka 'without disease and death' is applied. Cf. Yasht 23.7.

Q. Where is Peshotan at present?

A. In the Bundahishn it is said that he is in a cave called kangdiz, but we do not know at present where that cave is.

Q. Could Jamasp foretell coming events?

A. Yes. Zoroaster had blessed him well and so his knowledge increased greatly. Vishtasp asked Jamasp about certain things of the future which he answered. Cf. the Pahlavi book Jamaspi. It is said in the Dasatir that Dastur Jamasp knew all the mysteries of the sky.

Jamasp was a great astronomer. Astronomy is a science associated with pious dasturs.

Q. Was the body of Aspandyar really of bronze?

A. No, but with the blessings of Zoroaster his body became so strong and stout that a weapon could not hurt him. Rustam, while fighting Aspandyar, threw a forked arrow into his eyes and killed him. Cf. the Sharestan and Shahnama.

Q. Our people in the prayer tan-dorosti remember the name of King Kay Khosraw. Does this mean he is still living?

The prayer tan-dorosti is a prayer of blessing said on behalf of another person or for oneself.

A. Kay Khosraw entrusted his sovereignty to Lohrasp and journeyed in the direction of a mountain-cave and disappeared there. In Yasht 23[.7], Zoroaster, while blessing Vishtasp, says in Avestan: "Be without disease and without death like King Kay Khosraw."

Q. Where is King Kay Khosraw at present?

A. According to the Avestan scriptures we can say he is alive, but we cannot say where. Again in the Pazand prayer Afrin i Ardafrawash spoken after the afrinagans, the name of Kay Khosraw is remembered with the souls of the departed kings of Iran. From this benediction it appears he is dead, but as the Avesta states otherwise, we must believe he is alive.

An afrinagan is a ceremony of blessings, solemnized in honor of any spirit being (yazad). The Afrin i Ardafrawash is a benediction of the holy spirits of all departed ones.

Q. Who appeared before Vishtasp to prove [the truth of the] religion?

A. One day when Vishtasp was seated on the throne and Zoroaster was beside him, the gatekeeper came and announced that four majestic horsemen stood at the gate. The moment he said this the horsemen appeared before the king and said, "We are four fireshtes; God has sent us to tell you that the religion of Zoroaster is genuine. Accept it." Having said this, they disappeared. Seeing their majesty, Vishtasp fell unconscious. Afterwards when he became conscious, he asked Zoroaster who they were. He replied: fireshtes. Cf. the Denkard and the Zardusht Namag.

Fireshte is a Persian word referring to a spiritual being, sometimes applied in a generic sense to all agents of Ohrmazd's will, but more often used to refer to those countless spiritual beings for whom the tradition has no specific name. The hierarchy of spiritual beings in the Zoroastrian view is generally as follows: Ohrmazd, the Bountiful Immortals (amahraspands), guardian spirits (fravashi), yazads and fireshtes. Man is next in the order. Sometimes man himself is called a fireshte in the sense that he is a very good man who possesses piety, righteousness and virtue. Hence it is said of ***him, 'Oh, he is a fireshte!'*** *It would be a contradiction in terms to say a fireshte is bad. The truth about man is that he can be both a daeva [demon] and a fireshte.*

Q. What are the names of these fireshtes?

A. Zoroaster said: Bahman, Ardibehesht, Adar Khordad and Adar Gushnasp.

The Pahlavi writings mention only 3 fireshtes; Adar Khordad is omitted.

Q. How can you prove they were fireshtes?

A. Concerning this, see the Vishtasp Nask [Yt.24.32] and the 7th Book of the Denkard where it tells of the fireshtes witnessing before Vishtasp: "Oh, Zoroaster, **the religion was shown to us in the world by amahras**pands."

Q. What happened after Vishtasp and his family accepted the religion?

A. Vishtasp ordered an Atash Bahram (fire temple) built in every city, each staffed with priests (mobeds). He ordered the Avestan **Nasks** to be written down and sent to every city. Aspandyar propagated the religion and within a short time there was a great increase in the study of Avesta in the country of Iran and many became well versed in it. Cf. the Sharestan and Dasatir.

Q. How many Atash Bahrams were there in Iran?

A. It is written in Mir Mukhtar-e Tehrani's Makhzanu-'l Akhbar that King Vishtasp had sent to every city, numbering 12,000, a book of the Avesta written in gold and silver ink, and in the whole country of Iran there were 24,000 Atash Bahrams. The greatest Atash Bahrams were in the regions of Azerbaijan and Pars. It is said that there were no Atash Bahrams equal to the greatness of the one in the region of Pars, with 3000 mobeds always ready to serve. Cf. the Sharestan.

Even today Parsis remember in their liturgies the names of the ancient Iranian fires. Though these fires are physically gone, the spiritual powers (yazads) which presided over each of these fires continue to exist; hence their names continue to be invoked. Although the Bountiful Immortal (amahraspand) Asha Vahishta (Best Righteousness) is the primary purveyor over fire, separate fires have separate spirits (yazads) presiding over them. They are considered ***instruments*** *of Asha Vahishta and convey man's prayers to God. All aspects of the bountiful creation of God thus have their yazad, and the many names of yazads in the Zoroastrian tradition reflect both the rich diversity of spiritual life and the intimacy of spirit and matter as conceived by Zoroastrians.*

Q. Did learned persons from other countries also enter into discussion with Zoroaster?

A. Yes. When Aspandyar proclaimed the religion throughout the world, a learned man named Tutianus came from Greece to converse with Zoroaster. When he saw the face of Zoroaster he exclaimed: "This man cannot be a speaker of falsehood." Then Zoroaster told him: "Think to yourself what you are going to ask me. I will give you a reply before you ask the question." Saying this, he replied to the question that Tutianus was thinking. Hearing the answer, he [Tutianus] marveled. In the same way, two learned men from India, Changraghach and Vyas, came for discussions. Before they asked their questions, a disciple of Zoroaster read from the Avesta answers to their questions. Hearing that, they were wonderstruck and accepted the religion. Cf. the Dasatir.

It has been argued well that later disciples of Zoroaster invented stories about learned men coming and consulting Zoroaster in order to enhance the personality of the prophet. Such specific episodes seem very doubtful, since they cannot be verified in the earliest Avestan and Pahlavi sources. This does not mean, however, that the basic point of these stories is false. These stories are a way of pointing to the fact that Zoroaster was a prophet possessed of divine power, that of the Good Mind (Vohuman).

Q. Where did Zoroaster keep the fire which he brought from God?

A. Vishtasp installed that fire on the mountain Raevand, which is also called Pusht-e Vishtaspan ['the support of Vishtasp']. Cf. the Great Bundahishn.

Q. Where did he plant the cypress tree which he had brought from God?

A. He planted it in the region of Kashmir. After 1450 years had past, a king named Mutavakkil [847-61 A.C.] of the Abbasid dynasty of Iran heard about the tree from the praises of many people -- that there was no tree like it and that there would be no tree like it ever again. It was far away, so he ordered that the tree be cut and brought to him. The people were full of sorrow and requested that he not cut it, for below the tree thousands of animals rested and thousands of birds nested there. They even offered the king money. But the king refused and out of sheer force ordered his men to cut it down. A considerable amount of money was spent to cut it, it was so big, and much was spent to transport it to the king. When it was only one mile away the king was murdered at night by his slaves. He did not ever see the tree. Cf. the Dabestan.

In Parsi history books it says the king was murdered by his son. The oral tradition that Zoroaster brought the cypress tree from paradise was first recorded in the works of the chroniclers of the thirteenth and fourteenth centuries. The tradition is that two cypress trees arose from shoots brought by Zoroaster from paradise. One stood at Kashmar, near Turshiz (in Iran), the other at Ferumad in Khorasan. The Caliph Mutavakkil ordered the former to be cut and carried to Samarra, north of Baghdad, to be used in the construction of ***the J'afariya palace.*** *Kashmar is to be distinguished from Kashmir, within the borders of India and Pakistan.*

Q. What children were born of Zoroaster?

A. Three sons and three daughters. The sons' names were Isadvastar, Urvatatnar, and Khurshedcheher. The daughters were Freni, Thriti and Porochist. Cf. the Bundahishn.

Q. **What** was his wife's name?

A. Havovi. It is written in the Bundahishn.

Q. **What** was the name of his maternal grandfather?

A. Frahmurwag.

Q. Who was the first to accept his religion?

A. His cousin **Medyomah.** Cf. the Frawardin Yasht [Yt.13.95] and the Bundahishn.

Q. During the time of Vishtasp, how many years did the Zoroastrian religion prosper?

A. For 57 years during the life of Vishtasp the religion spread to all countries. Cf. the Denkard.

Q. How long did Zoroaster live after receiving the religion?

A. For 35 years. Altogether he lived 75 years. Cf. the Dadestan i Denig.

Q. On what day did Zoroaster die?

A. **He died on** the day Khorshed of the month Day. Cf. the **Dadestan i Denig.**

According to the Pahlavi text 'Selections of Zadspram' (Wizidagiha i Zadspram) Zoroaster died on the day Khorshed of the month Ardibehesht (the second month of the year). But because the traditional Zoroastrian calendar is only 360 days and an intercalation of a month is required every so many years, the day of Zoroaster's death has shifted to the day Khorshed of the month Day (the tenth month).

Q. How did Zoroaster die?

A. Some time after the Zoroastrian religion was proclaimed throughout the world, Vishtasp went to Sistan as the guest of the warrior Zal. At that time Vishtasp's son Aspandyar was imprisoned in the Diz-e Gumbadan fortress. Seizing this opportunity, Arjasp, the king of Turkestan, attacked Iran and conquered it. Zoroaster and Vishtasp's father, Lohrasp, were praying in the Atash Bahram of Balkh. Both died there together with many priests (mobeds). Great damage was done to the Atash Bahram. The conquerors tried to burn the Avestan books, but no damage was done to them. When the news came to Vishtasp, he set out at once for Iran and asked his son Aspandyar to defeat Arjasp. Aspandyar did so. Cf. the Sharestan and Dabestan.

Aspandyar had been imprisoned by Vishtasp in the mountain fortress Diz-e Gumbadan in Khorasan so that he would not take the throne prematurely.

Q. At whose hands did Zoroaster's death occur?

A. Zoroaster died at the hands of one of Arjasp's warriors named Turbaratur. At the moment when he was slain, Zoroaster threw a miraculous string of prayer beads on Turbaratur, which kindled into fire and caused the death of Turbaratur. Cf. the Dadestan i Denig and Dabestan.

The Dadestan i Denig holds considerable authority for Parsis because it preserves some solid tradition; there is, however, elaboration and color added to the stories. The story of the miraculous rosary is only found in the Dabestan. That Zoroaster died at the hands of the Turanian Bradrosh (Tur Baratur), is borne out by other Pahlavi works like the Zadspram, Denkard and the Iranian Bundahishn.

CHAPTER FOUR

Miracles of Arda Viraf and Adarbad Mahraspand, two priests of ancient Iran

Q. Who was harmful to our religion after Arjasp?

A. The Macedonian Alexander attacked Iran and conquered it. At that time he did much damage to our books and our religion. Cf. the Denkard.

Q. Who revived our religion after Alexander?

A. Ardashir **Babagan.** At his command Arda Viraf performed a miracle and convinced the people. Cf. Ardag Wiraz Namag.

*Ardashir **Babagan** was the first Sasanian King. He came from Pars where faithful Zoroastrians lived.*

Q. What miracle did Arda Viraf perform?

A. When Ardashir **Babagan** came to power he assembled 40,000 priests. From those he selected 4,000, from them 400, and then 40. From this last group he selected seven persons who were extremely pious. Among these seven, Arda Viraf was selected, the most pious of all. The king asked him to perform a miracle so that people would put trust in the religion. Arda Viraf went to the Atash Bahram called Adar Khordad and drank from consecrated wine. Then for seven days he slept on a couch surrounded by the 40,000 priests who were saying prayers. Because of his piety and the help of the yazads Vohuman, Ardibehesht and Srosh, the soul of Arda Viraf was able to perceive the condition of the (other) world. He returned to this world on the eighth day and woke up. Everything he had seen in that world he related to all present. Seeing this miracle, all had faith in the religion. This whole matter is written in the Ardag Wiraz Namag.

Q. What is written in the Ardag Wiraz Namag?

A. It describes such matters as the places called heaven (wahisht), hell (dozakh), purgatory (hamistagan) in the world above, the places that are given to the doers of different actions, what happens in heaven and what punishments exist in hell.

Ardag Wiraz Namag is a 9th century text. It was frequently given to Parsi adults in former times to teach them to desist from sins and to discriminate between good and bad. In those devout and religious times high standards of morality were kept and crimes such as the Ardag Wiraz depicts were not committed.

Q. What is miraculous about the fact that Arda Viraf slept, woke up, and then spoke about the other world?

A. For a person to sleep for seven days without eating and drinking is quite impossible and is considered a miracle.

Q. Did any other person perform a miracle after Arda Viraf?

A. Yes. During the reign of Shapur Hormazd [240-270 A.C.], Adarbad Maraspand performed a miracle by order of the king. Several persons poured molten metal on his breast but he did not suffer the slightest injury. People were quite astonished and had faith in the religion. Cf. the Denkard, Book 3.

Q. From whom was Adarbad Mahraspand a descendent?

A. His father was of the family of Zoroaster and his mother from the family of Vishtasp.

CHAPTER FIVE

The foundations of the Zoroastrian religion and sudre-kusti

Q. What is the foundation of our religion?

A. One can think of our Zoroastrian religion as being like a solid tree. Like a solid tree trunk our religion is strong. It has two large branches, three small branches, four main roots [Gujarati jad: 'far reaching.'] and five other roots. Cf. the Shkand Gumanig Wizar. Yasna 19[.16] states: "Ohrmazd has said that there are three measures [Pahlavi payman: 'golden means, moderations.'], four professions and five leaders."

Q. What is meant by the trunk of the tree?

A. The commandments of religion, the laws, and faith serve as the trunk of the religion. Thus we must lead our lives according to religious tenets. Cf. the Shkand Gumanig Wizar.

The difference between 'commandments' and 'laws' is that commandments are specific and moral in nature, such as 'do not lie or steal,' but laws are broader in scope and can be of many different types, such as laws of moderation or purification. 'Faith' refers to astwanih i den, which means 'steadfastness in religion.' 'Religion' (den) has to do with God and man's relation to the divine. Religion elevates man's soul. It enables him to live on a higher plane, to spread righteousness, to believe that there are many invisible forces that protect us, that the world is not only what we see with the naked eye, but also includes what is beyond our ordinary reach. Religion gives man consolation and courage, a consolation and courage that logic and arguments cannot give.

Q. What is meant by the two large branches of the tree?

A. To ever strive to do good deeds and to keep away from bad deeds are the two main branches of the tree (i.e. the religion). We should act accordingly. Cf. the Shkand Gumanig Wizar.

Q. What is meant by the three small branches of the tree?

A. To think the good, speak the good, and do the good. Cf. the Shkand Gumanig Wizar. Yasna 19[.16] states: What are the 'measures' [golden means]? To think, speak, and act well.

Q. What are the four main roots of the tree?

A. From ancient times in our Zoroastrian community, four separate estates have been distinguished: Athravan (the priests who serve and preserve the fire); Rathaeshtar (warriors, i.e. kings and heroes); Vastryosh (agriculturalists); Hutokhsh (traders and craftsmen). Those in the four estates should conduct themselves according to their own profession so that they do not damage the other professions. If they act accordingly then they do well according to their profession. Cf. the Shkand Gumanig Wizar and Yasna 19[.17], **the Denkard and Dabestan.** *A metaphor often used to illustrate the hierarchy of* *these different estates is that of a man. The priests are the head, representing intelligence; the warriors the upper torso and arms, representing physical strength; and agriculturalists, the middle stomach portion, providing food and nourishment; the traders and craftsmen, the legs, being those who journey and sell goods. Nowadays, however, Parsis do not think in terms of these four distinctions, but only of two, the priests and laity.*

Q. What are the five (other) roots of that tree?

A. The master of the house, the master of the street, master of the village, master of the country, and the prophet or his successors. These are the five roots of the religion. They have the privilege of guiding the people according to their status, thus providing strength and assistance just like the roots of a tree. Cf. the Shkand Gumanig Wizar and Yasna 19 [.18]: "Who are the leaders? The master of the house, of the street, of the village, of the country, and fifthly Zoroaster."

The master of the house is the one who has authority over the household, usually the oldest male member of the family. In former times they were joint families. The successors of Zoroaster are dasturs and the faithful. All pious Zoroastrians are successors of the prophet in that respect.

Q. What is the symbol of our religion?

A. Sudre and kusti, and by these symbols we are known as Zoroastrians.

The sudre is a sacred shirt of cotton, the kusti a sacred cord of fine lambs wool which is wound three times around the waist and tied with four knots. Every person receives his or her sudre-kusti, usually at the age of seven, when one becomes religiously and morally responsible for one's own deeds.

Q. Who commanded that sudre and kusti be worn?

A. Some say that Zoroaster initiated them, but according

to the Dadestan i Denig, the Saddar Nasr and Saddar Nazm, these symbols have been worn since the time of King Jamshed.

The sudre and kusti are the foundation of our religion. If one believes in God, and the Avesta as the word of God, but does not wear sudre and kusti, he is not a Zoroastrian. To lead a life of a true Zoroastrian, one must have sudre and kusti; without it, one's religious life ends. You cannot say prayers without sudre and kusti. If prayer is said without them, it is a sin. Even to loiter about without sudre and kusti is a sin. In every act of worship, the kusti prayer is the foundation. If one desires to pray, he must first do kusti if he wants to pray seriously, for by untying the kusti and then tying it, one is able to come fresh to the act. By tying and untying kusti you are beginning something which is divine, something elevated, and whatever you have done before, the kusti prayer (tying and untying) wipes out. It is a baj, a sacred act, the power of which safeguards the prayers which follow it.

Q. What is the Avestan name for kusti?

A. In Avestan kusti is called aiwyaonghana. The same word is also used for the date leaf which the priests use in their rituals in the fire temples.

This is referred to in Yasna, 9[.26].

Kusti means 'girdle' in Middle Persian. The date leaf used in the ceremonies is woven, like the kusti, and tied around the barsom, a bundle of consecrated twigs or metal rods.

Q. By what other names is the sudre known?

A. In Pahlavi it is called shabig, in Persian shib, nimak, namak, and payrahan. It is so stated in the Persian Rivayat of Nariman Hooshang and Kama Vohra.

Q. What is the meaning of the word sudre?

A. It means "beneficent path." We put on sudre in order to tread on the good path of the beneficent religion; the sudre is the symbol of that path. Cf. the Mojezat-e

Zartoshti.

Q. How can you recognize the sudre (i.e. the 'beneficent path')?

A. It can be recognized by the giriban.

Q. What is the meaning of giriban?

A. It means "trust" or "signs of trustworthiness." We are honest persons so we keep the sudre always as a symbol of honesty. Cf. the Mojezat-e Zartoshti.

The giriban is a pocket on the front neck portion of the sudre. A Zoroastrian should fill it with good deeds. In Persian it is called kissa-e kerfa, 'a bag of good deeds'.

Q. What is kusti and what does it mean?

A. Kusti is a belt for doing prayer and showing obedience to the religion. This means that those who put on the kusti are always prepared to pray and to remember God. Just as a man ties his belt in preparation for doing some work, so in order to pray, we always tie the kusti around our waist. By always having our waist tied with the kusti we are always, in every breath, remembering God. Cf. the Saddar Nazm.

Q. Of what material should the kusti be made?

A. It can be made of sheep's wool or camel's white hair. It should not be made of anything other than these. Cf. the Nirangestan.

Q. By whose hands should it be woven?

A. It should be woven by a priest or his wife. Cf. the Persian Rivayat of Kaus Kamdin.

That is, any woman of the priestly class can weave a kusti. Nowadays women of the lay class also weave kusti.

Q. How many threads are there in the kusti?

A. In all seventy-two threads.

Q. What is the reason for seventy-two threads?

A. It is equivalent to the text of the Yasna, which has seventy-two chapters. Whatever person of our good religion ties the kusti with piety, that person is said to have acquired the merit of performing the Yasna ritual. In the Ohrmazd Yasht, also, seventy-two names of God are written; it is also equivalent to that. Cf. the Mojezat-e Zartoshti.

Q. While weaving the kusti, the weaver makes six groups of twelve threads each. Why is this done?

A. In Pahlavi duwazdah means 12. There is one religious book called Duwazdah Homast, and there is the duwazdah homast ritual performed in honor of 12 yazads. He who puts on the kusti shares in the good merits of a performance of the Duwazdah Homast. Cf. the Mojezat-e Zartoshti.

Q. While weaving the kusti, the weaver divides 72 threads into six groups. What is the reason for this?

A. It relates to the fact that in the world there are six directions. One who puts on the kusti has the merit of the good deeds of all kusti wearers who exist in all six directions. Cf. the Gulshan-e Farhang.

The six directions are: north, south, east, west, up and down. All these explanations about kusti are rationalizations to ascribe some specific meaning to the way the kusti is made. Such thoughts or interpretations are not in the mind of the pious kusti wearer. The value of such explanations is that a modern Zoroastrian may think twice before discarding the kusti.

Q. Why are there six strands at the end of the kusti?

A. This relates to and is proof of the six gahambars [seasonal festivals] of the year. The wearer has the merit of associating himself with the good actions of the six gahambars. Cf. the Mojezat-e Zartoshti.

Q. Why does the kusti have two ends?

A. This is symbolic of and proof of the existence of the two worlds, this and the other. The wearer should have in mind, constantly, the thought of the next world of eternity.

All instructions of this nature must be taught to the Zoroastrian youth in their homes. What is taught in the home is of utmost importance.

Q. Why does the kusti have two layers, with the middle hollow?

A. The two layers of the kusti represent the sky and the earth. The hollow part in the middle is symbolic of the atmosphere between them. The meaning is that the wearer should always please all clean and pure things which exist between the sky and earth. It is so stated in the Mojezat-e Zartoshti.

Q. After weaving the kusti, it is turned inside out. Why?

A. We have come to this world for [the sake of] the other world, and we have to go back to the other. The wearer should always remember that we have come into this world from the other, and we have to give answers in the next world for our deeds in this one. Cf. the Gulshan-e Farhang.

Q. We hold the kusti in the middle and we tie it around our waist. What is the reason?

A. We wearers of the kusti are those who walk on the middle path in all worldly and religious thoughts, words and deeds. By putting the kusti around our waist, we gain benefit to our souls and protection to our body. Cf. the Nirangestan.

The middle path is the path of moderation.

Q. Why do we tie the three strands around the waist?

A. The three strands are a sign and proof of good thoughts, words and deeds. That is, we who tie the kusti should always be thinking well, speaking well, and doing well, and remain steadfast in this. Cf. the Mojezat-e Zartoshti.

Q. What should we remember while tying the three strands around our waist?

A. While tying the first strand we must think good thoughts, the second, good words, the third, good deeds.

That is, be intent on thinking good thoughts (not just thinking one good thought) each moment of every day.

Q. We tie the kusti with four knots. Why?

A. God has created the human body from four things: fire,

water, wind, and earth. The body of man is emblematic of these four things, and the wearers of the kusti must preserve all four of these elements. One who puts on the kusti has the merit of pleasing these four elements. Cf. the Mojezat-e Zartoshti.

The kusti is tied with two square knots. One square knot--which we count as two knots--is tied in front and one in back. First the middle of the kusti is placed across the front part of the waist, wound around the body once and then tied with a square knot in front. Then it is wound to the back of the waist and tied again with a square knot.

Q. What should we be thinking while tying the four knots of the kusti?

A. While tying the first knot we should think: God is one and He is the Creator of all good things which are his creation. While tying the second knot, think: Zoroastrianism is the true religion. While tying the third knot, think: Zoroaster is the real prophet sent by God. While tying the fourth knot, think: As far as it is possible I will do good deeds and only good deeds in this world. Cf. the Saddar Nasr.

Many pious Zoroastrians, when they tie the kusti, contemplate only the perfection of God.

Q. Can we put on the kusti without wearing the sudre?

A. We cannot put the kusti on the naked body. If we so do and tie it, we commit a sin. Cf. the Nirangestan.

Q. What direction should we face while tying the kusti?

A. In the morning while the sun is rising, face him [the sun]. At night, face fire, and if there is no fire, face the moon. If there is no moon, then face South. It is so stated in the Rivayat of Kamdin Shapur.

That is, face east up to 12 noon; face west in the afternoon. The moon itself is a nighttime qibla; it is a reflection of sunlight. South is called the mansion of Ohrmazd; the Zoroastrian is thus mentally facing the qibla of God's place. When there is no appropriate visible qibla, the invisible is the best. Young boys training for the priesthood are taught to face the wall, close enough that no one can walk in front of them and divert their concentration. At night, if some shining light is available, such as the stars, this is also good.

Q. When one is doing kusti, people do not cross in front of him. Why?

A. Whenever a person is doing kusti before a qibla it is not proper to walk between him and the qibla. If we walk three paces away from one who does the kusti, then it is proper, but never within three paces. Cf. the Persian Rivayat of Kamdin Shapur.

Kustis vary in length depending upon the size of the person. As noted above, the kusti should not be tied touching the skin, for a sudre must be worn under it. Also, there should be nothing between the kusti and the sudre. Garments must be worn over and outside the kusti. When the sudre-kusti is taken off, to be replaced with a clean sudre after a bath, it must be taken off ceremoniously with baj. The baj itself protects the person during the bath.

CHAPTER SIX

The twenty-one Nasks of Zoroaster

Q. Zoroaster brought 21 Nasks. What are their names in Avestan and Pahlavi and how many chapters does each Nask have?

A. According to the Persian Rivayat of Bahman Punjia, the Avestan and Pahlavi names of the 21 Nasks with their respective chapters are as follows:

	Avestan	Pahlavi	No. of Chapters
1.	yatha	studgar [sudgar]	22
2.	ahu	wahishta-mansr [warsht-mansr]	22
3.	vairyo	bag	21
4.	atha	damdad	32

5.	ratush	nadur [nadar]	35
6.	ashat	pazun [pazag]	22
7.	chit	ratushtayid [ratushtaiti]	50
8.	hacha	barish	60
9.	vangheush	kishsrub [kishkisrub]	60
10.	dazda	gushtaspad [wishtasp-sast]	60
11.	manangho	dad [washtag]	22
12.	shyaothnanam	chidrasht [chihrdad]	22
13.	angheush	spenta [spand]	60
14.	mazdai	bayan-yasht [bagan-yasn]	17
15.	khshathremcha	niyadam [nigadum]	54
16.	ahurai	dusrujid [duwasrud]	65
17.	a	husparam [husparum]	64
18.	yim	sakadam [sagadum]	52
19.	dregubyo	jud-dew-dad	22
20.	dadat	hadokht	30
21.	vastarem	yasht [stud-yasn]	33

The variant Pahlavi spellings inserted above are from the Denkard. The order of the 21 Nasks in both the Bahman Punjia and the Denkard is the same although in other Rivayats the order varies a little.

Q. What is the subject matter of these 21 volumes?

A. Descriptions of creation, both of this world and the next; descriptions concerning the praises of God and yazads, the knowledge of God, righteousness, prayer, and good works; details about the life of Zoroaster, his miracles; explanations about the tenets of the religion, astronomy, medicine; description of King Vishtasp and his kingship, and the arts and crafts of the world, etc. Cf. the Persian Vajarkard Dini.

The Vajarkard Dini has a summary of the Nasks. However, the Denkard would be the most authoritative and detailed summary of all 21 Nasks. The compiler of the Denkard had 19 of the 21 Nasks at his disposal, for he describes 19 of them in detail. We know his account is very trustworthy because his summary of the Vendidad, which is the only Nask we have in its entirety, is very precise. We have only fragments of all other Nasks; the Yasna and Yashts are taken from lost Nasks. Also the Persian Vajarkard Dini which Erachji uses as his reference should not be confused with the Pahlavi Wizirkard i Denig, composed by Dastur Edalji Dorabji Sanjana in the 19th century A.C. This last-mentioned Pahlavi text is of a doubtful nature; it was composed by the author to suit his own purposes. The doctrinal innovations which the author perpetrated during his dasturship determine the text, which is styled as being composed by Zoroaster's first disciple Medyomah. There was a great furor in the Parsi community when it was first published in 1848 A.C. by the trustees of the Sir J.J. Translation Fund. Subsequently, the trustees had to stop its distribution by keeping all copies in their custody.

Q. How were our religious books destroyed?

A. First King Arjasp sought to destroy all the Nasks. He attacked Iran and destroyed everything. At that time he threw all the books in the fire, but they did not burn and no damage could be done to the Nasks. King Vishtasp returned to Iran and he protected the religion. Cf. the Sharestan.

Q. How and when did our scriptures become scattered and lost?

A. The Nasks were safe up to the time of the last king of the Parthian dynasty, Darius. At that time Alexander attacked Iran and defeated it, destroying some volumes. Thereafter a great search was made and the volumes known by the dasturs were committed to writing. Later, in the time of Ardashir Babagan, founder of the Sasanian dynasty, Dastur Tosar [Tansar] was asked by the king to copy all the remaining books and send various copies to different cities of Iran. It is stated in the Denkard. The Persian Vajarkard Dini states that after Alexander a few chapters of four Nasks existed. Out of 50 chapters of Ratushtaiti (no. 7) 13 could be recovered; out of 60 chapters of Barish (No. 8) 12 could be recovered;

out of 60 chapters of Wishtasp-Sast (No. 10) eight could be recovered. Again, the Dabestan states that on the authority of Mobed Azar Khordad the Dasturs of Kerman have preserved 14 Nasks in their entirety, and seven others are lying incomplete with them.

The Darius Erachji refers to is Darius Codomanus (336-330 B.C.), known as Darius III, the last Achaemenian king (not a Parthian king). Firdausi and other Muslim writers have confused the history of the Kayanian and Achaemenian kings because of the lack of reliable sources in their time. Erachji further confounds history by making Darius a Parthian king although we know that the Parthian dynasty has no king of that name.

According to the summary account of the Nasks given in Denkard 8 and 9, 20 of the 21 Avestan Nasks and 19 of their Pahlavi translations were in existence as late as the ninth century A.C., when the Denkard was compiled. The description of the post-Alexandrian Avestan literature as given in the Persian Vajarkard Dini has as its source the Persian Rivayats. The Dabestan's observation that the Dasturs of Kerman are preserving 'lost' Nasks seems probable when we think about the Iranian Dasturs' secrecy in preserving manuscripts. Such secrecy, however, has also resulted in the destruction of many manuscripts through the carelessness of descendants who have not recognized their value.

Q. What is left of the Avestan Nasks at present?

A. Twenty-two chapters of the Vendidad, 72 chapters of the Yasna, 23 chapters of the Visperad, eight chapters of the Vishtasp Nask, three chapters of the Hadokht Nask; some fragments of Aogemadaecha; some fragments beginning with Vaetha; and the Khorda Avesta, i.e. the Niyayeshes and Yashts.

The Vendidad exists in its entirety; the Yasna is not a Nask, but a composition from various lost Nasks; the Visperad, like the Yasna, is not a Nask. The 23 chapters of the Visperad are surrounded by the 72 chapters of the Yasna, with some additions, repetitions, alterations and omissions. In manuscript F93 [Erachji's final draft of this catechism, now in the First Dastur Meherjirana Library] Erachji does not mention Vaetha; perhaps he doubted its authenticity. The Vaetha is not an original Nask. Its style of writing and diction indicate its late origin, and it contains heretical and un-Zoroastrian statements. For example, it says that a son born of a non-Zoroastrian mistress has the right of inheritance. Like the Pahlavi Wizirkard i Denig, it appears to have been written for personal motives.

CHAPTER SEVEN
The Avesta

Q. Why is the Avesta known by the words Gatha and manthra?

A. Gatha is created from the Ahunwar; manthra is different from the Gathas. Cf. the Denkard.

That is, the Gathic language is of the same meter and dialect as the Ahunwar. All the remaining Avesta which differs from this meter and dialect Erachji calls manthra. Not all Zoroastrians would agree with the distinction Erachji is making here. The distinction between Gathic dialect and manthra meter does not mean that the Gathas are not manthra, i.e., "glorious, powerful and health-giving" sacred sounds (cf. Yasht 1.1-3;2.6). The Gathas are manthras of the greatest efficacy. An old High Priest said once: To understand the meaning of the Gathas is like trying to measure the great pyramids with a foot ruler. The Denkard, Book 3, asserts that the manthras are created through the omniscience and power (harwisp-agahih ud kerog) of Ohrmazd.

The stress some scholars have placed on the Gathas as being the only true words of Zoroaster, the remainder of the Avesta not being considered so, is certainly open to question. There is a skepticism in this view which runs directly counter to the claims of our Pahlavi tradition where the whole of the Avesta is considered the authentic tradition derived from Zoroaster or from his early disciples. The Ardag Wiraz Namag (1.2), e.g., maintains that "for 300 years the religion was in purity and men were free from doubt." There is no conclusive evidence to cause us to doubt the integrity of the early tradition. On the contrary, evidence in the Denkard clearly states that holy manthras were composed by later disciples of Zoroaster. Sen Ahum-Stud, for example, was born in the 100th year of the religion, lived for 100 years, and composed holy manthras. A further point needs to be made. The Gathas and all Avestan manthra must not only be studied and understood from the point of view of philology; the Avesta must also be appreciated and understood for what it is to one who accepts and recites it as holy manthra. I ask: Is there not a place in modern discussions about the Avesta for what the priest can bring to the study of these texts? We seek to unravel the spiritual beauty of these scriptures, and we know, through experience, the quality of spiritual uplift they bring to our lives.

Some 'reformers' of Zoroastrianism have argued that because there is no mention in the Gathas of various religious practices we follow, such as certain laws of purification or exposure of the dead in dakhmas (places of exposure), these practices should no longer be followed because Zoroaster never instituted them. But such an argument again fails to understand the nature of the Gathas. You don't look for geometry in a poetry book. The Gathas, as hymns, have a different purpose. If one is looking for a description of the laws of purification or exposure, he should look in the Vendidad. They are all there.

Q. Is it compulsory to say the Avesta?

A. Yes, it should be recited every day. Yasna 50[.6] states: "O Ohrmazd, whoever recites the manthras becomes a friend of Zoraster."

During each of the five watches of the day there is an

appropriate prayer which should be said, according to Zoroaster.

Q. What is the injunction about not casting doubt on the religion and its Avesta?

A. We must be steadfast in our religion and we must recite the Avesta. As Zoroaster says in Yasna 13[.8]: "We praise the recitation of the Avesta which gives strength to the Zoroastrian religion."

Q. In what manner should the Avesta be said?

A. The Avesta should be said without idleness, and while reciting it one should not speak anything else. In Yasna 19[.5] it is said: "O Zartosht, we must say the Ahunwar prayer (i.e. the Avestan manthra) without negligence or interruption."

Q. If we forget the Avesta, then what?

A. A person who has learned the Avesta and then forgets even a small portion of it keeps his soul away from the best existence. Yasna 19[.7] states: "O Zoroaster, if anybody forgets the Avesta, I, Ohrmazd, will keep his soul away from heaven."

This injunction is intended for priests whose duty it is to learn by heart various volumes of the Avesta. In the time of Erachji it was necessary to know all of it. Because a priest performed rituals daily it was not difficult for him to remember it all. But there are different kinds of priests nowadays. Formerly, though one priest may have been more enlightened than others, all priests performed ceremonies. Now there are High Priests who are not seasoned in ritual performance and cannot give sound instruction in the intricacies and subtleties of the rituals. Today there has been a shift in emphasis from ritual to academic credentials. Trustees, for example, when seeking a priest for a fire temple, will first ask: Does he have a degree? Does he speak English well? They do not ask: Has he done rituals? They ask his views on religion. There is evidence that in former times this was not the case.

Q. What are the benefits for one who recites the Avesta?

A. Ohrmazd grants him paradise in the next world. Cf. the Vishtasp Nask [Yt.24.39]: "He who recites the entire collection of hymns reaches the highest heaven."
This means one should say prayers with a pure heart followed by good actions in daily life.

CHAPTER EIGHT
Concerning prayer

Q. What is meant by doing bandagi (prayer)?

A. We human beings are mortal. In order to show our servitude and humility before God, in order to plead before Him or thank Him for his gifts to us, being grateful for what he has given us, we do bandagi, i.e. prayer.
Bandagi is a Persian word meaning "service". We are in the service of God; we are banda of God, i.e. servitors. Though the term bandagi refers essentially to spoken prayers, in its wider meaning one could say that a good act is a sort of bandagi, as a good act always pleases God. Similarly, a bad act is doing bandagi to Satan.

Q. Whose bandagi should we do?

A. It is the commandment of the religion to do bandagi to God alone. He is the only one worthy of bandagi. Yasna 45[.7-8] states: "Ohrmazd is the Lord of the world, we must praise and worship him."

Q. Are we duty bound to do bandagi to God?

A. Yes. We must pay our debt to him through bandagi. It is stated in Yasna 13[.5]: "O Ohrmazd, in this way we bow down unto you, in this way we pay our debt unto you."

Q. In what language should we do our bandagi?

A. We should do it only in our Avestan tongue. Yasna 41 [.5] states: "O God, I do your bandagi with the manthra."
Manthra here means the holy spells in the Avestan language.

Q. Will we be rewarded for doing bandagi?

A. Whoever does bandagi to God receives rewards of various kinds from Him. Yasna 51[.21] states: "I yearn for bandagi so that God will give its reward."
The rewards sought here are of the following kind: that in all respects God protect me, so that I may live my life with respect and dignity. God is the giver of rewards, and will give them according to one's own competence.

Q. Is there any other advantage to bandagi?

A. By doing bandagi our wisdom increases. Vendidad 4[.45] states: "There shall be an increase of wisdom by doing bandagi."

Q. How should we do bandagi?

A. It is proper to do it keeping good thoughts in mind. Yasna 30[.1] states: "O God, I praise you and remember you through good mindedness."

Q. How do you perform bandagi?

A. To do bandagi we must hold our hands high and reverently. Yasna 50[.8] states: "In this way, to those who praise God, He gives the abode of heaven."

Q. Is it necessary to learn how to do bandagi?

A. Yes. As far as it is possible we must learn how to do bandagi well and how to perform good acts. It is stated in Yasna 28[.5]: "As long as I have power and strength, I shall teach the desire of holiness [i.e. good deeds]."
Every act of bandagi begins with a cleansing of one's hands, face and feet with water, and the untying and retying of the sacred kusti. These religious acts are always accompanied by manthric recitation, i.e., Avestan utterances. It is our firm belief that prayers should always be said in the divine speech of Avestan, and not in translated form. While praying we should concentrate on God alone and should have no bad thoughts in our mind. We should pray not because it is some external obligation imposed upon us by our religion; rather genuine prayer is a deeply natural response of gifts continually bestowed upon us by God. True prayer comes from within. When we say bandagi in front of fire, we first place a white handkerchief over the palm of our left hand. This is a

special gesture of reverence which suggests our own submission to God and also our reverent desire to establish a paywand or connection with all spiritual powers. While saying the Avestan phrase "Homage to thee, O fire, the son of Ahura Mazda", we bow our head, make an upward gesture toward our forehead with our right hand, and then bow deeply, touching our right hand to the ground. After straightening up, we again bow and pay homage to the fire with the gesture of the right hand raised to the forehead.

CHAPTER NINE
The qibla of fire, and related matters

Q. Since we cannot see God, how should we do our bandagi?

A. We must do our bandagi facing all shining things because the sun, moon, stars and fire are the natural lights out of the original light of God. Hence to stand facing them and do bandagi is very effective. In the Vishtasp Yasht [Yt.24:38] it is said: "You who do great bandagi should do it facing the shining things of the world."

Q. What is the commandment regarding doing bandagi in front of the sun?

A. During the daytime we must do bandagi facing the sun, and at dawn we must do bandagi when the cock crows. Yasna 50[.10] states: "O God, I do your bandagi facing the light of the sun during the daytime and at the time of dawn when the cock crows."

Q. Can we do bandagi without facing the light?

A. God is present in all directions, so it is proper to do bandagi facing any direction. But to face the light of the sun or the stars and do bandagi is very efficacious. Cf. The Dasatir.

Facing an object, like the sun, enables the worshipper to concentrate deeply.

Q. What is the command regarding the qibla of fire?

A. Yasna 36[.3-4] enjoins us to do bandagi to

God facing the fire. It is stated there: "Oh fire of God, we approach you with good thoughts and good bandagi."

Q. What is the advantage of putting incense and fuel on the fire?

A. Fire blesses the one who offers him fuel and incense. It is stated in the Vishtasp Yasht [Yt.24.38]: "Fire blesses him who brings frankincense for it, being pleased, unoffended and satisfied."

Q. What blessing does he [the fire] give?

A. He blesses thus: May there be increase of sons in your house, may there be increase of cattle. That means, may you have many children and much prosperity. Cf. the Vishtasp Yasht [Yt.24:38].

Q. What is another advantage of putting incense in fire?

A. Because of the fragrance, wicked persons and idolaters are kept at bay. For that see the Bahram Yasht [Yt.14:55]: "Whoever puts incense on fire, in an instant keeps wicked idolaters away."

He, the fire, is called the 'son of God'. He is the medium through which our prayers are sent to God, and it is through him that we receive benefits from God. When Hooshang saw the nur (light) of the first fire, he said: This is the divine light, a person who possesses wisdom will offer obeisance to him. Firdausi's Shahnama gives the full story. It is difficult for non-Zoroastrians to understand the function of fire. One cannot measure the benefits derived from fire.

The nur (light) and khwarrah (radiant glory) of a fire are part of the spiritual and material aspect of the fire, for we see it and it has an inherent spiritual strength. In the eyes of the faithful, this glow of fire and everything surrounding it would seem to be the presence of God. The most purified and consecrated of fires has the power to bestow the most blessings, and it is important that we approach him properly. For lay people, one must do kusti prayer before approaching the fire to pray. The priests who are tending the fire are required first to perform certain ceremonies so as to receive power before entering the sanctum sanctorum. When in a fire temple, there is nothing dearer to us than him (the fire). This particular qibla is most dear to our hearts; he is most precious, for from time immemorial he has been the medium through which we can send our prayers to God. This has been in our blood since the time of Hooshang. It is a pre-Zoroastrian practice. We have protected him in jungles, in the mountains, against robbers and thieves. Why is this? It is difficult to convey the 'son of God' idea. When a Zoroastrian leaves the fire temple he feels he has received some kind of aura or glory or energy that will sustain him. With a cheerful heart he will leave the fire; you can see it on his face.

Q. What sort of fuel should we offer unto the fire?

A. Use the logs of those trees which have good fragrance for fuel. Vendidad 19[.24] states: "Bring hard (dry) fuel unto the fire, also bring fragrance of different kinds unto the fire."

Q. What sort of fuel should we put on the fire?

A. Fuel which is dry and well-inspected should be put on the fire. It is stated so in the Atash Niyayesh [Ny. 5.16].

'Inspected' means that the bark should be scraped off, and the log should be clean and dry. The fuel should not be cleaned with water, for that would dampen the log and diminish the fire. In the highest type of fire, the Atash Bahram, the logs are placed horizontally around three sides of the fire. The priest who tends the fire watches the logs to make sure the fire burns properly.

Q. When we go to do bandagi before the fire, is it necessary to take sandalwood with us?

A. Yes, it is better to do bandagi by offering sandalwood to the fire. Just as a friend would take a gift to another friend, in the same way, fire looks to the hand of those who would approach him and desires the offering. Cf. the Atash Niyayesh [Ny.5.14]: "Fire watches the hand of all comers."

Q. Our people take with them hens and goats, etc., before the fire [in the temple]. Is this according to the law of the religion?

A. No. Such practices are an insult to our religion. We should not do them. We must offer him fragrance or things that can be used in the abode of fire, like ladles, pairs of tongs, plates of metal, bells, etc. Take them into the abode of fires and offer them. To do this is a good deed. Cf. Vendidad 14[.7].

The practice of bringing animals to the temple stems from an ancient mode of offering animals for sacrifice. In ancient times such acts were meritorious acts of devotion. Yet, some Parsis today say these people of old were wrong, absolutely wrong. Today it is customary to bring a gift to the fire, though not a gift beyond one's means. Small chips of fragrant wood can be purchased in shops near the temple. Some temples have shops adjacent to the compound which sell offerings to the fire. The offerings are placed on the fire and the fire consumes them.

Related to this whole matter of appropriate offerings to fire is an interesting discrepancy between the ms. F93 (p.44) and Erachji's published edition. In the manuscript Erachji introduces another question and answer:

Q. Is it proper to offer the fat of the gospand (sheep, goat) to the fire as our people do?

A. It is not proper to offer fat of the gospand to the fire since it extinguishes the fire. It is not proper to burn dead matter on holy fire.

Note that although Erachji is in the habit of quoting an authority to drive home his point on almost every other issue, he does not do so here. The practice of offering fat to fire was in vogue in Erachji's time and his outright dismissal indicates his awareness of this, but at the same time his answer shows the refinement and integrity of his ideas. The offering of fat to the fire has been abandoned totally in India among the Parsis for many decades.

Q. Is there any commandment regarding the preservation of the fire?

A. Yes, we must first serve him and preserve him so that we can reach God. Yasna 36[.1] states: "Oh Ohrmazd, we come near you through the service of fire."

Q. Since there is an injunction to preserve fire, if fire breaks out should we extinguish it or not?

A. Yes, of course. At that time we must extinguish fire because if we do not, much damage will result. In the 6th Book of the Denkard it says: "To extinguish fire is a sin, but to extinguish it at certain times is good." *The Shayest Ne-Shayest (20.15) states: "Notice this also that one should not extinguish fire, for it is a sin, yet sometimes one extinguishes it and it is good." In a Parsi kitchen there will be a fire the whole day. At night the embers are preserved and in the morning chips of wood are placed on them. We do not wish the fire to go out. If the embers do go out, we ignite the fire again, but it is not preferred. Because of our emotional attachment to fire, we question whether Parsis should belong to fire brigades--but then, fire can be a good servant but a bad master in such cases.*

Q. Should we keep a fire under the rays of the sun?

A. No. By doing that the strength of the fire [its glory] diminishes. It is a sin for anyone to keep the fire under the sun. Cf. the Saddar Nazm.

Q. When the Atash Niyayesh is recited, the priests touch the ladle to the fire vase (at certain points), and those outside the gumbad [the sanctum sanctorum] hold the iron bars of the window. What is the reason for this?

A. In the Avesta it is said: "Oh Ohrmazd, I hold your

fire." In the Atash Bahram [fire temple], when a priest performs the boy ceremony [feeding incense to the fire] he makes contact with the fire vase by means of a ladle. In this way we say we are holding the fire. At this point [in the ceremony] the priest says: "I hold thee, Fire, and I praise thee, with the offering of good thoughts."

Q. In the Atash Bahram we take fire ash and apply it on our forehead. What is the reason for this?

A. We go to the Atash Bahram to do bandagi to God. At that time we must show much humility and a sense of "nothingness". We must consider ourselves lesser than anyone, and we must consider fire as our superior and take his ash on our head to show that we are his real servants.

Q. What is qibla?

A. We have to face something to do bandagi: that is called qibla. It is an Arabic word. Cf. the Shamsu- 'l Lughat.

Q. How many types of fire are named in our religion?

A. In our scriptures there are in all nine types of fire:

1) Adar Gushnasp: It was manifest in the times of King Kay Khosraw.
2) Adar Khordad: It was manifest in the time of Jamshed.
3) Adar Burzin-Mihr: It was brought by Zoroaster.

These first three belong respectively to the three estates, viz., warriors, priests and agriculturists. In the Pazand benedictory prayer, the Afrin i Haft Amahraspand, Zoroastrians unite with the spirit of these fires to achieve well-being. The remaining six fires in this list are mentioned in Yasna 17.11 and are explained by glosses in Pahlavi which Erachji follows.

4) Atash Berezi-savangh: It is shining in the spiritual world.

That is, it is in the world of Ohrmazd and the amahraspands. It is there, always burning, yet it is not localized and is invisible.

5) Atash Vohu-friyan: It is in the body of man and

animals.

6) Atash Urvazisht: It is in the trees (plants, vegetation).

7) Atash Vazisht: It is the fire of lightning.

8) Atash Spenisht: It is the fire produced through friction.

9) Atash Nairyosangh: It is the fire in the body of kings and great ones.

The function of this fire is to guide the king to manage better the affairs of the kingdom. This fire is called the messenger of God.

Q. What is the injunction regarding making the moon qibla?

A. In the Vishtasp Yasht [Yt. 24.43] God commands: "Do your bandagi before the protector and guardian moon and the sun."

Q. Why should we do our bandagi facing water?

A. In Yasna 62[.11] it is stated that we must do bandagi facing water. There it is said: "Say your prayer before the waters. I [Zoroaster] desire you to do likewise, through this worship."

The ab-zohr (water-offering) ceremony begins with this verse of Yasna 62. This 'litany to the waters' (the Aban Niyayesh) the ordinary layman calls ab-zohr and recites the litany while facing running water. The term ab means water as well as lustre, for the character of water is lustre-giving. The main reason for reverence for water is its purificatory character. It purifies the semen of males, the womb of females, the very origins of life. Water which is flowing is worthy of praise. Every fire temple has a well with a good flow of water.

CHAPTER TEN

The duties which a man has to perform throughout his life

Q. What should one first prepare when a baby is born?

A. When a Zoroastrian baby is born, it is necessary to

give him haoma juice, because by doing that the baby receives an increase in intelligence and wisdom, and evil doers are warded off. Cf. Yasna 10[.6]: "Even by drinking the smallest amount of haoma juice, thousands of evildoers are smitten." Cf. also the Denkard. *Haoma (Pahlavi Hōm) is a plant (ephedra) pressed for its juice and is regarded as having great medicinal value. Once the haoma juice is consecrated, it can bring about the above mentioned effects. It is the same as soma, and its use dates from pre-Zoroastrian times. There are many Parsis today, however, who do not even know about the salutary benefits of haoma juice for a newly born child.*

Q. What should we keep in front of the child when it is born?

A. When the baby is born we must ignite a fire at once and maintain it for three days, offering fragrant fuel to it so that the fragrance wards off foul air and evil influence. In this way we can protect the child. Cf. the Denkard.

Q. How many months should the mother suckle her baby?

A. She is duty-bound to suckle her son 18 months and her daughter 15 months. Cf. the Persian Rivayat of Kamdin-Shapur and the Farziyat Nama of Darab Pahlan.

Q. What is the first thing we should teach the child when it begins to speak?

A. We must first teach him the name of God, and then the name of our prophet. Cf. the Farziyat Nama of Darab Pahlan.

Q. How many years should the parents look after the child?

A. For eight years they must look after the child and keep him away from sin. A child cannot understand what is bad and good, what are sinful and good acts. It is so written in the Denkard.

Q. When should we teach a child about the nature of religion?

A. When he becomes a full seven years of age he must be sent to a priest (mobed) to learn his duties toward the religion. Cf. Dadestan i Denig and the Farziyat Nama.

Q. At what age should a child be invested with sudre-kusti?

A. When he has completed his seventh year he should be invested. It is estimated that when a child is seven years and three months old he should be invested. It is so stated in the Persian Rivayat of Barzo Kamdin.
Zoroastrian custom adds the nine months a child is in the womb to his age. A child born seven years, three months ago, is considered eight years old.

Q. What is the reason for not putting on sudre-kusti before age seven?

A. After seven years, it is all right. But we must not put on sudre-kusti before that age because to put on sudre-kusti means to admit the child as a Zoroastrian, to ask him to accept the religion. After age seven a child can understand the goodness of religion (den) and of his own will accept the religion. Thus we must do it at that time, when he is mature. The injunction is to invest him then. Cf. the Rivayat of Burzo Kamdin.

Q. When our people put on sudre-kusti they call it navjote. Why?

A. Navjote means a new zaotar, a new initiate into priesthood. The word navjote is used erroneously for the investiture ceremony of the sudre and kusti, which should be called the ceremony (kriya) of taking the child into the Zoroastrian fold.
What Erachji says is quite correct. A priest's son, after completing the nawar ceremony, becomes a nozud, i.e. a new zot or officiating priest. He is thereby qualified to act as zot in ceremonies held outside a Zoroastrian temple. The Pahlavi and Persian texts use the words nawzud, nogzud, nozud in the same sense. The Irani Zoroastrians use the word sedra-pushun, 'putting on the sacred shirt' for the so-called Navjote ceremony of the Parsis.

Q. When are we duty-bound to do bandagi?

A. Beginning the eighth year we must do bandagi. Cf. the Dadistan i Denig.

Q. What should we do immediately upon getting up from bed in the morning?

A. As soon as we get up we must say ashem vohu. Said at this time it is equivalent to saying 10,000 ashem vohus. Then, standing there, do kusti; then apply bull's urine. If nocturnal discharge has occurred during the night one must take a bath immediately upon arising. Cf. the Saddar Nazm.

Ashem vohu is a sacred manthra meaning: 'Righteousness is good'. Kusti, or padyab-kusti, requires a fuller explanation than Erachji provides in this chapter. The most commonly practiced kusti is a short ceremony in which a Zoroastrian first washes the bare parts of his body with pure water after saying the ashem vohu manthra. Then he wipes his face and hands with a handkerchief and recites a prayer, after which he unties and reties his kusti. Next, with a small amount of bull's urine, the Zoroastrian first washes his hands, then touches it to his forehead and feet. There are two types of bull's urine used by Zoroastrians. One is consecrated, the other is not. The unconsecrated type is applied to the body and is called gomez. Consecrated urine has sacred power, and hence is called nirang (strength, power). It is consecrated by the chanting of Avesta and the bestowing of ritual upon it; in that way the yazads descend with power over it. Nirang is used only for drinking purposes. It heals from within. If gomez is not available, fire ash is used instead. In some country areas, men and women use cow's urine for application on the face, hands, and feet. But the urine of a bull is preferred. The bull is called gaw, and is the best creature of Vohuman (Good Mind) one of the seven great amahraspands. Nirang gives strength, purity and conscious satisfaction.

Q. Is there any injunction for applying gomez (bull's urine) in Avesta?

A. Yes, in the Vishtasp Yasht, [Yt. 24.31] it is said that King Vishtasp was given the order to wash his hands with gomez. He was asked to wash his hands first with gomez, then with water. The Avesta passage reads: "Vishtasp, your sons and brothers should first wash hands with gomez and then with water."

That is, when purifying hands soiled at night, he must first use gomez and then wash with water.

Q. How should one wash his hands and face before doing kusti?

A. First he must say: khshnaothra ahurahe mazdao ashem vohu [for the pleasure of Ahura Mazda; Righteousness is good], then he must be quiet. Next he must wash three times, first the exposed parts of his hands, then his face three times and the exposed parts of his legs. Next he must dry his hands and face and then he should begin untying and re-tying kusti. Cf. the Farziyat Nama and Saddar Nazm.

Q. How many times whould we do bandagi in a day?

A. Five times, in the five watches (gahs) of the day, namely:

1. Hawan: from early morning (sunrise) up to 12 noon.
2. Rapithwin: 12 noon to three.
3. Uzerin: three to sunset, or the time of seeing the stars.
4. Aiwisruthrem: from the time you see the stars to 12 midnight.
5. Ushahin: 12 midnight to dawn. Cf. the Rivayat of Kama Vohra.

One should pray in these five gahs (periods of the day). These gahs are essential for the priestly ceremonies. When the gah begins the priest does the compulsory prayer for that gah, and serves the fire. Thus at every interval the priest is made to stand near the fire and look after him. That is what enables the fire's existence to be permanent. Most other ceremonies are performed in the Hawan gah, when the sun is rising. This is the ideal time, and the fire temple is filled with activity, people coming in with offerings.

Q. How many months does the Rapithwin gah last and how many the second Hawan?

A. From the first day of the first month (Frawardin) up to the last day of the seventh month (Mihr), i.e., for seven complete months there is Rapithwin. From the first day of the eighth month (Aban) to the last Gatha day there is second Hawan. Cf. the Rivayat of Kama Vohra.

This question refers to the practice of substituting a second Hawan gah in place of the normal Rapithwin gah during the period of the year when the days are short. Since most ceremonies are performed in the Hawan gah, the short days of winter do not allow ample time for their enactment, so the time of the Hawan gah is extended into the second period of the day. Gatha days are the last days in the Zoroastrian calendar. According to our calendar each month has 30 days; 12 months equal 360 days. The remaining five days are each given the name of a Gatha. These five days are, in fact, five epigomena, and not part of the last month (Spandarmad) as some would claim.

Q. What are the five gahs named after?

A. They are the names of five fireshtes who preside over these five periods of the day. The word gah means 'time'.

Q. What is the advantage of saying prayers in all five gahs?

A. These five fireshtes recommend our merited acts and by saying the prayers of these five gahs, five things remain in our heart, namely: good nature, intelligence, friendship, moderation and justice. Cf. the Denkard [Book 6].

None of these references are connected with the meanings of the words designating the five gahs. Erachji's answer enumerates the five virtues which the faithful receive by being pious.

Q. What should we say in each of the five gahs?

A. In the Hawan gah we must say the following: Srosh baj [i.e., the opening prayer to Srosh], Hawan gah [i.e., the prayer appropriate to Hawan], litanies (Niyayesh) to Khorshed and Mihr, the Ohrmazd Hymn (Yasht), Ardibehesht Hymn, Srosh Hymn, the Vispa Humata and Nam Stayishn [prayers], and Namaskar [i.e., giving obeisance] to the four directions.

In the Rapithwin gah: the Srosh baj, Rapithwin gah, litanies to Khorshed and Mihr, and the litany to to Ohrmazd.

In the Uzerin gah: the Srosh baj, Uzerin gah, litanies to Khorshed and Mihr, and the hymn to Srosh called the Srosh Hadokht.

In the Aiwisruthrem gah: the Srosh baj, Aiwisruthrem gah, the long hymn to Srosh (Srosh Yasht Wadi), hymns to Ohrmazd, Ardibehesht, the hymn to Srosh called the Srosh Hadokht, and Patet [prayer of repentance].

In the Ushahin gah: the Srosh baj, Ushahin gah, hymns to Ohrmazd and Ardibehesht, and the hymn to Srosh called the Srosh Hadokht.

At every period of the day, if more Avesta is said, the merit is greater. Cf. the Persian Rivayat of Kama Vohra and the Farziyat Nama.

All the prayers Erachji mentions here belong to the Khorda Avesta, that is, the 'Small Avesta'. The Khorda Avesta is compiled from the Large Avesta (the Yasna, Yashts, Vendidad and fragments from the lost Nasks) and is used as a daily prayer book by the lay and priestly members of the community.

A devout Zoroastrian begins his daily devotions in each of the five watches of the day with padyab-kusti. His prayers then commence with the Srosh baj, that is, with a prefatory prayer to Srosh, the spirit being (yazad) who is the protector of the material world. Following this, the pious Zoroastrian says the prescribed prayer appropriate to the watch or time of day. This is called the gah prayer and bears the name of each gah. These two prayers, the Srosh baj and the appropriate gah prayer, constitute a person's minimum obligatory prayers (farziyat) for the day. As Erachji notes, one can do as many prayers as he wishes in addition to these prayers, with the merit increasing proportionately.

In the daylight gahs (one, two and three) the litanies to the yazads Khorshed and Mihr are ordinarily done. In addition, a few other small prayers, like the Vispa Humata (an eulogy of good thoughts, words and deeds) and the Nam Stayishn (a Pazand prayer in praise of Ohrmazd) are included as appropriate prayers. They are also to be found in the Khorda Avesta. The Hymn to Ardibehesht (Best Righteousness) is in praise of the Holy Immortal presiding over the fire which is his visible sign.

There are two hymns dedicated to Srosh. One is called the Srosh Yasht Wadi, or the long Srosh hymn--taken from Yasna 57, and the Srosh Yasht Hadokht, which is taken from the Hadokht Nask.

Finally, the Namaskar to the four quarters of the earth is an Avestan prayer taken from Yasna 1.16 and is a prayer in praise of God's creations. In his ms. F93 Erachji calls this prayer namaz i chahar nemag 'obeisance to four directions'. It is said four times, each recital facing one of the directions. In the first watch of the day, the order is East-South-West-North; in the second and third gahs the order is West-South-East-North. It is not recited during the night gahs.

Q. At what time should the prayer of Hoshbam [Ph. 'dawn'] be said?

A. The prayer Hoshbam should be said at dawn because there are good blessings in it. For this reason when we invest a child with sudre and kusti we say this prayer also.

Erachji is saying here that a young person's investiture with sudre and kusti should properly be performed at dawn. Practice has now shifted to after dawn, i.e. the Hawan gah, and even as late as the third gah of the day.

Q. When should we pray the litany to fire (the Atash Niyayesh)?

A. It should be done specially during the following five days of the Zoroastrian month: Ohrmazd [first day], Ardibehesht [third day], Adar [ninth], Srosh [seventeenth] and Bahram [twentieth]. If it is done daily it is of great merit. It is so stated in the Persian Rivayat of Shapur Bharuchi.

Q. When should we pray the litany to water (Aban Niyayesh)?

A. It should be done during the following five days of the month: Spandarmad [fifth day], Aban [tenth], Den [twenty-fourth], Ard [twenty-fifth] and Mahraspand [twenty-ninth]. If it is done daily, there is even more benefit. Cf. the Farziyat Nama.

This should not be done during the night hours, however, because the Avesta says that if you do this (either the litany or hymn to water) at night, it will reach the daevas (demons). Do not disturb the waters, the spirit of waters, during nighttime. The Khorshed and Mihr litanies are also for daylight gahs only. In our fire temples, moreover, if it is absolutely necessary to draw water for ceremonies at midnight, we say yatha ahu vairyo, clap loudly, and then fetch the water from the well.

Q. On what days should we pray the litany to the moon (Mah Bakhtar Niyayesh)?

A. Three days during the month: New Moon day, Full Moon day, and the Dark of the Moon day. If it is done daily, it is better. Cf. the Nirangestan.

The third litany, the Mah Bakhtar Niyayesh (Phl. mah, 'moon'; bakhtan, 'distribution') is the litany of the moon. This Niyayesh is usually said during the night-time gahs, but can be said anytime. It is said of Mah (the moon) in the Pahlavi commentary that when the moon waxes for 15 days it means that the moon is gathering glory (khwarrah) and blessings (afrin) from yazads. For the next 15 days that it wanes the moon acts as a distributor (bakhtar) of those blessings on deserving holy people.

Q. What are the Avestan names for the New Moon, Full Moon, and Dark of the Moon?

A. Antare-maongha; pereno-maongha; vishaptatha. Cf. the Mah Niyayesh [Ny. 3.6].

Q. What is the reason for doing patet?

Patet, in Pahlavi patit, means "confession" and comes from the Avestan paitita meaning "expiation". A patet, in other words, is a confession of sin and is usually spoken in a set formula.

A. If we have done sinful acts it is necessary to do patet. According to Vendidad 3[.21]: "If anyone commits a sin, patet is required of him."

Q. If one does not commit a sin, should one do patet or not?

A. If one does not commit any sin, even then one should do patet. He may have committed a sin of which he is not conscious. Vendidad 3[.21] states: "If a person does not commit sin, still he should always say patet."

Q. In what language is the patet written which we now say?

A. We have today four pieces of patet which are in Pazand and written by our ancestors: 1. patet pashemani or patet of Adarbad -- believed to be composed by Adarbad Mahraspand, 2. patet irani, 3. khud patet, 4. patet rawani.

The Adarbad patet is usually said in first person, for oneself. It is said during all barashnom ceremonies (a nine-night ritual of purification) and prior to the commencement of the navjote ceremony. If this patet is said on behalf of someone who is deceased, then certain modifications are required, namely inserting the name of the deceased in appropriate places. Then the patet is called patet rawani, 'patet for the (departed) soul'. If a ceremony is performed for the departed soul on the anniversary day of his or her demise, then the patet rawani is usually said. This patet must be said in each of the five gahs during the first three days after death. The patet irani came from Iran but is not frequently recited by Parsis. It is said in the early morning, has a ring to it, with good sounding words. The khud patet is exclusively said for oneself, but has fallen into disuse and is seldom recited.

Q. What is the Avestan patet?

A. The Avestan patet is the passage of the Avesta which begins with frastuye ('I ardently praise'). This patet of frastuye was brought by the prophet, and if we do not know the recitation of the other four patets, we must say this Avestan patet three times.

It is a short patet and frequently occurs in the Khorshed and Mihr litanies. It is usually said every day as the Pazand prayers are long.

Q. What is the meaning of patet, and does God pardon our sins if we say it?

A. Patet means first to repent of all bad deeds and thereby atone for them and desire forgiveness. If we have committed a sin unconsciously and we do patet God forgives us. If we sin every day and then we seek forgiveness God does not accept it. Cf. the Denkard.

The meaning of this last statement is that if we do patet but continue to commit that sin, God will not forgive us. One must take a solemn vow to try one's best not to commit the sin again. God has given us the will power, and if one wants to, he can avoid doing the sin again. The blessings of God are there to be obtained. but man has to obtain them.

Q. If we do not know any Avesta, then what should we pray?

A. Our prophet has enjoined us to do bandagi even when we do not know Avesta. He has given us the Ahunwar and ashem vohu to repeat certain numbers of times as equivalents to different Avestan prayers. The list of Avestan prayers given in the Denkard and Persian Rivayat of Bahman Punjia is as follows:

For the	Khorshed litany	: 103 Ahunwars
	Mihr litany	: 65 Ahunwars
	Mah Bakhtar litany	: 65 Ahunwars
	Aban litany	: 65 Ahunwars
	Atash litany	: 65 Ahunwars
	For each of the five gahs	: 65 Ahunwars
	For patet	: 121 Ahunwars and 12 ashem vohus
	Ohrmazd Hymn	: 103 Ahunwars and 12 ashem vohus
	Ardibehesht Hymn	: 65 Ahunwars
	Srosh Hadokht Hymn	: 75 Ahunwars
	Srosh Wadi Hymn	: 103 Ahunwars
	Afrinagan	: 121 Ahunwars and 12 ashem vohus

This injunction may be due to illiteracy among a large section of the people in former times. Such an attitude should not be encouraged when full prayers are available. I consider this practice good only for the sick and the infirm.

Q. Should we say grace before eating our meals?

A. Yes, God is the provider of our daily bread and meals, so when we eat we must first be thankful to him for all his gifts. Thus we first say grace (take the baj) and then eat our food. Cf. Yasna 8[.4]: "Those who are of the Zoroastrian faith, who do not say the Avesta for the baj, will have bewitching thoughts, that is, their nature will be full of deceit."

Q. Should we 'take the baj' before answering the call of nature, and also 'leave the baj' after answering it?

A. Yes. We must take the baj by standing three paces away from the place, and after saying one Ahunwar, then answer the call of nature. Thereafter, again standing three paces away, we must leave the baj. It is so stated in Vendidad 18[.43]: "After answering the call of nature, the person should stand three paces away and leave the baj and utter three ashem vohus, two humatanam [Yasna 35.2], three hukhshathrotemai [Yasna 35.5], four ahunwars and the prayer yenghe hatam."

As we noted previously (above, p.22), baj is a spoken Avestan formula (manthra) which precedes, accompanies or follows an action. The purpose of reciting a baj is to encircle the action with the power of holy speech. When the baj manthra is said before the act, it is referred to as 'taking the baj'; when it follows the act, it is called 'leaving the baj.'

The yenghe hatam is one of the great Zoroastrian prayers which praises all beneficent divinities. It is usually said at the conclusion of the recitation of litanies and hymns, its content being basically Yasna 51.22.

Q. When should we say the Ahunwar and how many times?

A. We should say one Ahunwar at the following times:

When we go to work,
when we finish any work,
when we go out of the house,
when we converse with anyone,
when we begin any work,
when we approach nobles and governors,
when we receive any loan,
when we repay any debt,
when we perform any work and while returning from it.
While giving blessings or asking for blessings [we should say] two Ahunwars;
when doing any good work for our children, six Ahunwars;
when we argue with anyone, six Ahunwars;
when we become victorious in that conversation, six Ahunwars;
when we plant seeds or anything in the ground, nine Ahunwars;

when we marry someone's daughter, and when we give our own daughter in marriage, or while arranging any sort of relationship, 11 Ahunwars;
while buying four legged animals or making an enclosure for keeping animals, 11 Ahunwars;
while climbing a mountains, a fortress, a bridge, or any such high place, 12 Ahunwars;
while climbing down to lower places, while entering a city or village, or going astray on the road, 12 Ahunwars;
while traveling, 21 Ahunwars.

The matter of reciting a number of Ahunwars is written in the Persian Rivayat of Bahman Punjia.

The prescription regarding the recital of a number of yatha ahu vairyos while undertaking certain activities is also mentioned in the Denkard and the Supplementary Texts to the Shayest Ne-Shayest (ch. 19).

Q. What advantage and good merit do we receive through the saying of ashem vohu?

A. Whoever keeps in his heart the manthra of ashem vohu, and recites it, benefits the world and praises God. For that, see chapter one of the Hadokht Nask [Yt..21.3]: "Whoever says ashem vohu and thinks of it in his heart is the promoter of the world and one who praises Ohrmazd."

Q. How does the world increase through the saying of ashem vohu?

A. In the ashem vohu prayer there is the intention of doing all that is true and good. Thus a person who always thinks about truthfulness and piety will not harm the world but will bring prosperity into the world.

Q. At what times and places is the saying of one ashem vohu equivalent to saying many ashem vohus?

A. When we take the baj at the time of meals, we say three ashem vohus at the conclusion of the baj. Each of these three ashem vohus is equal to [the merit of saying] ten ashem vohus. After finishing our meals we leave the baj and say four ashem vohus. Each of these four ashem vohus has the merit of saying 100 ashem vohus. Saying one ashem vohu when going to bed is equivalent to 1000 ashem vohus; when getting up from bed in the morning, one ashem vohu is worth 10,000 ashem vohus. And if a dying person is able to say one ashem vohu just before he dies, it is a very great merit. Cf. chapter one of the Hadokht Nask [Yt.21.6-15].

Meal time is a special time to merit these equivalents because a meal is representative of the whole creation. Saying an ashem vohu at that time makes us think about God and our sheer gratitude to him; we praise Ohrmazd who has given us the meat, the flour, water, vegetables, etc. It is an appropriate time to remember the whole creation of God. Such a remembrance should precede the meal.

Q. What are the advantages of the Ahunwar?

A. The Ahunwar prayer is the protector of our body and the giver of victory. Thus at every place, in every task, one should recite it. The Avesta states [Yt. 11.3]: "The Ahunwar is the protector of our body; the words of the Avesta are victory-giving."

Q. According to our religion, if someone is guilty of a crime, who should punish him?

A. By the command of a dastur or a judge, any person can punish the guilty. But while punishing him he must be careful that there should be no wound inflicted on him. Cf. the Denkard [Book 3].

The person should not be made to bleed.

Q. What are the duties of a Zoroastrian when he reaches the age of 15?

A. His first duty is to choose a fireshte for help and recommendation in this and the other world. He must always praise him [the fireshte] so that his case will always be recommended. Cf. the Farziyat Nama.

Q. What is his second duty?

A. He should choose a dastur of the religion as his contact with the religion. In this way he can do all his religious activities in accordance with the advice of the dastur and he should not disobey the dastur's directions. Cf. the Denkard [Book 6].

Q. What is his third duty?

A. In order to do his duty and work in this world he must choose a wise friend and act in this world according to his advice. It is so stated in the Denkard [Book 6].

Q. After 15 years of age, what are the other necessary duties?

A. Every year there are six duties which we should perform. By doing them our soul goes with ease to heaven after death.

1) perform the six gahambars [seasonal festivals of the six creations] of each year;

2) consecrate Rapithwin;
That is, when the period of Rapithwin begins, attend the temple and perform the appropriate ceremonies.

3) perform the worship of Srosh;
Srosh is the yazad who is Ohrmazd's vice-regent on earth, and man's chief protection. The worship of Srosh refers to the zinda-rawan (soul of a living person) ceremony which a Zoroastrian of means is advised to perform every year.
Cf. chapter 25 below.

4) remember the fravashi of the departed on the Frawardigan days;
As stated previously, fravashi are the guardian spirits of the souls of the dead, and protectors and guides of the souls of the living; remembrance is due them on All-Souls day (Frawardigan). These days are festivals dedicated to the fravashis.

5) say the litanies to Khorshed [the sun] and Mihr three times a day;

6) recite the litany to the moon (Mah Bakhtar Niyayesh) three times a month.

Q. What is the commandment for keeping faith in the

religion?

A. Whoever maintains a genuine faith in the religion should be considered a truly religious man. Not from his outward appearance or from his clothes should he be judged. A religious man should have unflinching faith and believe in his religion without doubt. Cf. the Avestan passage [Yasna 12.9]: "This Mazda-worshipping religion is without doubt."

Q. What is the advantage of maintaining faith in the religion?

A. A person who keeps faith in the religion and performs the duties enjoined by the religion is given happiness by God. Yasna 49[.5] states: "Oh Ohrmazd, whoever is a leader of the religion through the Good Mind (Vohuman) is given abundance and prosperity by God."

CHAPTER ELEVEN

Ceremonies for the deceased: from the moment of demise to the placement in the dakhma

Q. When a man is about to die what should we do?

A. First we must wash him and clothe him with clean clothes. If he still has some consciousness and can say ashem vohu and patet it is of very great merit. If he does not have the strength to do that, his children or relatives should say one ashem vohu near him and also patet. Cf. the Farziyat Nama.

Q. What should we do after putting on clean clothes?

A. Two persons should do padyab-kusti and Srosh baj. The dead person should be seen first by a dog. Then the dead person should be clothed in old garments and placed in the area made ready for him. Cf. the Farziyat Nama. *If the area made ready for the body is soil, a furrow must be dug around the area and gravel placed on top of the soil. If it is a stone floor, a gravel furrow has to be made all around the area in which the dead body is placed. Present day practice is to use two or three stone slabs joined together and placed on the floor. The body is then placed on the slabs. These stone slabs are removed after the body is taken away.*

Concerning the practice of a dog viewing the corpse during each period of the day, it is Zoroastrian belief that there is some power in the dog's eyes that wards off evil influence. It may also be that the dog is a means of ascertaining if any life remains, as some writers have suggested.

Q. What sort of clothes should we put on the dead person?

A. As far as is possible, very old clothes which are washed and made clean should be put on, but never new clothes. Putting on new clothes is prohibited in our religion. The lesson being taught to the people of the world is that at the time of death we cannot take anything with us but old clothes. Hence when we are living we must keep our hearts solely on the performance of good deeds. Cf. the Persian Bahram Firuz Nama.

Q. How much clothing should be used?

A. As far as possible use clothes very parsimoniously and no more than required. To put more clothes on a dead person than is necessary is prohibited according to chapter 8 of the Vendidad. One should not waste what one has.

Q. Our people offer the corpse to birds. What is the reason for this?

A. It is absolutely necessary to dispose of the corpse as soon as possible, to be eaten by vultures. If this is not done, a foul wind exudes from the corpse and harm comes to other persons. Thus it is the command of God that it be devoured by flying creatures. Vendidad 6[.46] states: "In this way the dead should be taken near the corpse-eating birds."

Q. What sort of place in the house should we prepare for the dead?

A. If the floor is earth then a place the size of the deceased should be dug out, gravel spread over it, and the corpse placed there. Cf. the 5th chapter of the Vendidad.

Q. When will that place become pure again?

A. The earthen place upon which the dead body has been laid will become pure after nine nights during the time of Rapithwin [i.e., summer]. In the time of second Hawan [i.e., winter] it will take 30 days. Cf. 5th chapter of the Vendidad.

Q. What is the reason for sagdid [being seen by a dog]?

A. When a person dies, foul and demonic air (druj i nasush) comes from the body as it begins to decay inwardly. Whoever approaches that body or goes quite near it will be attacked by that foul air. According to our religion, such a person should wash himself and make his body clean. But in the eyes of the dog there is some quality that wards off the demon of putrefaction (druj i nasush) when the dog sees the corpse. Thus according to Vendidad 7[.3], sagdid should be performed. There it is said that "the dog should see him or corpse-eating birds should fly over him so that the druj i nasush retreats."

Q. If there is no dog, whose sagdid should be done?

A. If a vulture, crow, or other corpse-eating birds see him or fly over him, this is equivalent to sagdid. It is so stated in the Pahlvai commentary to the 7th chapter of the Vendidad.

The Pahlavi commentary names three birds: the mountain buzzard, black crow and eagle.

Q. After the dead body is placed [on the slab], what should be done next?

A. A fire should be lit there and fragrance burned. For three days the fire should be kept burning and the Avesta and penitentiary prayers (patet) should be recited there. The fire should be kept burning for three days near the dakhma (place of exposure) so as to give solace to the soul. Cf. chapter 8 of the Vendidad, the Dadistan i Denig and Bahram Firuz Nama.

A fire should be kept burning in the home and in the sagri. Sagri is a technical term (Guj. 'brazier') for a room at the site of the dakhma (place of exposure) where a fire is burning. Nowadays most sagris have a permanent fire and also have prayer facilities. Ancient sagris were very small vault-like structures without permanent fires. The priest would have to bend low to enter and would place an oil lamp in a specially made niche. The outer side of the wall of the niche was glass studded which would reflect the rays of fire light toward the distant dakhma, some 300 paces away. There are still sagris of this old type without permanent fires. And even our sagris with ever burning fires contain this special reflective device. Ceremonies conducted in the sagri give relief to the souls of the departed.

Q. Why are the Gathas recited before the dead person is carried to the dakhma?

A. The foul demons (druj i nasush) putrify the body of the dead person and attack living persons and pollute them. The recitation of the Gathas keeps the demons of putrefaction (druj i nasush) away. Thus the soul of the departed receives comfort, and the living receive solace. Therefore we must say the Avesta of the Gathas. In Vendidad 10[.3] Zoroaster asks Ohrmazd: "How can I keep back the druj i nasush who rush at the living from the dead? Thereupon Ohrmazd replied: Those passages of the Gathas which are to be said twice, say them." *At the end of each chapter of the Gathas there are passages which are repeated. The above quotation is referring to such passages.*

Q. Why is the body put on the bier halfway through the chanting of the Gathas?

The bier is a flat iron grid on which the body is carried.

A. When the priests start the chanting of the Gathas (gehsarnu), the first portion of the Avestan chant is for the bier, and the remainder is for the corpse. This means that the Gathic chanting (gehsarnu) keeps the demons of putrefaction (druj i nasush) away from both. Cf. the Persian Riyayat of Kamdin Shapur.

Gah (geh) sarnu means chanting of the Gathas. Generally the procedure is for two priests to go to the entrance of the home and stand at the door. First the priests look at the bier and begin chanting the first half of the gehsarnu to bless the bier. Then they turn around until the corpse is placed on the bier and sagdid is performed. Women assembled in the room also turn their heads at this point. The reason is that when the corpse is placed on the bier, the corpse shakes and invisible germs of pollution spread. So they all turn around to avoid this. Once the corpse is properly placed and sagdid has been performed, the priests turn around and face the corpse and chant the second half of gehsarnu for its sake.

The starting time for this ceremony is fixed by the family in consultation with the priest. In orthodox Navsari families, if a death occurs in the morning the preference is to take the body to the dakhma that same day. Hence they arrange for it to be taken in the Uzerin gah (3:00 in the afternoon). But if more time is needed for relatives from a distance to come, then the funeral is held the next day. If the death occurs in the evening, the earliest the funeral can be held is the next morning, the latest, that afternoon. The ceremony is never held at nighttime, for with so much pollution involved one needs the purifying rays of the sun to proceed safely.

Q. Where should the dead body finally be placed?

A. According to Vendidad 6[.45] it should be placed on a high mountainous area. Ohrmazd said, "the corpse should be placed on a high place."

Q. What should the dead body be placed in?

A. A dakhma should be built on a mountain and the corpse should be placed in it. In Vendidad 8[.2] Ohrmazd says:

"for the corpse of the departed, one should seek a high dakhma." In other words, we should seek a dakhma on a high place.

"Dakhma is a controversial word: the original meaning appears to be 'grave'. But in this passage it is a technical term. Some believe it is derived from daz 'to burn', burning through exposure to the sun.

Q. Of what material should the dakhma be built?

A. It should be built of stone and lime. If it is not possible to build it that way, then it can be built of bricks and mud. But it should be built in such a way that the putrid secretions of the corpse should not enter the ground. If they do, it is a grievous sin according to the Persian Rivayat of Nariman Hooshang. If such putrid secretions are absorbed in the soil, it will make the wells and stream nearby impure.

To make anything impure is a grievous sin. By mingling such filthy matter with the elements of nature you are ultimately playing with the life of the living. The natural work of the vultures is to eat all these things. Thus, when God created them for this function, so long as life is in them, they do away with impurity without becoming impure. That which they eat they digest properly.

The dakhma can be constructed of bricks, mortar or stones, as resources dictate. Solid stones are less porous than the other two materials, hence are better. In India Parsis have built dakhmas of all three materials without any reservation according to the means at their disposal.

Q. What is the reason for building a dakhma on an elevated place?

A. The reason seems to be that by taking the corpse to an elevated place the 'foul air' coming out of the body will not influence the living but will go from that high place up into the sky and not harm the health of the people.

Q. Why do the people attending the funeral walk in pairs with paywand when they go to the dakhma following the corpse?

Paywand means 'connection'. Those who walk in the procession which accompanies the corpse to the dakhma hold a handkerchief between them. No one is allowed to walk alone.

A. When a corpse is taken to the dakhma, it should be at the head of the procession. A dog should follow and should look here and there three to nine times in all four directions so that the foul demons (nasush) are kept away. The priests, having taken the baj of Srosh, walk with paywand behind (the dog). Vendidad 8[.19] states: "After first saying the victorious words of yatha ahu vairyo up to ashahe, the priest walks on the road."

The Vendidad is very terse here. It is referring to the baj of Srosh which begins with five yatha ahu vairyos and concludes with the kem na mazda prayer (a prayer for protection) which ends with the word ashahe. This is a good example of how priestly rituals are abbreviated in the Avestan text.

To walk together with baj and paywand gives us an added strength against the foul demons (druj i nasush) because in some places the dog does not follow the corpse to the dakhma. In Bombay all possible care is taken. The dog is brought to the vicinity of the dakhma and the corpse bearers also proceed with paywand to insure greater strength and unity between them.

Q. Is there any merit for one who follows the dead person to the dakhma?

A. Yes it is of great merit. By doing that we are giving great respect to the deceased, and as we follow behind him holding paywand and taking baj, every pace that we take is equal to the merit of one tanapuhr (one good deed). Cf. the Persian Bahram Firuz Nama.

The Pahlavi word tanapuhr (Av. tanu-peretha; Pers.

tanafur) is commonly used to refer to a mortal sin, but it can be used in the context of good deeds also, in which case it means an extremely good deed which vitiates a tanapuhr sin.

Q. Is it proper to lament after the death of someone?

A. No. Whether he is young or old, God calls him of His own will. Endless lamentation is equivalent to going counter to the demand of God and thus committing a sinful act. By over-lamenting one makes the soul of the deceased unhappy because the soul is very happy to proceed to the realm of eternal bliss from this frustrating world. Therefore we should not be excessively sorrowful. When we bewail too much, both that place where the body rests and its lord who is the Bountiful Immortal (amahraspand) Spandarmad, [the one who presides over earth] become very unhappy. Cf. the Persian Bahram Firuz Nama and Vendidad 3[.11]: "Ohrmazd replied: O Zoroaster, the land on which holy men, women or children pass away and become dust and dry-up--from that time whoever bewails and bemoans such an event displeases the amahraspand of earth."

The most important thing to understand is that we should make the soul happy and ease his journey, keep his memory fresh, perform ceremonies on his behalf, and do charitable deeds. Grief does not promote health, but a charitable deed such as using the money of the deceased to educate a young orphan pleases the soul and promotes his well-being.

Q. When someone dies, should we keep on mourning for him?

A. No. Death and life are not within our power, so we must be content with death. In this world we are like a foreign traveler and our body is just like a hired shell which we are in. From it a man goes to his original abode. There should be no deep mourning for that. Everybody dies; others go before us, and we have to follow. Thus to be mournful is a sinful act. It spoils our health, also, and if one keeps on mourning, then sorry episodes will occur in his household. Cf. the Persian Bahram Firuz Nama.

CHAPTER TWELVE

The soul's passage from this world to the next and the eventual destiny of the soul

Q. Where does a person's soul go when he dies?

A. The soul stays in this world for three days, in the house in which he died and in the vicinity where the body is kept. The 8th chapter of the Vishtasp Nask [Yt. 24.54] states: "The soul remains around the head."

Q. When does a person's soul go to the other world?

A. At the time of dawn in the Ushahin gah of the third night, the soul approaches Mihr yazad in the direction of the rising sun. Cf. Vendidad 19[.28]: "In the direction of the holy mountain where the sun rises, the soul approaches Mihr yazad at the time of the shining dawn in the Ushahim gah of the third night."

Q. What happens to the soul while in the presence of Mihr yazad?

A. Whether it is a holy soul or a sinful soul, it reaches the Chinwad bridge and a judgement is made before Mihr yazad. Vendidad 19[.29] states: "The soul of either a holy man or a sinner reaches the Chinwad bridge for judgement."

The Chinwad bridge joins this world with the next, and commences from the heights of the Alburz mountain.

Q. What is done to the soul after judgement is made?

A. It is given a reward or retribution according to its deeds in this world. A holy soul is ordered to go to heaven and a sinner to hell. Cf. Vendidad 19[.29]: "Consciousness and soul receive [their] reward according to the deeds done in the material world."

Q. Where does a sinful soul go?

A. He is given a place in dark hell. Cf. Vendidad 19[.30] which states: "The wicked soul of an evildoer goes to the dark place (i.e. hell)."

Q. Who takes the sinners, i.e. the sinful souls, to hell (dozakh)?

A. The head of hell is a demon (daeva) called Wizaresh. He drags the soul of evil-doers to hell. Cf. Vendidad 19[.29]: "Oh Zoroaster, wicked idol worshippers and those who live their life in sin, souls of such men are taken bound by the demon called Wizaresh."

Q. What are the sinners given in hell?

A. Those who do evil, speak evil, think evil, and are of evil faith are given evil food in hell. Cf. Yasna 49 [.11]: "Thus those who are of evil power, evil thought, evil speech, evil action and evil religion are fit for hell and evil food is brought before such souls." *'Evil food' is filthy, bad food. 'Evil faith' refers to one who has no faith in his own religion and is an idolater. The Zoroastrian religion is against idolatry.*

Q. Where does the soul of a holy man go after it is judged?

A. It crosses the Chinwad bridge by way of Alburz mountain. Vendidad 19[.30] states: "The soul of the pious proceeds by way of Alburz, crossing the Chinwad bridge."

Q. What is his destination upon crossing the Chinwad bridge?

A. He approaches the place of the spiritual yazads and the Bountiful Immortal Vohuman [Good Mind]. Cf. Vendidad 19[.31]: "The holy soul approaches the spiritual yazads where Vohuman is seated on a golden throne."

Q. What does it do in the presence of Vohuman?

A. Vohuman says to that soul: From the mortal world [you have come], you are welcome here in this blissful, eternal world. Cf. Vendidad 19[.31]: Vohuman tells the soul: "O holy one, you are welcome in this world full of happiness, [having come] from the world of misery."

Q. After approaching Vohuman, where does the soul go?

A. Rejoicing, the soul proceeds toward Ohrmazd and the amahraspands. Cf. Vendidad 19[.32]: "Being pleased the souls of the holy proceed toward Ohrmazd and the amahraspands".

Q. After approaching Ohrmazd, where does the soul go?

A. The soul proceeds to the highest heaven (garothman behesht) of Ohrmazd and dwells there in ever-lasting peace. Cf. Vendidad 19[.32]: "That exalted heaven (garothman behesht), which is the mansion of Ohrmazd, the Bountiful Immortals, and the pious, he goes there." *Garothman means 'the house of songs', i.e., where the chanting of Avesta is continuous.*

CHAPTER THIRTEEN

Ceremonies to be performed during the first year following a person's demise

Q. The Zoroastrians, when some death occurs in the family, do not eat flesh. What is the reason?

A. According to our religion eating flesh seems to be improper and Zoroastrians do not eat flesh for three days after death. Cf. the Pahlavi commentary of chapter 8 of the Vendidad, and also other religious books which say that for three days one should not eat flesh. *Religious books prohibit eating flesh for three days after someone's death. But it is not accurate to say that in general eating flesh is improper. The reasons for the three day restriction are probably these: bringing flesh into a house where death has occurred would attract more pollution, for it too decomposes with the passage of time and thereby would affect people's health; a second reason may be that flesh is looked upon as a delicacy; it is for feasts.*

Erachji's reply in ms. F93 differs considerably from the one above which appears in his published work. On pp. 117-118 of the ms. Erachji adds a comment to the above reply. He cites the Avestan quote, Vendidad 8.22, which states that after disposing of the corpse in the dakhma Zoroastrians may eat wine and meat. Erachji then honestly says that it does not appear from this reference that one should abstain from meat and wine for three days after the corpse is placed in the dakhma.

As in Erachji's time, however, contemporary Zoroastrians follow the general practice of abstaining from meat for three days.

Q. What ceremonies (kriyas) should be performed for a person who dies?

A. As soon as someone dies we must order the Yasna ceremony of Srosh, and if there is not enough time for doing the Yasna, then a Dron of Srosh should be consecrated in each watch (gah) for three days and nights. Cf. the Vaetha: "Then they should adore Holy Srosh for three days and three nights."

As mentioned previously, dron is the name of sacred bread prepared from wheat flour and having nine cuts on its surface. A Dron service is a short service of offering performed in the fire temple, in this case dedicated to the yazad Srosh.

Q. What is the reason for saying litanies (niyayesh) and penitentiary prayers (patet) for three days on behalf of the soul?

A. When a man is alive in this world, it is his duty to do bandagi during the five watches of the day. When a man dies his soul remains in the world for three days. Thus it is our duty to do bandagi on his behalf during the five watches of the day, and that duty should be performed by his relatives, family members, friends and near and dear ones. Cf. the Farziyat Nama and Bahram Firuz Nama.

The soul is still in this world for three days, so when the relatives do bandagi on his behalf they are fulfilling his duty as well as producing merit for him. Such merit will reach him at the Chinwad bridge.

Q. If someone dies, why is a ceremony of blessings (Afringan), dedicated to Srosh, performed on behalf of the deceased in the Aiwisruthrem gah [late evening to midnight]?

A. When a person dies, Srosh yazad cares for him in this

world for three days. There is no religious injunction to perform any ceremony except in honor of Srosh. The Aiwisruthrem gah is the time related to the soul (rawan). For this reason we do an Afrinagan of Srosh at that time, so that Srosh can look after the soul. Cf. the Farziyat Nama.

Srosh protects the material world with special vigilance after sunset. It is during this watch, the Aiwisruthrem gah, that the soul of the deceased requires more attention from Srosh. That is why Erachji says the Aiwisruthrem gah is the time related to the soul.

Q. On the third day in the Uzerin gah [3:00 p.m. to sunset] we do the Uthamnu ceremony in honor of the dead. Why?

A. It is the duty of relatives and friends to say prayers (niyayesh) and penitentiary prayers (patet) for the deceased during the first three days. On the third day, in the Uzerin gah, we assemble and say prayers [the Khorshed and Mihr litanies] and patet for the deceased.

Prayers in honor of the sun (Khorshed) and the yazad Mihr (who accompanies the sun across the heavens) are said in the Uzerin gah of the third day. These prayers constitute the Uthamnu ceremony. At the end of the ceremony, priests and relatives assemble, and if the deceased has passed away without an heir, an heir is proclaimed in the assembly. This means that though the man may have died childless, someone is now there to look after his soul (rawan) and to perform ceremonies in his behalf. Usually the one adopted is a family member. One can even adopt during his lifetime, once he knows he will have no heirs of his own. The person selected for adoption must agree to it. Nowadays, however, a legal will is necessary.

Q. When someone dies we also do Uthamnu at dawn in the Ushahin gah [12 midnight to dawn] of the third day. Why?

A. On the third night, at the time of dawn in the Ushahin gah, the soul goes to the other world. At that time it is our duty to say prayers in honor of the soul and to do patet. Doing this gives relief and comfort to the soul.

In all, then, there are two Uthamna: one during the Uzerin gah, the other in the Ushahin gah. There is a controversy over which Uthamnu is correct. The majority say the Uthamnu of the Ushahin gah is the proper one. However, it appears that in very ancient times only the Uthamnu of the Uzerin gah was performed because that was the time when the whole anjoman (local assembly of all adult Zoroastrian men) could attend, i.e., in the evening. In the presence of the anjoman the adoption could take place when the soul of the deceased was still in the house. The Uthamnu of the Ushahin gah occurs at dawn, a time when the soul has already started its journey, and the four dron ceremonies appropriate to the soul have already been completed. Very old orthodox families of Navsari, even to the present day, perform only the Uthamnu of the Uzerin gah. Of course this is very rare now, because the high priests (dasturs) recommend that it be performed in the Ushahin gah, an ideal time for prayers. The best advice to the laity is to do both Uthamna. Then there is no place for doubt. Ninety percent of the people now do both. Praying for the soul is the focus of the ceremony and it is appropriate at both times.

Q. What constitutes an anjoman (assembly) and what is the advantage of the anjoman participating in ceremonies (kriyas)?

A. The minimum number for an anjoman is three, and an anjoman can participate in all kinds of ceremonies (kriyas) with one heart and one opinion. Such kriyas are more effective and God approves of them very much.

Q. What ceremonies (kriyas) are conducted in the Ushahin gah of the third night in honor of the soul?

A. In the Ushahin gah we must consecrate four Dron ceremonies [also called baj, a ritual consecration of unleavened bread] in honor of the yazads Rashn-Ashtad, Mino Ram, Srosh, and all the holy spirits of the departed (ardafrawash). In the Dron ceremony in honor of the departed spirits, syaw ('clothes') should be consecrated. At the very beginning of the fourth day, a ceremony of blessings (Afrinigan) in honor of Dahm yazad should be performed. Thereafter hymns (yashts) to Khorshed and Mihr should be recited. It is so stated in the Persian Bahram Firuz Nama.

Syaw means 'clothes', referring to the clothes which the soul is supposed to put on when he presents himself in priestly garments before the fireshtes. These clothes consist of all priestly vestments, i.e., a full gown, sash, padan (mouth veil), white cap and turban, trousers, sudre, kusti. Syaw in the Persian Rivayats is called jama i ashodad, i.e., a garment or dress of clothes to be given away as alms to a priest. Such alms are still given to family priests today.

The four Dron ceremonies are performed in order to help the soul in his sojourn to the other world. The yazads Rashn and Ashtad both preside over true justice and take account of the deeds done by the soul in this world. Mino Ram is the good air (way i weh) who assists the soul as it ascends to heaven and prevents the bad air (way i wattar) from doing any harm. The yazad Srosh and the holy spirits of the departed (ardafrawash) guard the soul. Dahm yazad is the custodian of the souls of the pious, hence his invocation on the dawn of the fourth day. Benedictory prayers (afrins) are said on behalf of the soul of the deceased and also the living for the first time at the conclusion of the Afrinagan of Dahm.

Q. While consecrating the dron (sacred bread) and performing the ceremony of blessings (Afrinagan), what things should be offered?

A. We must offer especially dry and green fruits, flowers, milk and water. Our people, however, place meat, fish and chickens alongside dron. This does not seem to be proper because such things should not be placed alongside dron. Our religious commandment requires that we offer only four drons, [together with] clarified butter, dates, pomegranate and water. If one has the means he may offer something in addition and consecrate it with the drons. Cf. the Persian Bahram Firuz Nama. *The dron is brought to the ceremony on a tray from the household. Items such as chicken, fish, etc. were previously put on this tray at times, but that no longer occurs today. If one wishes to add more offerings, then one can prepare some sweet dishes made of wheat and add these. Also it should be noted that rather than speak of four drons, it is more accurate to say four bread cakes, two of which are marked with nine cuts and are called dron and two of which are unmarked and are called frasast. They are made out of unleavened dough by women who have clean hands and are cooked without a ladle in a large, slightly concave frying pan, and turned over by hand. They are white, flat and round, about the size of a person's hand, and should have no puffed or burnt spots. After the ceremony, the dron, frasast and syaw are taken from the fire temple and sent, with other things (e.g., a sweet dish), to the family of the deceased.*

Q. What ceremony should be performed on behalf of the soul on the fourth day?

A. On the fourth day in the Hawan gah, one Yasna, Dron (baj) and Afrinagan ceremony in honor of all holy departed spirits (ardafrawash) should be performed. And at lunch time [about 11 a.m.] one Stum should be performed over the meal. This meal should be given away to pious, deserving persons or poor helpless persons so that their hunger can be satisfied and their good wishes for the soul of the departed reach God who will be kind and merciful towards the soul. These same ceremonies should be done on the tenth day in honor of the soul. It is so stated in the Persian Bahram

Firuz Nama.

The Yasna ("act of worship") service is the principal liturgy performed daily in the precincts of a Zoroastrian fire temple. Its most distinctive feature is the consecration of the haoma (hom) drink, which together with the dron (wheat cake) is tasted by the officiating priest as sacramental food and drink.

The Stum (so called because the appropriate prayer begins with the Avestan staomi 'I praise') is a very short kriya, lasting about 15 minutes at most. In this ceremony the food is prepared in a clean way, placed in front of the priest and prayed over. The real merit of this service lies in the giving of the food in charity.

The Afrinagan ceremony, like the Stum, can be conducted outside the fire temple, in a clean place. It is a ceremony of blessings (afrin) and may be solemnized in honor of any of the yazads for their favor and blessing.

Q. What is meant by siruza, and what ceremonies are to be performed on that day?

A. Siruza refers to the 30th day after the day of demise. On that day, the Yasna, Dron and Afrinagan ceremonies are performed on behalf of the soul and are dedicated collectively to the 33 fireshtes with their khshnumans.
The term khshnuman is from the Avestan root khshnav meaning 'rejoice'. It is a dedicatory formula which names the yazads or fireshtes for whose pleasure the ceremony is performed.
Zoroastrians on that day also consecrate 33 boiled eggs and 33 chaptan [a fried round wheat pastry]. This appears in the writings of the Persian Rivayats.
The Persian Rivayats also give the prescription for using walnuts as substitutes for eggs. Vegetarian Parsis may follow this advice for the Siruza and Fireshte ceremonies.
On the 31st day, i.e., exactly one month after the day of demise, one Yasna, one Dron, and one Afrinagan

ceremony should be performed in honor of all departed souls (ardafrawash), and syaw ('clothes') should be consecrated with the dron. Stum should be performed at meal time, and every month on the day of demise one Yasna, Dron, Afrinagan and Stum should be performed. And just as these ceremonies are done on siruza day so they should be done on the day prior to the first anniversary day [365th day, also called siruza] and on the day following the siruza day [366th day]. Cf. the Persian Rivayat of Kama Vohra and Bahram Firuz Nama.

Q. Our people perform the ceremonies as required for siruza on the day prior to the sixth month day. Does our religion so require?

A. This does not seem to be the case according to the religious books, and what the source of this custom is I do not know. But the writer of the Farziyat Nama says that it is the command of the ancients.

All Parsis conduct ceremonies for the first four days after someone's demise. It is even better to continue to remember the soul afterwards for a full year and even longer if you wish. Thus the high liturgies for four days are fixed. The soul needs relief and comfort, and the ceremonies help him. Souls crave for praise and bless the living when satisfied.

Q. If a small child passes away, what ceremony should be performed?

A. If a child passes away at any time between the day of birth and seven years, we must have three Yasnas to Srosh and an Afrinagan to Srosh performed in the Aiwisruthrem gah [sunset to midnight]. In the Ushahin gah [midnight to dawn] on the third night we must consecrate four baj (Dron) ceremonies and also offer a small sized syaw. On the 4th, 10th, and 31st days, on the anniversary day, and also the monthly day of demise, the Dron and Afrinagan ceremonies should be performed and all things used in the ceremonies should be small in size. In the Pahlavi commentary of the Vendidad, the 8th chapter, it says that the ceremony for small children is not different. This is also said in the Persian Rivayat of Shapur Bharuchi.

Q. What ceremony should be performed for a child who dies after seven years of age?

A. A child is invested with sudre-kusti after the seventh year and the duty of bandagi becomes his responsibility. Thus after his death all ceremonies should be performed on his behalf, just as they would be performed for a grown man. It is so stated in the Pahlavi commentary of the 8th chapter of the Vendidad and also in the Persian Rivayat of Shapur Bharuchi.

Q. Is there any authority for doing the 'ceremony of the pair'?

Ceremonies for man and wife performed side by side, even when one is still living, are called 'ceremonies of the pair'.

A. There does not seem to be any reference to that in the religious books. But it is stated that a living person must have his zinda-rawan (living soul) ceremony performed every year. Since it is not always possible to perform this every year, when a person dies, the zinda-rawan ceremonies for the wife who is still living may be performed at the same time [as the ceremonies for the deceased]. The expenses are less when it is done this way.

The zinda-rawan ceremony is comprised of ceremonies dedicated to Srosh for the first three days, and to all departed souls (ardafrawash) on the fourth day. These ceremonies can be performed side by side with those performed for the dead. In this way living persons carry out an injunction of the religion.

Q. A person dies in some foreign land, and no ceremony is performed for him because no one knows to do so. After one month the news comes. How shall we perform that person's ceremony?

A. On the day the news arrives a Yasna to Srosh should be

performed immediately. On the same day an Uthamnu ceremony should be performed, and that night, in the Ushahin gah, four dron (baj) should be consecrated, with syaw. The following day at dawn, in the Hawan gah, an Afrinagan in honor of Dahm yazad should be performed, and in the same gah, ceremonies for the fourth day should be performed. In the Rapithwin gah the ceremony of the tenth day should be performed; in the Uzerin gah, the ceremony of siruza. In the same gah, Dron and Afrinagan ceremonies in honor of all the holy departed souls (ardafrawash) should be performed just as they are on the 31st day.

In other words, all the ceremonies are finished in a couple of days. If, for some reason, the soul is wandering in the world the ceremonies will help him. There is not a single example of a ghost in our community, for the ceremonies insure that the soul will not be wandering helpless in this world. They help him go to the other world.

Q. If a person dies during the Gatha days [five additional days at the end of every year], what day should be kept as the day for his monthly ceremonies?

A. If anyone dies on a Gatha day, his 4th, 10th, siruza (30th) day and 31st day ceremonies should be done by counting from the day of his death. After that every monthly ceremony should be performed on the day Frawardin.

Since the Gatha days occur only at the end of the year, the day Frawardin (19th day) of each month has been selected.

The ceremony for the anniversary day should be performed exactly one year after the day of demise. Cf. the Pahlavi commentary to Vendidad 8[.22].

Nowadays this is not strictly followed. If one dies on the first Gatha day, for example, the ceremonies through the first 31 days are performed as stated by Erachji. But the second monthly ceremony is performed on the first calendar day of the next month. Likewise, if a person dies on the second or third Gatha day, his second monthly ceremony is performed on the second or third calendar day of the next month. This is not the correct way, according to the Vendidad, but it does give an extra ceremony to the priest, as ceremonies are generally performed on each Frawardin day during the year by the Parsis in India.

Q. When someone dies, a metal pot full of water and flowers is kept near the place where he dies. Why?

A. Wherever there are water and flowers, the holy souls of the departed (fravashis) happily come. When a man dies, his soul stays in the vicinity for three days, and therefore water and flowers are kept there and an oil lamp fire is also present.

Water and flowers give such comfort and joy to the soul, it is as if the soul were in heaven. Fire protects the soul from bad spirits and gives it a sense of security. Avestan recitation of the Gathas, or the saying of patet and other manthras, gives the greatest joy and protection to the soul. It is best if those dear to the deceased recite such prayers.

Q. If one does not know the name of the deceased, how can his ceremony be performed?

A. In place of his name we must say wahman. If a name is not given to a child before he dies, we must also say wahman. Cf. the Persian Rivayat of Kamdin Shapur.

Wahman is a Pahlavi term meaning 'such and such' or 'so and so'.

Q. If a Zoroastrian is converted to some other religion, then whose name should be used in the ceremony of his son?

A. That son should be adopted by another Zoroastrian who should remember his name because in our religion the name of the son is remembered with his father's name. If this is not possible, then we can say wahman.

The name of the son is said with the name of the father,

maintaining the paywand, i.e. a connection of lineage.

Q. What is the merit in saying the Yasna, Vendidad, and other ceremonies?

A. If the Vendidad is performed with ritual activity (kriya), its merit is 100,000 tanapuhrs, and the act does away with 200 tanapuhr sins. In weight 1200 drahm (a silver currency or weight) is equal to one tanapuhr. If the Vendidad is recited without ritual accompaniment (kriya), it is equivalent to 10,000 tanapuhr merits. If the Yasna is performed with kriya, its merit is 1,000 tanapuhrs. If recited without kriya, 100 tanapuhrs. If the Visperad is performed with kriya, a merit of 10,000 tanapuhrs is earned; without kriya, 1,000 tanapuhrs. If the Frawardin Yasht is performed with kriya, 60 tanapuhrs; without kriya, six tanapuhrs. If a dron service is performed with kriya, ten tanapuhrs. If one says or asks another to say litanies to Khorshed, Mihr, Mah Bakhtar, Aban and Atash, it is one tanapuhr merit. If one takes baj before partaking of a meal, it is one tanapuhr merit. If one takes baj before answering the call of nature, it is one tanapuhr merit. Cf. the Persian Rivayat of Bahman Punjia and also the Avesta-o-Zand.

CHAPTER FOURTEEN

Zoroastrian morals: the good life man should live

Q. We are believers in one God. What, then, is the reason for reciting litanies (niyayesh) and hymns of praise (yashts) to shining things (nur)?

A. It is a religious injunction to bow down to shining things and praise the fireshtes. This does not mean that we worship them, but God has created all good things and has put qualities and virtues in them. From these qualities we receive many kinds of benefits. Therefore we must praise these good things and the fireshtes who preside over them. In that way we recognize the power of the creator and his wonderful nature. It is the command of God that we should praise all creation. Cf. Vendidad 19[.14]: "Oh Zoroaster, this creation which is of Ohrmazd, do you yourself praise it."

Ohrmazd is the supreme being; the fireshtes do their allotted work under Him. They depend on God for their existence; they are not self-created, but are worthy of praise as beneficent spirit beings.

Q. What is of primary importance in life?

A. From birth on we must be righteous and pious. In Yasna 48[.5] God says "Piety is the best thing for man from (the time of) his birth."

Q. How can we attain paradise?

A. We attain it by good thoughts, good words, and good deeds. It is said in the Avestan fragment called Vispa Humata [so called from its beginning words]: "All good thoughts, good words, and good deeds lead man to paradise."

Q. What deeds lead us to hell?

A. Evil thoughts, evil words and evil deeds. It is said in the prayer Vispa Humata: "All evil thoughts, words and deeds lead man to hell."

Q. Does the religion teach us to always be truthful?

A. We must cling to the truth and be steadfast in it. It is very advantageous. Yasna 31[.19] states: "A truth-speaker receives honor and is a master without fear."

Q. What do we receive in return for truthfulness?

A. In every task we become victorious. One who speaks the truth is never defeated in any task. Cf. the Srosh Yasht Hadokht [Yt. 11.3]: "By speaking true words we receive many victories."

Q. What is the teaching concerning charity?

A. God considers a man dear to him if he has showered wealth on him. It is necessary for him to aid a helpless man and give charity. Vendidad 4[.44] states: "If anyone approaches with the hope of receiving charity it is the duty of the rich to fulfill his wish."

Q. What advantage do we receive by nourishing the poor?

A. God gives greatness to him who nourishes the poor that walk on the path of God. Cf. the Ahunwar prayer: "Whoever nourishes the poor, God gives him greatness."

Q. What benefits are there for a doer of good deeds?

A. It is our duty to be good to everyone. If we are good, our name remains in this world forever, and in that world we attain happiness. Cf. Yasna 43[.1]: "He is a good man through whom goodness reaches other persons in all places. God gives such a person greatness." *Good deeds are not done out of self-interest. The good reputation one acquires by doing good deeds is merely another word for the fragrance of one's good deeds which endear him to others.*

Q. What is the teaching regarding industriousness?

A. An industrious and hard working man is loved by one and all. Such a person is considered one of good faith and everyone loves him. Concerning that see the Visperad [7.1]: "We praise industry and courage."

Q. What is the injunction for increasing prosperity in the world?

A. We must keep all the good creations of the world prosperous and all good men should keep their bodily limbs intact and in good strength. This is the work of the worthy. Cf. Yasna 46[.12]: "Those who make the world prosperous through good thoughts and honest endeavors are those who live a virtuous life in good thought."

Q. Should we get angry or not?

A. We should not. By getting angry we damage many activities. The man who has no intelligence and is foolish arouses his anger. Cf. Yasna 49[.4]: "Those who promote wrath and jealousy are of evil intellect." *When we are angry, we do not accomplish our work with any success. Thus we damage our activities.*

Q. Should we think evil or not?

A. We should not think evil of others. He who thinks evil of others first makes himself ill and in the end goes to hell. Cf. Yasna 49[.11]: "An evil thinker is a man worthy of hell."

To think ill of others has a reverse effect; others in turn come to think ill of you.

Q. Should we teach evil to others?

A. If we teach evil to others, they will walk on a bad path and act sinfully. This will result in much damage to the world and the responsibility for their damage is on him who teaches them to sin. Cf. Yasna 45[.1]: "An evil preacher is the spoiler of your life."

Damaging actions are those which bring harm to others and impede the progress of the world. If one lies to another, animosity results, and eventually there is chaos everywhere. This is spiritual damage. It is better to lead a person on the right path and save his soul.

Progress has to do with whatever good things are produced and used for the benefit of mankind. If one does not work and becomes idle, he invites poverty. In that way he impedes the progress of the world. Instead, one should seek to create a prosperous, advantageous atmosphere all around. Any endeavor, whether it is specifically moral or purely technological or scientific, if it is undertaken with a good motive, gladdens the soul, and thus helps one's fellow human beings and brings satisfaction to oneself. It promotes general goodness.

Q. How bad is it to tell lies?

A. Telling lies is the work of a very mean person. No one gives any weight to the utterances of such a person, and it is necessary to keep away from him. Cf. the Ardibehesht Yasht [Yt. 3.16]: "May the most lying of liars be smitten."

Q. What happens if one has greed?

A. A greedy man has no prestige. Greed is the work of a mean man. Cf. Yasna 16[.8]: "Keep away from the greed of a wicked man."

Q. What happens if one is idle?

A. An idle man lives in this world in eternal poverty and lives his life miserably. In the next world he goes to hell. Cf. Visperad [18.2]: "A man who is idle is worthy of hell."

Q. What punishment is there for a miser?

A. If a wealthy man behaves like a miser, he is a slave to wealth in this world and it seems as though he is created this way. In the next world he goes to hell. Cf. Yasna 18[.5]: "He who avoids doing unnoticed charity is a man worthy of hell."

Q. What is the sin in stealing?

A. Stealing is a very sinful act. No one likes his [a thief's] presence. We must protect others from him. Cf. Yasna 12[.2]: "From the Zoroastrian streets I prevent the harm done by thieves and robbers."

Q. Is arrogance bad?

A. Many people become arrogant because of money or knowledge. This is a sign of ruin. Therefore, prudent men do not become arrogant. In our religion an arrogant man is hated. It is so stated in the Ardibehesht Yasht [Yt. 3.8]: "Keep away from those who have arrogant thoughts."

Q. Should we be vengeful?

A. There are many persons who, out of the slightest enmity toward another, are forever vengeful in their minds. God disapproves of that. Cf. the Ardibehesht Yasht [Yt. 3.15]: "May those who remain vengeful be smitten."

Q. Is it proper to find fault?

A. One should not find fault with any man. By doing so we spoil the good work of that person. We must keep away from a person who finds fault in others. The Ardibehesht Yasht [Yt. 3.8] states: "Keep away from those who find fault."

We are referring here to those who are spitefully finding fault, i.e. slanderers. This is not an injunction against discernment in human matters.

Q. Is it good to have an evil eye?

A. It is very bad. Upon seeing the world and everything around us we must thank God for what he has given us. He who sees these things with an evil eye is hated in our religion. Cf. the Ardibehesht Yasht [Yt. 3.8]: "Stay away from those who cast an evil eye."
When a person, for example, sees you enjoy something that he cannot, and his heart burns inside him and he thinks 'why should you have this and not me' and he wishes your ruin, such a man casts an evil eye. It is a mental attitude, and it has a physical effect. If one looks at you with such intention, your health decreases. The glance itself has some sort of power; meanness is there and he transmits his meanness in his glance. If we are out with our children, and we see such a person coming, we quickly call in the children. Our Zoroastrian way of looking at things is the opposite. If we see you happy, we hope that God may keep you like that. And when we see an unhappy man, we try to make him happy. Avoid the person with the evil eye.

Q. Should we be jealous when we see another's prestige, wealth, learning or other such assets?

A. No. It is like burning ourselves up without fire. Our religion teaches us to avoid jealousy. Cf. Yasna 48[.7]: "Forever and ever, always avoid anger and jealousy."

Q. Should we live in peace with everyone?

A. Yes. It is the work of a worthy man to live in peace with everyone. God approves of one who lives in peace and courage. Cf. Visperad [7.1]: "We praise peace and courage."

Q. Should we be friends with wicked persons?

A. By being friends with wicked persons we learn wicked acts, and proceed to hell. We must keep away from them. That is the teaching of our religion. Cf. the Srosh Yasht Hadokht [Yt. 11.2]: "He who is a friend of wicked persons is more wicked than the wicked."

Q. What about deceivers?

A. Those who deceive others by giving false explanations are the opponents of religion. Thus they become wicked. Cf. Yasna 53[.8]: "Those who adopt wickedness cannot comprehend the religion but are deceivers."

Q. What is the merit of cultivating land?

A. To adopt the profession of an agriculturalist is to work at increasing the world. Hence to promote that work is equivalent to promoting the religion. Vendidad 3[.31] states: "He who plants grain plants goodness and is the increaser and propagator of the Mazda-worshipping religion."

Q. Is it meritorious to help another marry?

A. Yes. If a person who is about to marry comes to you with the hope of being helped, you should help him according to your means. It is a meritorious act. Cf. Vendidad 4[.44]: "If one comes to you with a desire to marry a woman, help him do that."

The kind of help referred to could be either financial or help in kind, giving the poor some furniture, for example. This is not a reference to wedding presents, but gifts before the marriage. The parents of the woman also give a dowry, the idea being that because the man will look after the woman for the rest of his life, initially some amount should be given to him to help him look after her. It is not a matter of extorting money by way of dowry, as some people practice. The Parsis help the couple in very practical ways.

Q. Should we use our money like the idle rich?

A. We must produce wealth with our own labor and enjoy it. It is better to eat little from your own earnings than to eat well from unearned wealth. We ask God in the Mah Niyayesh [Ny. 3.10]: "Give me food from my own labor."

Q. What is the religion's teaching about keeping promises?

A. It is the virtue of a true gentleman to keep a promise and we should not recognize a promise-breaker as a religious man. Thus we must keep away from one who breaks promises. Cf. Yasna 61[.3]: "Keep away from a covenant breaker and from one who tampers."

A promise-breaker is not a religious man because he does not keep his word, and therefore is unreliable. If he is unreliable to man, how can he be reliable to God? The Avesta will have no efficacy when he prays.

Q. Is idol worship a sin?

A. Yes. To believe in images and idols and to give respect to such things is a very heinous sin. We must keep away from such actions. It is so stated in Yasna 32[.3]: "If you worship daevas [male demons] and drujs [female demons] you will be ruined."

Images and idols are lifeless. We adore nature which is full of life, something that grows, that promotes, that has a beneficent effect on mankind. The sun, for example, gives life and emits light; happiness surrounds it. A flowing river running eventually to the ocean speaks of the magnitude of God and his greatness.

Q. Should we have faith in another religion?

A. No. Our religion is very holy. We should not have faith in any religion except our own. Vendidad 15[.2] states: "If a person, being a member of the good religion, willingly accepts the commandments of another religion and speaks pejoratively of our religion, he becomes a tanapuhr sinner."

Q. What about adultery?

A. Adultery is a sinful act according to our religion, and a person committing such actions displeases God. In Vendidad 18[.61-62] Zoroaster asks God: "Oh Ohrmazd, who is vengeful toward you and who harms you most among those who cause harm?" Ohrmazd replied: "An adulteress."

Q. Should we squander money?

A. To earn money man has to undergo a variety of difficulties. It is with great labor that he earns money. To squander it in wrong ways is not approved by God.

Vendidad 5[.60] states: "God has not given treasures and goods to be spent on the wrong path."

Q. Should we lie down for long periods of time?

A. We should not sleep for excessive periods of time and become idle. We must stay away from [excessive] sleep so that we can perform many good deeds and beneficent works. Vendidad 11[.9] states: "May the demon of slothfulness which increases idleness depart."

Q. Who created sleep?

A. God has created sleep for the rest and comfort of men and animals. Visperad [7.3] states: "We praise the sleep which Ohrmazd has created for the joy of all men and animals."

Q. Then how long should we sleep?

A. In a 24 hour day, one-third of it we should sleep, and not more than that. Cf. Atash Niyayesh [Ny. 5.11]: "I sleep for the third part of a whole day. May God give me no more sleep so that I can wake up on time."

Q. What does the religion teach about preservation of cattle?

A. From cattle we receive various kinds of benefits; therefore, we must nourish them. We must give them fodder and shelter. This is the commandment of our religion. Cf. Yasna 10[.20]: "[Give] fodder, shelter and care to the cattle because they increase our food."

Q. Should we take a bribe?

A. It is a sin to tell a lie and spoil the work of a truthful man by taking a bribe. It is prohibited in our holy religion. In Yasna 32[.13] it is said: "Those who crave greatness by taking a bribe are evil thinkers and spoilers of the world."

Erachji paraphrases the Avestan quotes rather than translating them as modern philologists do.

Q. Should we give to bad persons?

A. No. Those who shower gifts on bad thinkers become bad thinkers themselves. Yasna 18[.6] states: "It is prohibited to give gifts to bad persons. Those who give gifts to bad persons always have thoughts of bad deeds in their minds."

Q. Should we seek knowledge?

A. Yes, everyone should yearn for knowledge because through learning the advantage of both worlds is gained. Through knowledge of all religious matters and of the world one follows the right path and increases his wisdom. Yasna 9[.22] states: "Those who go to school to learn, Hom yazad increases their intellect."

Hom is the giver of wisdom, both religious and worldly.

Q. Should the rich establish schools?

A. The rich should establish schools so that the children of poor families can learn. It is a great meritorious act and also a commandment of God. Cf. Vendidad 4[.44]: "If anyone approaches you with the desire to learn knowledge, you should teach him knowledge."

Real knowledge does not come in conflict with religion. Ours may be the only religion which has survived only in fragments, so many historical and geographical truths of the Avesta are lost beyond redemption. But from what remains we can say there is no conflict between science and religion. Science has to do with the secular. What is right one day will be wrong the next. But religion is based on the solid rock of faith which is infused with holiness. Science has no means of evaluating the sacred. Religion tells us what the responsibility of the soul is, so that we can attain heaven. Holiness is beyond the scope of science.

Q. Should we educate girls?

A. Yes. God loves women who are holy and whose thoughts are good. Therefore if they acquire knowledge they will understand their duties. To educate them is approved by God. Cf. Aiwisruthrem Gah [Gah 4.9]: "We praise the holy women who are advanced in good thoughts, good words, good deeds and who are holy and learned."

Q. What is the advantage of acquiring an education?

A. Education increases our knowledge. Through it we come to understand well what are the proper duties pertaining to religion and the world. Thus we can attain happiness in both worlds. Cf. Yasna 46[.3]: "Acquiring knowledge benefits our intellect."

Q. Is there another advantage?

A. Our first duty is to acquire knowledge. By learning we acquire all types of help and joy. Yasna 15[.1] states: "By learning we acquire help and joy." *'Help' in this context means that we are able to think, produce, solve problems, make out our own way.*

Q. What time of the day should we seek knowledge?

A. According to God's command it is better to seek knowledge in the morning, or in the evening or during the first period of the night, or the last period of the night. By this method we can acquire knowledge in good quantity. Cf. Vendidad 4[.45]: "There is an increase of knowledge during the first part of the day, the last part of the day, the first period of night or the last period of the night."

Q. Under whom should we learn?

A. According to the commandment of our religion, we must learn under a perfect teacher so that he can give us good knowledge. Vendidad 4[.45] states: "One must learn under an adept [i.e. proficient] teacher."

Q. Should we be respectful of elders?

A. Those who do not show respect to elders and insult them will not gain any greatness. Cf. Yasna 29[.6]: "He who does not show respect to an elder will never receive honor."

Q. Should we remain honest?

A. Honesty is a very good virtue and everyone loves an honest man. It is stated in Yasna 48[.5]: "Whoever acts with honesty is a man of good intelligence."

Q. Should we be merciful?

A. It is the teaching of our religion to show mercy to everyone. In our religious books a man without mercy is given the title of daeva. Yasna 45[.11] states: "Those who are cruel toward man are daevas without mercy."

Q. What advantage does one gain by cleaning the soil?

A. If we remove bad polluting things from the soil and keep it clean, it gives health to mankind. If we do not do that, we spoil the health of people and so are guilty. Cf. Vendidad 5[.4]: "Those who throw very dirty things on this earth are smiters of purity and thereby become guilty and cause their souls to lament."
Purity here refers to cleanliness. For a thing to be pure it has to be clean.

Q. Should we keep water clean from dirty things?

A. Yes. Water is one of the best gifts given by God to mankind. We must keep it clean and use it. If we do not keep it clean and use impure water, then it spoils the health of men. That is why our religion commands us not to allow any dirty things in water. It is so stated in Vendidad 6[.29]: "One should not throw or keep bones, hair, flesh, urine, or blood in water. If one does so he is guilty."
There are proper places to dispose of these things. One must take the baj of Srosh, for his protection, and then dispose of them in a desolate area so as not to pollute the soil, water, etc., that are necessary for the continuation of life.

Q. What punishment is received by one who injures mankind?

A. To injure persons and cause them pain is a very sinful deed. A person who does so is worthy of hell. Cf. Yasna 65[.8]: "He who injures mankind is a cruel person worthy of hell."

Q. Should we hear and learn all matters relating to religion?

A. Yes. It is a great advantage to hear and learn all

matters relating to religion. By doing this we gain happiness in both worlds. Cf. Yasna 49[.9]: "Hear and learn the religion, it produces great benefit."

Q. What kind of person should a religious instructor be?

A. A religious instructor should be one who always treads on the right path. It is stated in the Nirangestan: "We must have a religious instructor who walks on the very good path."

Q. What is the benefit of trying to earn merit?

A. He who toils to perform a meritorious act acquires happiness in that world and a good reputation in this world. Cf. Yasna 30[.10]: "Those who endeavor for the sake of God and for the sake of meritorious deeds earn very good fame." *The fame or reputation Erachji is speaking about here has nothing to do with publicity. He is referring to the performance of good deeds without noticing people's opinions about them. People may have immense respect for you in private; they love and praise you secretly. This is the type of reputation he is referring to, not the kind where persons flatter you to your face and do not say what they really think.*

Q. What is the benefit of acting justly?

A. If a man comes to us seeking justice we must be just to him, because to give a true verdict is like doing and learning bandagi to God. Cf. the Denkard.

Q. What is the religious teaching regarding speaking good words?

A. To keep sweetness in the mouth and then speak good words is like doing the Yasna ceremony in honor of amahraspand Vohuman. Cf. the Denkard.

Q. What is the religious teaching about performing works of merit?

A. When a person learns to do good and meritorious deeds of all kinds, and practices them, God resides in his heart. Cf. the Denkard.

Q. Should we obey our parents or not?

A. Those who act in accordance with the wishes of their

parents and respect them do the equivalent of bandagi to God. Cf. the Denkard.

Q. Who receives honor in both worlds?

A. He who desires to earn his livelihood through his own profession receives honor in both worlds. Cf. the Denkard.

Q. How should one behave as a worshipper of Ohrmazd?

A. If one behaves in accordance with the command of Ohrmazd with good intention and willingness, it is like doing Yasna in honor of Ohrmazd. Cf. the Denkard.

Q. What benefit does one gain by loving the Zoroastrian religion?

A. God himself will take care of a person who loves the Zoroastrian religion and trusts his whole being to God. Cf. the Denkard.

Q. What benefit does one gain by giving to a holy person?

A. One should love those who are deserving and holy. It is equivalent to smiting and keeping away bad persons. Cf. the Denkard.

Q. When should one do meritorious deeds and bandagi?

A. Meritorious deeds and bandagi to God should be done today, and never left for tomorrow. That means one must do good acts as soon as possible. Cf. the Denkard.

Q. Who should be considered a disciple of Zoroaster?

A. A man or woman who respects the teachings of Zoroaster should be considered a disciple trained under him. Cf. the Denkard.

Q. What benefit does one receive by being charitable to the dervishes?

A. Being charitable to the dervishes, meaning "those who are walking on the path of God," is like bringing increase to the world. Cf. the Denkard.

The term dervish comes from the Pahlavi drigosh, meaning the poor or needy. They are the pious poor who live a very simple life and sing hymns in praise of God. They bring blessings to all and depend upon alms for subsistence.

Q. What is the advantage of giving to devout people?

A. Those who give things in charity to holy persons of our religion perform actions equivalent to promoting the Mazda-worshipping religion. Cf. the Denkard.

Q. How should one earn money?

A. One should not earn money by doing sinful deeds. If one earns money by a sinful act and keeps it in his home, the money which he has earned by good means and by the sweat of his brow decreases. Cf. the Denkard.

Q. What is the punishment for one who afflicts other persons?

A. There are bad thoughts residing perennially in the body of a person harming others. He goes to hell in the other world. Cf. the Denkard.

Q. What principles should a person observe?

A. He should consume only that which he has earned; he must keep his promise; he must do his duty; and he must love only his wife. These are good acts. Cf. the Denkard.

Q. What things should every person remember?

A. We must always remember these five things in our hearts:
1) Am I a man or a demon?
2) Do I belong to paradise or hell?
3) Am I walking on the path of God or the devil?
4) Am I following the good or the bad?
5) Shall I go again to heaven or proceed to hell?
Cf. the Denkard.

Q. What deeds are best in our religion?

A. There are five things which are [considered] best in our religion: truthfulness, charity, skill, endeavor and giving encouragement to others in good deeds. Cf. the Denkard.

Q. Should we abuse [others] or not?

A. It is a sinful act to abuse anyone and to say bad words. Abuse is a sin equal to telling lies. Cf. the Denkard.

Q. What works should a man do?

A. Man must keep three things in mind: He must make enemies his friends; he must purify the sinful; he must make the ignorant well-informed. Cf. the Denkard.

Q. How does a man learn to do good deeds?

A. By sitting in three places his would becomes full of goodness: sitting in the house of a wise man, in the house of a good man, and in a fire temple (Atash Bahram). Cf. the Denkard.

It is said that everyday the yazads and amahraspands hold assembly three times in an Atash Bahram and bestow their virtue and righteousness. The more often a person goes there the more virtue and righteousness become inherent in him.

Q. Should we give charity to bad people?

A. No. To give anything to bad people is equal to doing damage to good people. Cf. the Denkard.

Q. How much should we speak and how much should we eat?

A. By eating in moderation our body gets strong. By speaking in moderation our soul receives benefit. Cf. the Denkard.

If you speak too much, your words become dead, and you increase the possibility of lies.

Q. Who is a friend of the other world?

A. Whoever does good deeds for the sake of the other world, desires blessings from spiritual beings and does not care for this world is a friend of that world. Cf. the Denkard.

Q. What happens if one associates with a bad person?

A. When one does this he becomes bad himself by learning bad characteristics. It is better to avoid such a person. Cf. the Denkard.

Q. Should we tell our secrets to anyone?

A. We must not tell our secrets to many persons because if we do our secrets are revealed. Many persons cannot keep our secrets. This in turn harms our work. Cf. the Denkard.

Q. What things are advantageous to man?

A. A good nature, wisdom, skill and religion are advantageous to man. Good behavior is the weapon of nature. Bandagi to God and doing goodness to people is the weapon of wisdom. Following the right path is the weapon of skill and being steadfast in the religion is the weapon of religion (den). Cf. the Denkard.

Skill, here, refers to proficiency in one's chosen profession.

Q. What possessions are better, those of this world or the other?

A. If we use the possessions and wealth of this world only for the sake of goodness, then they are called real possessions of wealth. Otherwise possessions of this world are of no avail. But good and meritorious deeds which are the possessions and wealth of the other world give us happiness forever. These will remain forever. One possession of that world is better than 1000 possessions of this world. Cf. the Denkard.

Q. What is the advantage of living a righteous life?

A. To live in righteousness is much approved by God. God gives twofold to him who lives in righteousness. Cf. the Denkard.

There is a Pazand prayer which says if you go one step forward toward righteousness it comes 1200 steps to meet you.

Q. What benefit does a charitable man receive?

A. One who does charitable acts receives a place in garothman ('house of songs'). It is always better to be charitable to good people who believe in God. Cf. the Denkard.

Q. Which sinner is a margarzan sinner according to our religion?

A. A margarzan sinner, according to the Denkard, is anyone who extinguishes the fire of an Atash Bahram, who throws dead matter into a fire or water, or who inters a corpse in the earth. A margarzan sin means a sin worthy of death. Cf. the Denkard.

Q. What are the spiritual aspects of our being?

A. There are five spiritual aspects: 1) life (gyan: 'vital force'); 2) soul (rawan); 3) conscience (axw);

4) consciousness (boy); 5) guardian spirit (farohar). The function of life is to take care of the body and give it joy, purity and strength to walk about. It strengthens the fire of the body so that misery can be removed. The function of the soul is to keep us from doing bad deeds and direct us to do everything with intelligence and thought. It shows us in dreams heavenly things and directs us to do good deeds. The function of conscience is to admonish the body and soul to do good deeds and to avoid bad deeds. It tries to keep away wrath, jealousy and other such vices. The function of consciousness is to take care that the intellect has its role in every act so that one is engrossed in his work. It also gives strength to the body and bodily joints. The function of the guardian spirit is to give strength to the body and every joint of the body through food. It takes out bad things from the body and removes pain. Cf. the Saddar Bundahesh.

When Erachji says that consciousness gives strength to the body, he is thinking of the fact that when one is unconscious the body has no strength, it is not alert. Not all Parsis would agree with the functions ascribed by Erachji to all five spiritual aspects of the body, especially the last mentioned, i.e., the farohar. Farohars give us divine guidance in all matters and help us follow the right path.

Q. How can one attain happiness in both worlds?

A. Recognize as our equal one who is inferior to us, and one who is equal to us recognize as greater than us, and one who is greater than us, recognize as our leader. Do not worry about every action because by doing so our body becomes weak. The strength of our soul to do merited works also diminishes. We should not commit sin out of a sense of shame (sharm) and we should not perform immoral acts. By doing so we damage our wealth, body and soul. The greatest sin is adultery. It is also wrong to be a partner to a greedy person.

Concerning these matters see the Menog i Khrad. Hereafter [for the remainder of Chapter Fourteen] you will find quotes from the Menog i Khrad and admonitions from Adarbad Mahraspand and Adar-Farnbag Farrokhzad.

Adarbad Mahraspand was High Priest and prime minister of Shapur II (309-379 A.C.). The composition of patet, nam stayishn, and other Pazand prayers are ascribed to him. Adar-Farnbag Farrokhzad was a learned commentator of the post-Sasanian times. He was one of the compilers of the encyclopaedic Pahlavi work, the Denkard. Erachji states that one should not commit a sin because of sharm. Sharm in modern Persian connotes 'modesty, bashfulness, shame'. By translating the term with the English word 'shame', we intend to convey the basic sense of committing a sin out of fear of being disgraced or shaming someone. An example used to explain its meaning is as follows. Suppose a judge calls you as a witness in some legal case involving your superior. The judge asks a question and although you know the correct reply which would go against your superior, you don't say it in order to protect him. You do not have the moral courage to speak the truth in public. This is committing a sin for the sake of a reputation, or out of a sense of shame to avoid disgracing someone.

Q. How does our body remain healthy?

A. By eating only when we are hungry, by eating in moderation and by keeping our body active.

Q. What kind of work should we do?

A. We must do that kind of work which does not put us to shame and which is not without prestige.

Q. In what things should we not put our trust?

A. We should not put our trust in this life, possessions, prestige, honor and high office. We should not be proud of these things because they do not remain forever.

Q. What are the best things in this world?

A. For the benefit of the soul it is best to be charitable to the pious. For receiving honor in both worlds it is best to adopt truthfulness. It is also best to be thankful to God for his gifts, to be humanitarian, and to have fortitude in all activities. In order to be healthy it is best to be happy. We must also be content with happiness and unhappiness.

To be content with happiness and unhappiness means that we must accept whatever God gives us.

Q. Which merited works are best?

A. To be charitable, to walk in truthfulness, and to practice khwetodas in order to safe-guard our family virtue. To be at one with our co-religionists, to praise God, to build dharma-shalas for the devout and religious persons, to wish good for everyone, and to look favorably upon good people.

The Phl. term khwetodas has been understood by Parsi dasturs to mean marriages between relatives (the nearest being first cousins) so that family virtues can be preserved.

Dharma-shalas are places of refuge and shelter. Basically they are free rooms, or rooms with nominal fees at most, where Parsis can stay for several days. In a small village they are probably near the fire temple or in the same compound and the priest manages them.

Q. Whose help and protection is the strongest?

A. Except God's, all other help and protection are weak.

Q. Whom should we recognize as our best friend?

A. One who is our child and who is religious, wise, of good reputation, and a doer of good deeds.

Q. From whom do we receive much happiness and joy?

A. From one's own wife who has a good disposition, good nature and good thoughts, and who is the preserver of her reputation, the house and her husband. From such there is external happiness.

Q. What things give joy?

A. Health, a state of fearlessness, purity, piety, and good fame.

Q. What type of wealth gives joy?

A. Wealth which has been earned honestly with the sweat of our brow, and is spent only on the right path.

Q. Which is better, poverty or wealth?

A. It is better to earn a little money through the virtuous path and remain poor than to amass wealth and enjoy becoming a rich man by telling lies and cheating. To make the body happy with ill-gotten wealth is a sinful act.

Q. What things should we always keep in mind?

A. We must remember the following: first, nothing of this world will remain forever; second, death does not spare anyone; third, after death the soul has to give an account; fourth, if we commit sinful acts we shall go to hell.

Q. What is better, to live or to die?

A. It is better to die rather than pass through this world telling lies, cheating, being deceitful and doing other bad deeds. In that way one would be spared more pains in hell.

Q. What is the end for a person who ridicules?

A. While he is living, the glory of his face and body is diminished, and after that his soul is not placed in a high position, but receives a place in hell.

Q. What sort of friendship should we avoid?

A. Avoid that friendship in which there is vengeance and which damages whatever work is done.

Q. Who is eternally unhappy?

A. A jealous man remains full of sorrow because he cannot see any good in others. Hence he causes misery for himself and consumes himself with his own fire [of jealousy].

Q. Who should be recognized as a worthy man?

A. He who does not crave for things of this world, but loves the other world and craves always for good deeds is a worthy man.

Q. Whom should we not trust?

A. We should not trust a man who has no fear of God and who does not honor others, because he who has no awe of God would not hesitate to do bad deeds.

Q. Whom should we understand to be a very strong man?

A. He who with piety keeps bad traits from his body and always puts good traits to work.

Q. What is better than wealth?

A. Intelligence, wisdom, learning, skill and health are very great gifts. The learned man is like gold; wherever he goes he is esteemed and receives honor.

Q. What activities are equal to <u>bandagi</u> to God?

A. According to the teaching, to live in truth and goodness and not harm any person in any way and always try to perform good deeds is considered equal to great <u>bandagi</u>.

Q. How should we perform prayers of penitence (<u>patet</u>) for delivering our soul?

A. We should not commit sin knowingly. If it is committed unknowingly, then we must affirm that we will not do such a sin again. If we have committed such a sin, we should not become hopeless [fearing] that God will not give us heaven. Rather we must atone for our sin because the soul of a sinner is purified by doing <u>patet</u>. *No person can claim to be sinless. Therefore, <u>patet</u> is essential for one and all, even for those who might claim to be 100% pure, for one can commit a sin unconsciously. <u>Patet</u> is the remedy for an unconscious as well as a conscious sin.*

Q. Whom should we understand to be a good man?

A. He who keeps company with virtuous persons and learns their virtues is a good man.

Q. What should we consider as dear to us?

A. We must always think about doing works of merit and also avoiding sins. We must not leave for tomorrow good deeds which we should perform today because these good deeds are the wealth of that world and we cannot be sure that life [will be ours] tomorrow.

Q. What matters should we not think about?

A. If there is anything we are not able to get in this world, we should not worry about it, because this thing cannot accompany us to the other world. Rather we must be steadfast in trying to attain the things of that world.

Q. What sorts of things will we be sorry about?

A. We will be sorry and regret it very much if we do not educate our wife and children, if we tell certain stories to others which we have heard from someone but do not evaluate or verify, and also if we reveal secrets to a foolish man.

Q. What is there that is shameful in both worlds?

A. We shall be ashamed in both worlds if we keep all kinds of vices within ourselves and if we perform immoral acts.

Q. Who is a senseless man?

A. He is senseless who maintains a friendship with a wrathful man and also who quarrels with a madman.

The seriousness of wrath or anger is that through it one can perform the most heinous, cruel sins which cannot be amended. When angered, one does not listen to wise counsel.

Q. How does one acquire ill-fame?

A. If you borrow money from a lowly-born man you will be harassed by him unfavorably.

Erachji's point here is that a good man, however destitute he may become, should always approach another good man for help and never a mean person, that is one whose mind is always on money, not on help. The latter type of person would relentlessly pursue the good man indebted to him and destroy his reputation.

Q. What type of man should be befriended?

A. You should befriend the man who is wise, of good disposition and discerning. Many advantages will accrue from his friendship.

Q. How does a man remain sorrowful?

A. By quarrelling with others and entering into other's quarrels.

Q. How can one attain goodness in both worlds?

A. By endearing oneself to a wise and prudent man, considering him greater than oneself, remembering his admonishments and acting according to them.

Q. How does a man lose his fame?

A. By telling lies, taking false oaths, by giving false evidence. All these are great sins.

Q. How does one acquire a good reputation in this world and deliverance in the other world?

A. By being charitable according to one's means to those who walk the good path.

Q. How can one attain greatness?

A. By respecting the leader and superior of our own community, by obeying his words and honoring all persons according to their status.

Q. To whom should we give most respect?

A. We must give respect to old people and should not ridicule them, for tomorrow we too shall become old.

Q. What are the duties of parents toward their children?

A. Parents should give them an education in their childhood so that they will be able to understand the goodness of both worlds. The man without knowledge is like a blind man. If parents do not fulfill their duty to children they become sinful.

Education is our long-standing commitment. We encourage high standards and an eagerness to keep on studying. Many Parsis have encouraged non-Parsi children to attend schools, paid their fees and enabled them to climb to very high positions.

Q. How does one lose his prestige?

A. By going to an assembly and instead of taking a seat

equal to one's status, taking a higher seat.

Q. How does one acquire an evil reputation?

A. By not respecting one's parents and by injuring them. We should not be friends with such a person.

Q. How does our bodily strength diminish?

A. Overeating increases sickness. Eating in moderation increases our health. It is the work of cattle to eat immoderately.

Q. How do our wishes get fulfilled?

A. In every task we must be patient and content and we must be pleased with what God has in store for us.

Q. How does one bring ruin on himself?

A. Through pride, as this is the attitude of a senseless and haughty man.

Q. What leads to defamation?

A. Greed. A greedy man loses his prestige even for a mean thing. One also loses prestige by talking too much and speaking without thought.

Q. How does one become bad?

A. By becoming a friend of a bad man. A wicked man stings like a serpent and one cannot expect goodness from him.

Q. How can we ward off wickedness?

A. Goodness comes to a person through learning, skill, and intelligence, which [in turn] drive wickedness, poverty, difficulty and pain away.

Q. Whom should we understand to be our friend?

A. He who helps us in our difficulty, sorrow, and helplessness is our real friend. In good times we can have many friends, but one should not trust them.

Q. Who is a fortunate man?

A. He who maintains righteousness and purity, who has genuine trust in God and religion, and who avoids those of bad faith.

Those who are of bad faith, such as cheaters, idolaters, fakes and charlatans, are worse than those with no religion.

Q. What is the faith of God and what is a wicked faith?

A. To think, speak and do good; the opposite is a wicked faith.

Unfortunately Erachji has given a very incomplete answer here. The Zoroastrian faith does not restrict itself to ethics. One must also refer to the spiritual exercises which make up the life of a true Zoroastrian, that is, the holy ceremonies, manthras, and the wide variety of customs and practices of our tradition.

Q. Who are the enemies of our soul?

A. There are vices in our body which lull us and lead us astray. As a result our soul suffers in the next world.

Vices such as enmity and vengeance are functions of the body that affect the soul. The soul is ultimately responsible for all actions, however, because the soul directs the body.

Q. Whom should we consider a man of good lineage?

A. A man of good family, in whom we find humility, obedience, a sweet tongue and good manners.

Q. What is the best act of merit?

A. To be pleased over whatever God gives us, no matter how little or how much, being happy over it and showing gratitude to God for it.

Q. Who has the best knowledge?

A. He who administers the affairs of the world very well and performs actions in a moderate way so as not to damage religious or worldly affairs is the one with the best knowledge.

One who advances the society as well as the religion in a measured, moderate way, with equal attention to both, is a man of true knowledge.

Q. What is our greatest enemy?

A. Our greatest enemy: the vices in us which cause pain and damage.

Q. Who is a person of misfortune?

A. He who is aware of the teachings of the religion but does not act according to them and goes on the path of wickedness and praises other faiths.

It is good to appreciate other religions, no doubt, but not at the expense of one's own religion.

Q. Who is a man worthy of praise?

A. A person who is wise and learned and who promotes the name of his father is a man worthy of praise. Also a woman who always walks on the path which makes her husband happy.

Q. Who is our friend to the very end?

A. Our good and virtuous deeds which get us to heaven.

Q. Who is our enemy to the very end?

A. Our bad actions and sinful acts which follow the path to hell.

Q. What is going to last forever?

A. Good actions and merited deeds which give us a good name in this world will accompany us to the other world. Excepting these, nothing else will accompany us.

Q. What is most powerful?

A. Truthfulness: to be honest and speak the truth. This will give us success and increase our fame.

Q. What is the most precious thing?

A. Friendship with the wise and elderly men, and following their admonitions.

Q. How many sins are mentioned in our religion?

A. There are many sins mentioned in our religion. Some of them are enumerated in the patet. A few great sins are:

agrift: when a person holds a weapon in his hand with the intention of striking (another person), it is called the sin of agrift;

owirisht: when one turns the weapon upon another person;

ardush: when one inflicts such a wound that the cut of that wound pains for three days;

xvar: when the wound is over a spread of two-fingers and a half;

<u>bazay</u>: when a wound is made on the hand so that it is fractured and covers a spread of three fingers;

<u>yat</u>: when a foot is wounded so that it is fractured over a spread of three or four toes;

<u>tanapuhr</u>: when a person is wounded in such a way that he becomes lame or incapacitated.

Erachji does not list the greatest sin: <u>margarzan</u>, a sin worthy of death. Examples of <u>margarzan</u> sinners are as follows: one who does not regard Ohrmazd as peerless, or Zoroaster as a genuine prophet; who does not obey the commands of his father, mother, or teacher, but learns witchcraft and practices unnatural intercourse, heresy, deceit, or falsifies the Avesta; who is polluted with <u>nasa</u> (dead matter), throws <u>nasa</u> on fire, in water, or conceals <u>nasa</u> under the earth; who extinguishes an <u>Atash Bahram</u>; who takes away the property of other persons by unjust means and oppression; who casts an evil glance on a strange woman and seduces her; who approves of the religion of wickedness, who gives false evidence against an innocent person, a holy man, a spiritual leader or <u>dastur</u>, leading to their death; who beats an innocent man and permits injustice; who exacts gold from men by foul means; a woman who does not remarry after a year has passed following the death of her husband and sleeps with another man; one who eats bodily refuse with drugs and medicine, or causes them to be consumed by others; who, as a <u>mobed</u> or <u>dastur</u>, does heretical things; or an ignorant woman who causes injury to the fetus or aborts or causes miscarriage. The margarzan sins are enumerated in the <u>Patet</u> and <u>Saddar Bundahesh</u>.

<u>hamemal</u>: a sin in which a false accusation is levelled against someone;

<u>pulshahod</u>: the failure of a living person to perform the six religious duties every year. If

these were not undertaken, the soul is prevented from crossing the bridge. So says the Patet.

CHAPTER FIFTEEN

Women and marriage

Q. At what age should men and women marry, according to our religion?

A. The minimum age for marriage is 15. At this age youth may commence (marriage) according to the Avesta. Cf. the Dadestan i Denig.

Present day practice is usually after 18 years. If marriage is sought prior to that age the father of the girl has to sign his permission.

Q. Should a girl of 15 years marry of her own will or according to the will of her parents?

A. She should marry of her own will. Even when she is 12 years of age she can marry according to her own will. If her parents make her marry without making her happy [i.e., against her will], then that marriage is not proper. Cf. the Rivayat of Shapur Bharuchi.

It is proper to marry at 15 years of age, but even at 12 the girl may select a husband herself and tell her parents about her choice. The point is, the girl should have the dominant role in the selection.

Also, marriage should be understood here in the proper context. A woman can marry at 12 years of age, but she remains with her parents until she reaches puberty and is fit for married life. Then she joins her husband.

In the time of Erachji both boys and girls were marrying very young, even before their Navjotes were performed, i.e., before the age of seven. In such circumstances a temporary sudre-kusti was put on by the marrying couple and it was taken off after the marriage ceremony. The real Navjote ceremony was performed after they had reached seven years of age.

Q. How should we tie the marriage knot?

A. At the marriage ceremony the hands of the couple are tied with a thread and our people understand this to be the marriage knot. But this is incorrect. While the priest blesses the couple at the beginning [of the ceremony], questions are asked of witnesses and their answers are heard. Likewise the marrying couple is asked questions and they reply. This is what should be understood as the marriage knot.

The questions that occur in the ceremony are in Pazand. The couples do not know the meanings of the terms, they simply bow and say yes when given the proper cue. In so doing the witnesses and the marrying couple take the following oaths. The priest first asks the father or guardian of the bridegroom whether he agrees to receive a certain amount of gold and silver (in coins) from the bride, thereby accepting her as new kin in accordance with the superior law and custom of the Mazda-worshipping religion. The bridegroom's father or guardian says: Yes, I agree. Then the priest asks the father or guardian of the bride: Do you swear to welcome the bridegroom with truthful thought, for the increase of good actions and progeny, so long as you live? The bride's father or guardian responds: Yes, I promise. Finally, the priest asks the marrying couple whether they agree to abide by these promises with truthful intent throughout their lives. They both reply: Yes, we approve of it.

Zoroastrians consider the marriage bond important. It is recommended that one should think 100 times before marrying. If a divorce occurs, a divorcee can marry again, as can a widow. But divorce is a legal matter and has nothing to do with a priest. Priests do not encourage divorce. Marriage should be understood as a life partnership and should be maintained throughout life.

Q. Why is the question "Do you approve?" (passand kardid) asked of the marrying couple?

A. Our people understand the phrase passand kardid to mean that the husband is being asked whether he likes his bride, and hence approves of her. But this is the wrong idea. In the oath-taking ceremony the couple is being asked by the priest whether they approve of the oath taken by the two witnesses at their sides. Thus the chief priest asks the question passand kardid of the couple, to which they individually respond passand kardam, "I have approved of it."

Q. What sort of woman should she be?

A. A woman who is willing to give happiness to her husband and who likes to walk on the path of gladness, who takes care of the household and keeps her body pure, such a woman makes a good wife. Cf. the Denkard.

Q. What is the reason for marrying a woman?

A. Marriage at the proper time gives us children so that in this world our lineage remains intact up to eternity.

Q. How does a man become very happy?

A. When his wife does what he likes and loves him he becomes very happy. Cf. the Denkard.

Q. How many classifications of women are enumerated in our literature?

A. There are five kinds:

shahzan: a woman who married with her parents' sanction;

ewagzan: a daughter who has been permitted to marry on the condition that her child be kept as the adopted child of her parents and their wealth be given to that child.

The child, in other words, is the grandchild of the maternal grandparents.

saturzan: a woman who in name is made the wife of a man who died without marrying. She is given whatever wealth he had, by his relatives. When that woman (saturzan) marries another man, the son born of that marriage is given as an adopted son to the deceased.

chakarzan: a woman whose husband has passed away and has remarried another person;

khudrahzan: a woman whose marriage has been arranged by her father but she is not pleased with that arrangement and by her free will marries another person. Cf. the Persian Vajarkard Dini.

These are ancient classifications of women which are not used today. Now we say all women are shahzan.

Q. Is marriage to a widow permitted?

A. Yes. Our prophet Zoroaster had two wives, one shahzan and the other a widow (chakarzan). The name of the shahzan was Havovi and that of the widow is not known. His two sons Urvatatnar and Khurshedcheher were born of the widow and the remaining children were born of the shahzan. So says the Bundahishn. From this we can see that one can marry a widow.

This is a sensitive topic for many Parsis, but Ercahji is an honest man and states his view boldly. In general the tradition does not claim more than one wife for Zoroaster. The Pahlavi text, the Bundahishn, states that Zoroaster had three wives, but this claim is not borne out either in the Avesta or in authentic Pahlavi texts like the Denkard and Zadspram. The last chapters of the Bundahishn, where one finds the reference, are regarded as a later addition by most scholars, probably written in Abbasid times. It is possible that a Zoroastrian convert might have interpolated the reference to Zoroaster as having three wives in order to make his new religion at par with his old one in this respect. Another text which claims Zoroaster had three wives (all alive during Zoroaster's lifetime) is the Pahlavi Wizirkard i Denig. This text is clearly a deliberate elaboration on the part of the author to suit his own purpose. Pahlavi words were wrongly read as names of Zoroaster's wives, and the author had a Parsi friend who sought to marry a second woman while his first wife was alive.

Q. After the death of her husband, when should the wife remarry?

A. Our religion states emphatically that if a woman is pregnant she may marry after four months and ten days; if she has a suckling child she can remarry after 18 months. Cf. the Persian Rivayat of Kaus Kamdin.

Q. If a woman is betrothed and her husband-to-be dies, should she marry as a widow?

A. She should not be considered a widow. Such a woman should be married to another person and the marriage knots should be tied because she was only betrothed and her marriage knots were not tied. Cf. the Persian Rivayat of Kaus Kamdin.

Q. If a Zoroastrian is converted to another religion should his wife marry another person?

A. The woman should not marry another person for one year. Within that period if that man returns to his religion with genuine faith it is better. Otherwise, following that period the woman should be married to another person. Cf. the Persian Rivayat of Shapur Bharuchi.

CHAPTER SIXTEEN

How women in menses should maintain themselves

Q. What should a woman do at the time of menstruation (dashtan)?

A. Shortly before the time approaches, the place (in the home) where she is to sit should be cleared off. Cf. Vendidad 16[.2]: "From the path [where she is to be] the Mazda-worshippers shall take away shrubs and wood and put them in a dry place."

In former times people used to live on the muddy soil so that small shrubs might have grown in the house itself. In order that no living things would come in contact with a menstruating woman they were removed. Such contact would pollute them, and the power of their growth diminished. Pollution is stagnation, decomposition, degeneration, the opposite of growth, increase, prosperity.

Q. What is to be done at the time of menstruation?

A. As soon as a woman feels the effect of menses, she should at once put on clothes kept separate for that purpose. She should sit apart and not touch anything at all. Cf. the Persian Rivayat of Kama Vohra.

Q. Where should a woman in menstruation sit?

A. She should sit in her house where the earth is elevated a little. It is stated in Vendidad 16[.2]: "In that house a high place should be made and she should sit on that."

Q. Should a woman in menses sit on an iron couch?

A. It is better to sit on iron but from the Avestan quote above it appears that in the time of the Avesta in ancient Iran, women used to sit on an elevated place on the soil itself. In various villages in India today they sit on such places because of poverty.
The mound of earth separates the woman from the earth itself. In addition, the mound is a signal to others that this place should not be touched.

Q. What things should a woman in menses keep away from?

A. She should keep away from all things, but mostly from fire water, barsom and holy men. So says Vendidad 16[.4]: "She should keep 15 paces from fire, 15 from water and 15 from barsom, and three paces from a holy man."
Barsom is a bundle of consecrated twigs or metal rods. The mention of fire, water and barsom together indicates that these are liturgically consecrated things. Therefore she should stay 15 paces away from any area where liturgy is being prepared or performed. A holy man is not a consecrated thing; nevertheless she should keep three paces away from him for her very touch would

diminish his glory.

Today, with women employed in various jobs, they must observe these rules the best they can. For example, if a woman is a teacher and is devout, she will sit in a separate place in the home, on an iron bed, and when she leaves and enters the home going to and from work some member of the family will open the door for her so as to preserve the home. The ideal, of course, would be for her to stay home from work.

In the home she should be fed on a metal plate placed on the floor a short distance in front of her. After she eats, she herself should clean the plate with water. A special provision to use water is made for her. If there are non-Parsi servants in the house, they may clean the plates. For them this is not important.

Q. How should she eat her meals?

A. She must put on gloves and then eat with a spoon. Cf. the Persian Rivayat of Kama Vohra.

Here in India women do not use gloves or a spoon, but in Iran the practice continues in some instances even today. These Rivayats Erachji quotes are discussions between Irani Zoroastrians and their Parsi counterparts of past years, but this is not our practice.

Q. Should such women perform kusti?

A. They must partake of food. Therefore, after washing their hands with gomez, they should do kusti.

Gomez, bull's urine, is a strong cleansing agent. On the matter of doing kusti, there are contradictory answers to this question in the Rivayats. Ladies in India do not say any prayers at this time and for that reason are called zan-e binamaz, 'a woman without prayers, i.e. in menses.'

In order to understand an issue where the Rivayats contradict each other, one must first understand the context in which the Rivayats were written. The Indian dasturs were asking questions of their Iranian counter-

parts in order to increase their knowledge and learn other points of view. This is not to imply that the Indian dasturs *were ignorant and asking for advice. Rather, it was an exchange of knowledge. The result was that sometimes they adopted the Persian custom and sometimes it was set aside entirely. The questions came from Navsari, Broach and Surat, from learned people. The questions were being asked of their Iranian brothers of the same class.*

Q. Should a woman in menses touch another woman in menses?

A. No. While in menses they should not touch each other. It is also a sinful act to walk barefoot. Cf. the Persian Rivayat of Kama Vohra.

The prohibition of going barefoot applies to everyone, male and female. When the body is clean and fit for prayers a person must keep his feet protected from directly touching the ground so that the person's ᶜamal *(ritual power) remains intact, i.e. so that his purity is contained. Even in the temples where we take off our shoes there are carpets on the floor. Hence* paywand*, the binding connection you must keep with purity, is retained.*

Q. Should any person touch a woman in menses?

A. No. No one should touch that woman, nor should she touch anything. The regulation is that a woman in menses should be given her meals only at a distance of three paces. From this it follows, even today, that contact is prohibited. Cf. Vendidad 16[.6]: "Thus said Ohrmazd, take meals for a woman in menstruation by standing three paces away." That is, one should give her meals by standing three paces away.

Q. How can a woman in menses purify herself?

A. When the time of dashtan stops, three stones should be placed in the bathing area. Standing on two stones she should purify her body with gomez; on the third stone she should purify her body with water. Cf. Vendidad 16 [.12]: "The Mazda-worshipper places three stones on the earth. On two stones she should apply bull's urine, and on another she should purify her body with water."

Q. Can our kusti remain intact if we see a woman in menses?

A. If a woman in menses is 30 paces away from us, our padyab-kusti remains intact. It is written in the Denkard.

CHAPTER SEVENTEEN

How women should conduct themselves during maternity

Q. What observances should a woman in maternity follow?

A. For a woman who gives birth to a dead child or gives birth to a live child naturally, a separate place in the house must be kept for her from one to ten months. That place should be clean and dry and some distance from fire, barsom and the path of holy men and animals. She should sit in that place. Vendidad 5[.46] states: "In the house of Mazdayasnans a clean and dry place should be prepared. A place removed from cattle and the fire of Ohrmazd, tied barsom and the place where holy men walk."

Whether the woman gives birth to a live child or a dead one, her condition is the same, a condition of pollution, as something which is internal to the body has come out.

Q. What should be done at the time a woman gives birth?

A. At the time when a woman is to give birth to a child, ten other women should be present. Among them, five should treat her with care, and five should hold her. Among the last mentioned, one should hold her belly on the right, another on the left, the third should hold her waist and the fourth her neck. The fifth must care for the child when it comes. In this way she should be cared for as stated in the Pahlavi Rivayat.

Birth is a purifying process. In order for the world to increase and become pure, it has to pass through certain processes in stages. Thus, though birth involves pollution, blessings can come through it and purification can be reestablished through the ritual of barashnom.

Q. What should be done in the area where women give birth?

A. Immediately at the time of birth, a small distance away, fire should be kindled and for three days fragrance offered to it. The fragrance will make the foul air disappear. Cf. the Denkard. Our people do not do it this way, but instead kindle an oil lamp at a distance. This is also a good practice.

Q. Why do our people keep a curtain all around the area?

A. It is necessary so that the woman can rest, have privacy, and people can know that she is there and they should not disturb her. Cf. Vendidad 5[.48].

Q. Should a woman in maternity sit apart from others?

A. Yes, she should sit in an excluded place, should not touch anything, should not leave the house, and should remain 30 paces from fire, water and barsom.

Q. After maternity, how many days is it before the mother becomes purified?

A. After completing 40 full days the woman becomes pure by washing herself with gomez and water. Cf. the Pahlavi commentary to Vendidad 5[.49] and also the Pahlavi Rivayat.

On the 40th day she is completely dry. On the 41st day she is given a purification bath. All Parsis do this.

Q. What should be done when a woman gives birth to a stillborn baby between the first and fourth months of pregnancy?

A. There is no evidence of life in a baby of four months; therefore no ceremony (kriya) is to be performed and it should be put in the dakhma. If the baby comes after four months and ten days, when life comes, then kriya should be performed and afterwards it is put in the dakhma. One service (yasna) to Srosh and four baj ceremonies with a small set of clothes (syaw) should be consecrated on the dawn of the fourth day. Cf. the Persian Rivayat of Shapur Bharuchi.

CHAPTER EIGHTEEN

Dress and food

Q. What sort of clothing should be worn?

A. While doing bandagi, especially, we must wear clothes of white cotton. According to our religion white dress is an emblem of piety and the Mazda-worshipping religion. It is stated in the Menog i Khrad that cotton is produced through the elements of water and soil and is therefore natural and of great merit. *'Natural' means that cotton is produced through nature's work; hence cotton dress is well suited to our religion which has so much to do with nature.*

Q. Can we wear cloth other than that of cotton?

A. There is nothing wrong with wearing clothing of wool, so if we wear cloth of wool it is quite proper. Nor is there anything wrong if we put on silk or gold clothing, because we wish the same for the souls of the departed. That is, in the Pazand Afrin i Ardafrawash we read: "May the Holy Immortal Bahman give dress of gold and silk to the souls of heaven." From this it is clear that we recommend gold and silk dress for our souls. Hence there is nothing wrong if we wear the same.

Q. What sort of dress did our Kayanian kings wear?

A. It is certain that especially at the time of prayer (bandagi) they wore white dress. King Kay Kaus had a son named Syawakhsh. Syawakhsh's step-mother made false allegations against Syawakhsh. In order to establish his truthfulness, Syawakhsh walked through burning fire mounted on a horse. When he did so he was wearing white clothes. Also, when there was a battle between King Kay Khosraw and Afrasiyab, both Kay Khosraw and his grandfather Kay Kaus prayed in the

Atash Bahram of Adar Gushnasp in Pars. They were wearing white clothing then. Again, when Kay Khosraw killed Afrasiyab and renounced the world to do bandagi, he put on white dress. Examples are taken from the Shahnama of Firdausi.

Q. Which is the best food?

A. It is stated in the Menog i Khrad that food prepared from the milk of cattle is best.

Q. Which grain is the best?

A. According to our religion, the best and most precious grain is wheat, and that is the reason why we prepare dron from wheat only. For the greatness of wheat see the Nirangestan and the Menog i Khrad.

Q. Which is the best fruit?

A. According to our religion the most precious fruit is the date. It is written in the Menog i Khrad. Pomegranates and grapes are also precious fruits.

We use these foods in our ceremonies. We use the dron in the baj ceremony and in the high liturgy of the Yasna. Wheat is given this high status because it is so useful to life. There is also the injunction that if dates are not available we should use pomegranate seeds or grapes. Hence these are also precious fruits. Originally the intrinsic quality of the grain or fruit must have been the reason for their selection in the ceremony as representative of the plant kingdom. In the course of time they came to be talked about as the most precious foods. However it may be the other way around: because they are in the ceremony they are considered precious. The pomegranate and date trees are always green throughout the year, thus always suggesting continued productiveness.

Q. Which type of bird should we eat?

A. According to our religion it does not seem proper to eat meat. Nevertheless, that kind of bird which eats grain, corn, and such things should be eaten. The bird that eats decomposed and dead matter should not be eaten. Cf. the Persian Rivayat of Nariman Hooshang.

Erachji's personal preference is vegetarian; this is not necessarily Parsi. What Erachji wants to say is that birds like vultures, kites, and crows, which eat decomposed food, should not be eaten.

Q. What kind of fish should we eat?

A. It seems, according to our religion, that it is improper to eat fish. In the Nariman Hooshang Rivayat it says fish grow in the ocean by eating various kinds of bad things. The Rivayat especially prohibits the eating of big fish because big fish often eat dead things in the ocean.

Erachji is right. We eat small fish. However, the law of nature is such that the big eat the little, kites eat crows, etc., and you cannot really make rules that fit all situations. These are only cautionary notes.

Q. Should we drink liquor?

A. It is proper to drink liquor moderately, but it is a sin to drink it beyond a certain limit. So says the Denkard.

Q. What happens if we drink liquor in excess?

A. Many vices result from drinking in excess. The Denkard says: "Five types of evil result from drinking liquor in excess: bad nature, bad thoughts, spite, enmity and apostasy."

CHAPTER NINETEEN

Adoption

Q. What is adoption according to our religion?

A. When a man who has no male issue adopts some other male as his son, this is called adoption. In the Pahlavi and Persian language the word for adoption is stur.

Stur is also variously translated "trustee, guardian, curator."

Q. What is the minimum age when one can adopt a son?

A. A man who reaches the age of 14 years and three months and then dies should be given an adopted son. If we consider that he was nine months in his mother's womb, then he is 15 years old. He can be a father to a child at this age and if he has no male issue at that time or thereafter someone should be given to him as stur. In this way his lineage and succession (paywand) can continue in this world and the adopted son can fulfill all prayer duties incumbent on the departed. The son can act according to the testament of the deceased. Cf. the Saddar Nazm and the Persian Rivayat of Shapur Bharuchi.

Men who have not married also can adopt. A son is considered one who can fulfill the duties and proper ceremonies for the departed. There needs to be someone in the material world who will remember the deceased always. This brings comfort to his soul when the time comes to pass over the Chinwad bridge. In former times this rule was very rigid; it is more flexible today. Other terms used for the adopted son in orthodox Zoroastrianism were: palaka (Skt.), meaning "guardian, protector," the son, by performing duties for his father, was his guardian in that sense; dattak putra (Skt.), meaning "given away, presented, made over," refers to one of the 12 kinds of sons in Hindu law, this one being the adopted son; dharma-putra (Skt.) meaning "lawful son", i.e., a son begotten from a sense of duty and not from lust or sensual pleasure.

The need for an adopted son does not arise for a woman because her name is always linked with her husband's in ceremonies, or, if she is not married, with her father's.

Q. At what age should one adopt?

A. A man who is young and still has hope of having a son should not adopt anyone. But a man who has reached old age, has no son, and has no hope of having a son, should adopt a person during his lifetime.

It is interesting to note that the first Dastur Meherji Rana who went to the court of Akbar in 1578 A.C. was adopted by his uncle Vatcha Jesang during the latter's lifetime. This fact is borne out by a document of 1534 A.C. wherein Meherji Rana is called Meherji Vatcha.

Sometimes it happens that the wish of the deceased who is childless is not carried out by his surviving wife. That is, sometimes the wife declares a male from her own family as the adopted son of the deceased, contrary to the wishes of the deceased. Because of such cases, the anjoman (assembly of the faithful) of Navsari resolved in 1676 A.C. that a person can adopt a male of his choice as palaka during his lifetime. The anjoman also resolved that the assembly would not disperse following the ceremonies on the third day after the person's demise (the uthamnu ceremonies) until a palaka was publicly proclaimed.

Q. When does a palaka [guardian, protector] become necessary?

A. The night of the third day after a person dies, his soul craves for a son. If he has no male issue it is necessary to appoint some other male person as his dharmaputra (lawful son). Cf. the 8th chapter of the Vishtasp Nask [Yt. 24.55]: "At the end of the third night, one desires to have a son like Frashostar."

This specific reference is not totally clear. If one does not have an adopted son, relatives will perform the necessary ceremonies. But it is better to have an adopted son because in the ceremonies the name of the son and father are always uttered together. In this way, a definite paywand or connection is established and maintained.

Q. Who should be adopted as palaka? What kind of person should he be?

A. A palaka should be selected from among relatives of the deceased. Generally speaking, his age should be less than the deceased. Cf. the Persian Rivayat of Kamdin

There is no objection to an adopted son coming from a different family, but it rarely happens. The brother or nephew of the deceased is usually the first preference for a palaka of the deceased. The hereditary priestly class adopts persons from its own class, and the laity from its own class.

This elaborate system of adoption practice is likely responsible for the misunderstanding of khwetodas on the part of some scholars who suppose it to refer to actual marriages between members of an immediate family. Khwetodas is derived from Av. khvaetvadatha, 'giving of oneself,' or 'self-dedication', and is much better understood in the context of the responsibilities of an adopted son in fulfilling the duties and proper ceremonies for the departed.

CHAPTER TWENTY

Consecrated fires, the Bountiful Immortals, heaven, hell, the Chinwad bridge, Good Mind and Bad Mind

Q. How many fires are required for consecrating an Atash Adaran?

A. We must incorporate the fires from four estates, namely: priests (athravan), warriors (rathaeshtar), agriculturalists (vastryosh), and artisans (hutokhsh). Out of these four estates we must take those fires which have endured much hardship, especially the fires of blacksmiths, goldsmiths, tinsmiths and potters. We must keep these fires from the four estates separate and perform the Yasna and Vendidad ceremonies for three days. On the fourth day we must bring these fires together, perform one Yasna service and thereby enthrone the Atash Adaran.

There are three degrees of consecrated fires, the Atash Bahram, Atash Adaran and Atash Dadgah. We are speaking here of the middle grade fire. Fires are gathered from the four estates so that all walks of life are merged into the Atash Adaran. A consecrated fire has his own being, his own existence, just like a living man. He comes into existence through extensive ceremonies, prayers and manthras. These give birth to a fire, and once he is enthroned his anniversary is celebrated just like a man's birthday is remembered. Each of the fires from the four estates is purified; only the essence is taken. The priest approaches the blacksmith's fire, for example, with a perforated ladle bearing sandalwood. He holds the ladle a distance above the blacksmith's fire until the sandalwood ignites, capturing the essence of the fire. Fires of hardship are taken because the consecrating process is one of purifying them. Thus the spirit of the fire is gladdened. A blacksmith's fire is used to heat iron red hot, and then the iron is beaten. Gathering the essence of such a fire and consecrating it counterbalances the situation, making it purer to advance the creation of God.

Q. How many fires are required for consecrating an Atash Bahram?

A. We incorporate 16 types of fires from 16 different places. We make many fires from each of these fires at the outset, and in this way collect together more than 1000 fires. Of these we first take a cremation fire from which 91 fires are made;

For example, if we take the essence of a fire used for cremation, the injunction is to make 91 fires in succession from this. The wind blows the flame and ignites chips of wood from one to the next, in succession, until the 91st fire, which we preserve. This is a purifying, sifting process involving physical labor. Throughout, we consecrate the fires with brief manthras and ceremonies and make sure that only good, dry wood fit for the consecration is used. In the final stages the priests take complete charge of the process.

second, a dyer's fire made into 80 fires; third, a public bath fire made into 70 fires; fourth, a potter's fire, made into 61 fires; fifth, a brickmaker's oven-fire made into 75 fires; sixth, a fakir's or kansara's fire made into 50 fires;

The Gujarati term kansara refers to one who makes bronze vessels and utensils; a fakir is a non-Zoroastrian mendicant who has the name of God on his lips and who eats only what others give him. When options of fires are given it generally means that opinions of dasturs vary somewhat on specifics.

seventh, a goldsmith's or alchemist's fire, made into 60 fires; eighth, a minting fire for coins, made into 55 fires; ninth, a blacksmith's fire made into 61 fires; tenth, a weapon-maker's fire, made into 61 fires; eleventh, a baker's oven fire made into 61 fires; twelfth, a brewer's or idolater's fire made into 61 fires; thirteenth, an army chief's fire or the fire of a departed army made into 35 fires; fourteenth, a shepherd's fire or one from a stable for horses and camels, made into 30 fires; fifteenth, a fire caused by lightning made into 90 fires; sixteenth, a fire from the house of a priest (athravan) or a layman (behdin) [a pure and pious person of the Zoroastrian religion] made into 40 fires, or a fire made from flint or two logs rubbed together, made into 144 fires. If the last two are done together, then 184 fires are made.

Variations may be found among dasturs regarding the various sources of fire. For example, J.J. Modi, in his book, Religious Customs and Ceremonies of the Parsis, states that the third fire should be from that of a king, and the thirteenth from a traveler's fire.

We must perform Yasna, Vendidad and other ceremonies for one year, according to the injunctions of our religion, and then enthrone the fire. Concerning these 16 types of fire we find a description in Vendidad 8 and in the Persian Rivayat of Kamdin Shapur.

It takes about a year to do all this. The Vendidad gives a description of how to purify the 16 types of fire.

There are individual ceremonies with each fire. When combined in the final ceremony, the 16 fires are placed on a very large fire vase, embers and all, and in this way merged into one. The ceremonies for establishing an Atash Bahram are found in the Rivayat.

There are nine Atash Bahrams in the world, eight in India and one in Yazd, Iran. The Atash Bahram in Yazd appears to be the oldest. The oldest in India is the Sanjan Atash Bahram which is now located in Udvada. We do not know what procedures were followed, but we presume that the consecration of the Sanjan Atash must have been done in accordance with ancient Iranian practices. The second oldest fire in India is in Navsari. This Atash was consecrated in 1765 and its whole history is known. Of the remaining six Atash Bahrams in India, four are in Bombay and two in Surat.

Q. What is a Bountiful Immortal (amahraspand) and how many are there?

A. There are six fireshtes who are called amahraspands: Vohu Manah [Good Thought], Asha Vahishta [Best Righteousness], Khshathra Vairya [Dominion], Spenta Armaiti [Bountiful Devotion], Haurvatat and Ameretat [Health and Life]. The meaning of the word amahraspand is 'bountiful immortal', and this is the title for these six fireshtes. They are understood as having a high position. Some of the other fireshtes are called yazads, a word which means 'worthy of adoration.' Some fireshtes have the title menog, meaning 'invisible.' Thus are the titles conferred by God. The six amahraspands are written about in the Persian Rivayat of Darab Hormazdiyar and in the Pazand prayer Nam Stayishn.

We speak of 33 yazads (from 30 days in the month, plus three), a reference which includes the six mentioned amahraspands. One Pazand prayer calls all 33 yazads amahraspands, as does the Yasna itself in the first chapter. Thus in some ways the terms yazad and amahraspand are interchangeable; yet they also designate differences. The term fireshte is applicable to both categories, i.e. yazads and amahraspands. The latter category includes Ohrmazd who, as the foremost one, brings the list of amahraspands to seven. There are also co-workers (hamkars) for each of the seven amahraspands.

Q. What is heaven (behesht)?

A. Heaven is that comfortable dwelling place in the other world which we attain after our life of good deeds in this world is finished. That dwelling is for the holy souls and farohars especially. Cf. Yasna 16[.7]: "We adore the lofty mansion of the pious full of light and happiness in which the holy farohars and souls live."

Q. Is there only one heaven or many?

A. There are in all seven stages of heaven. A man attains a [certain] stage according to the good deeds he has performed. All [persons] do not get one and the same stage. The stages of heaven are:

1) Starpay: star station
2) Mahpay: moon station
3) Khorshed pay: sun station
4) Garothman: abode of songs
5) Pashum: best
6) Akhvan: existence, being, world
7) Anagra Raochah: endless lights

Cf. the Persian Rivayats.

According to the Dadestan i Denig the seven stages of heaven are: Humat (Good Thoughts), Hukht (Good Words), Hwarsht (Good Deeds), Starpay, Mahpay, Khorshed-pay and Garothman. The other terms, Pashum Akhvan (the Best Existence) and Anagra Raochah (Endless Lights) are descriptions of the highest heaven, Garothman.

Q. What is hell (dozakh)?

A. Hell is that dwelling place full of pain and difficulties [in the other world] which a man attains after a life of bad deeds in this world. It has three stages:

1) dush-mat (evil thought),
2) dush-hukht (evil words),
3) dush-hwarsht (evil deeds).

Cf. Yasna 46[.11] and the Menog i Khrad. The Yasna states: "Those who spoil the people of the world by their bad deeds remain forever in hell."

Q. Who are the leaders of heaven and hell?

A. The leader of heaven is the Bountiful Immortal Ardibehesht [Best Righteousness]. The leader of hell is the demon Wizaresh. Cf. the Ardibehesht Yasht [Yt.3.3] and Vendidad 19[.29].

Q. What is hamistagan?

A. It is a dwelling place between the star station (starpay) of the sky and the earth, given to a man who has performed good deeds and bad deeds equally in this world; his acts of merit and acts of sin are equal. After his death he arrives at this place where his soul will get less punishment than in hell. Cf. the Denkard.

The Phl. term hamistagan literally means 'a place of the mixed'.

Q. What is the Chinwad bridge?

A. It is the name of the place reached by the soul of a man on the dawn of the fourth day after his death. There Mihr yazad examines the account of his deeds performed in this world, and gives him either the reward or retribution due him in accordance with his good or bad deeds. Cf. Vendidad 19[.29]: "Near the holy Chinwad bridge created by Ohrmazd the soul craves for the reward of the deeds done in this world."

Q. Who is Vohuman and who is Akoman?

A. Vohuman is good thoughts; Akoman is bad thoughts. Theireshte called Bahman [Pers.] is Vohuman [Phl.] who promotes intelligence and peace among men. Any characteristic which hinders the way of the intellect or peace is known by the name Akoman. A man possessing such characteristics is also called Akoman. The other

Bountiful Immortals and their works also have their antagonists who have bad natures and perform bad deeds.

Q. Who are these antagonists of the Bountiful Immortals (amahraspands)?

A. The work of Bahman [Good Mind] is to give peace to mankind and promote wisdom. Akoman [Bad Thoughts] opposes him; his work is to create discord among mankind. The work of Ardibehesht [Best Righteousness] is to encourage men to do good deeds. His antagonist is Spozgar [Disorder] who teaches man to do the opposite. The work of Shahrewar [Dominion] is to increase the knowledge of kings and to instill in their hearts the desire for justice. His antagonist is Bushasp [sleep, sloth] who teaches the opposite. The work of Spandarmad [Bountiful Devotion] is to exalt man to do good deeds with good thoughts. His antagonist is Astwihad [Death] who teaches man to do the opposite. The work of Hordad [Health] is to increase sweetness and cleanliness in water. His antagonist is Az [Greed, lust] who teaches the opposite. The work of Amurdad [Life] is to promote sweetness and growth in trees, leaves and fruits. His antagonist is Tishn [Thirst] who teaches the opposite. The work of Srosh is to protect and care for this world. His antagonist is Kheshm [anger] whose work is to produce wrath and vengeance in man. It is so written in the Afrin i Ardafrawash and the Rivayat-e Dini.

CHAPTER TWENTY-ONE

Good spirits and evil spirits

Q. The Avesta often speaks about the yazads or fireshtes of this world. Who are they?

A. The yazads of this world are the sun, moon, and stars. Through them this world remains full of light and receives thousands of advantages. We also understand fireshtes to be those persons who, like the prophets or others, possess many good virtues, qualities and characteristics. Cf. the Dasatir.

There are both getig (material) and menog (spiritual) yazads. Getig yazads such as the sun, whose function is to promote this world, can be seen with our eyes. They bring increase to this world and are worthy of adoration. The Avesta speaks of the sun as the most excellent body of Ohrmazd, visible in this world. It is the source of eternal light. The menog yazads, on the other hand, are imperceptible to us but their blessings are evident all about us.

Q. What type of virtuous persons should be considered fireshtes?

A. Those persons who pray to God daily, live a pious, restrained life, who are humble, soft-spoken truth speakers, who wish good to one and all, are pure of heart, patient, and avoid wrath, who are not tempted by the things of this world, live at peace with one and all, who give due respect to superiors and inferiors, keep promises, and have no greed for drink and food.

Q. Who is an evil spirit (dew)?

A. An evil spirit is a person of vicious characteristics. A person who does bad deeds is himself an evil spirit. Cf. the Persian Rivayat of Shapur Bharuchi.

Q. What vices can make one an evil spirit?

A. One who has the following vices is an evil spirit: anger, greed, jealousy, forgetfulness, enmity, pride, sloth, derision; one who refrains from good actions, who lies, steals, is treacherous, possesses an evil eye, wishes ill of others, ridicules, remains idle, procrastinates, and is obstinate.

CHAPTER TWENTY-TWO

Festival of the six creations, ceremonies for Rapithwin and Srosh, and the commemorative days for All-Souls

Q. What is the meaning of gahambar [festival of the Six Creations]?

A. Gahambar means "to assemble with one another in a work of merit," or "the period for receiving merit," or "to assemble at one place at one time." There are six gahambars in a year.

The term gahambar literally means "the time of storing." It is a time for storing good deeds through the performance of ceremonies in honor of Ohrmazd, the Creator. For each gahambar the community comes together for prayer to commemorate the six aspects of creation and shares a communal meal, thereby nurturing brotherhood.

Q. Give the names of the gahambars with their duration.

A. Each gahambar lasts for five days. The first, called maidyozarem [mid-spring], begins on the day Khorshed of the month Ardibehesht and lasts until the day Day-pa-Mihr. The second, maidyoshahem [mid-summer], begins on the day Khorshed of the month Tir and lasts until the day Day-pa-Mihr. The third, paitishahem [(feast of) bringing in the grain], begins on the day Ashtad of the month Shahrewar and lasts until the day Anagran. The fourth, ayathrem [(feast of) the home-coming of the herds from pasture], starts on the day Ashtad of the month Mihr and ends on the day Anagran. The fifth, maidyarem [mid-winter], starts on the day Mihr of the month Day and ends on the day Bahram. The sixth, hamaspathmaidyem [the meaning of this term is not clear], is held during the five Gatha days. Cf. the Pazand Afrin i Gahambar.

The popular etymology of the Avestan term hamaspathmaidyem, as given in the Bundahishn, is: ham-spah rawishnih, 'coming of the whole group (of farohars)'.

Q. What did God create during the six gahambars?

A. In the first gahambar he created the sky; in the second, water; the third, earth; the fourth, vegetation; the fifth, animals; the sixth, man. This means that God created all these creatures and fixed a time for remembering them in the gahambars. Cf. the Pazand Afrin i Gahambar.

Q. What is the merit in celebrating each of the gahambars?

A. For celebrating the first gahambar the soul receives merit in that world equivalent to the merit accrued by giving 1000 ewes with lambs to a holy person. For celebrating maidyoshaham gahambar, the merit is equivalent to giving 1000 cows with calves to a holy person. For paitishahem the merit is equivalent to giving 1000 mares with colts to a holy person. For ayathrem the merit is equivalent to giving 1000 camels with foals. For maidyarem the merit is equivalent to giving 1000 cattle; for hamaspathmaidyem the merit is equivalent to giving fresh food to a holy person.

Parsis today do not think in such a specific way about merit. The references quoted above refer to ancient times when the grandeur of our kingdom meant there might be 500 to 1000 priests attending the large Atash Bahrams of Azerbaijan. Kings and persons of wealth might dedicate cattle and sheep for the needs of those priests and other holy persons. The priests needed animals for their subsistence: for milk, meat, the ploughing of fields, etc.

Similar to our Hindu brothers, a Parsi today might give a live cow to the family priest, in payment for services rendered or as a gift to benefit the soul of a departed one. In this way the cow is a source of income for the priest. It should also be noted that such cows are not slaughtered for food by the Parsis. When the cows become old, they are used for some lighter form of work. Zoroastrianism teaches that tamed animals should be properly fed and cared for.

Q. What is the meaning of each gahambar?

A. Each gahambar is named on account of its time and season. Maidyozarem means the "period of full greenness and spring"; maidoshahem means "full heat" during which the grass, etc., grow well; paitishahem refers to the period when grain and fruits are abundant; ayathrem refers to that period at the end of summer when there is an increase in strength in man and animals; maidyarem refers to the time of coldness and leisure; and hamaspathmaidyem refers to the time when day and night are equal and heat and cold are also the same [the temperate time of the year]. Cf. the first chapter of the Visperad.

There is controversy over the meanings of these terms. Some say they are seasonal festivals of Iran, others regard them as days of remembrance for the creations of God. We should consider the gahambars therefore as commemorative both of the days when God made the various creations and of the six seasonal festivals.

Q. Who commanded us to celebrate the gahambars?

A. King Jamshed of the Peshdadian dynasty gave us the injunction. Cf. Saddar Hazm.

Q. How should one celebrate the festivals (jashans) of the gahambars?

A. It is best to celebrate the festival (jashan) with as many persons in attendance as possible because the meaning of the word indicates that we should. Gahambar means the time of meeting together with one another in an act of merit.

Q. What kinds of meals should there be at the gahambars?

A. Our religion requires that the meals should be cooked sweet. In the Afrin i Gahambar it is stated: "They should prepare a sweet meal from the milk of the gospand."

To cook sweet means the meals should be made with the milk of cattle. Gospand is the generic term for all beneficent animals. Erachji is deviating here from the Pahlavi translation of the Avestan text. The Pahlavi translation states that fatted cattle should be slaughtered. Erachji is translating the Avesta, quite naturally, in a way which supports his vegetarian philosophy. Other scholars, however, have largely agreed on the Pahlavi translation of the Avestan passage.

Q. On what day should we consecrate Rapithwin?

Rapithwin is the yazad of noon and the lord of summer.

A. The Rapithwin period begins on the day Ohrmazd of the month Frawardin. We should do the Yasna, Dron and jashan ceremonies in honor of Rapithwin on the day Ardibehesht of the month Frawardin. If this is not possible, we can consecrate Rapithwin on any day within the period of Rapithwin. Cf. the Saddar Hazm.

The Yasna of Rapithwin, i.e., the service in honor of Rapithwin, is just like the ordinary Yasna of 72 chapters, except that the emphasis is on the lord Rapithwin. Consequently, certain phrases which invoke the yazads of other gahs are omitted. The number of barsom tays (metal wires) used in the ritual are 15 for Rapithwin rather than the usual 23. The reason why priests celebrate Rapithwin on the third day of the new year, i.e., the day Ardibehesht of the month Frawardin, rather than on the first day, is that immediately preceding the new year the ten-day Frawardigan (All-Souls) festival is held. In other words, the Frawardigan festival is held during the last five days of the month Spandarmad and the five Gatha days which conclude the year as epigomena to the last month. The priests need some respite before celebrating Rapithwin, which would normally be on New Year's day. Also, the dedicatory formula (khshnuman) of Rapithwin is more or less the same as that of the day Ardibehesht; hence the third day is preferred. The boywara (priests tending the Atash Bahram fire), however, cannot forego the consecration of New Year's day, so they celebrate the Yasna of Rapithwin in the Atash Bahram on the first day. By so doing, they acquire the ritual power ('amal) which qualifies them to perform the boy ceremony (offerings of fragrant wood to the fire) during the seven month period of the Rapithwin gah.

Q. Rapithwin starts on the day Ohrmazd of the month Frawardin. Why do our people consecrate it on the day Ardibehesht?

A. In the consecration of Rapithwin we say a dedicatory formula (khshnuman) to the Bountiful Immortal Ardibehesht. So it seems the day Ardibehesht is proper.

Q. What is the reason for honoring Srosh?

A. The fireshte Srosh is always looking after us in this world. When a man passes away, his soul remains in this world for three days and at that time Srosh also protects it. Thus it is our duty to perform ceremonies in honor of Srosh every year. The ceremonies performed before our death are called ceremonies in honor of zinda-rawan (living soul) and are done in the name of Srosh. Then at the time of our death Srosh can instantly come to help our soul. Cf. Saddar Nasr. In the Srosh Yasht Hadokht [Yt. 11.20] it is also stated: "We adore Srosh who takes care of all houses."

'All houses', here, means all families, i.e., the whole material creation.

Q. What are the All-Souls days (Frawardigan)?

A. The holy fravashis [guardian spirits] of those who have departed from this world visit the houses of their relations and stay for a certain number of days. These are called All-Souls days (Frawardigan).

Q. How many days are there in Frawardigan?

A. There are ten days, beginning with the day Ashtad of the month Spandarmad and ending on the Gatha day

Vahishtoishti. Cf. the Frawardin Yasht [Yt. 13.49].

Q. What should we do on the Frawardigan days?

A. First we should set aside a place in our house which is clean and pure. It is so stated in the Nirangestan.

Q. What should we put in that place?

A. Everyday we must place pure water, fresh flowers and fruits there. The holy farohars happily stay where such things are kept. Cf. the Frawardin Yasht [Yt. 13.147]. "In that house in which clean and pure water and vegetation is placed, the holy farohars agree to move about."

Q. What do they desire from us?

A. They desire [those] "who will praise us," "who will adore us," and "who will give offerings to us." Cf. the Frawardin Yasht [Yt. 13.50].

That is, they desire the uttering of manthras, the performance of ceremonies (kriyas), and offerings of cooked food and fruits. The Yasht also says that they desire those "who will welcome us with syaw (clothing)". We do all these things because of the Avestan injunctions.

Q. What ceremonies (kriyas) in honor of the holy farohars should we do during the Frawardigan days?

A. Every day for the first five days we should perform the Yasna in honor of all holy farohars [Ardafrawash] and Srosh, and Dron and Afrinagan ceremonies. On the day Mahraspand [the fourth day of the Frawardigan and the 29th day of the month Spandarmad] the Yasna, Dron and Afrinagan ceremonies in honor of the Bountiful Immortals (amahraspands) should be performed. During the Frawardigan days we must also do the geti-kharid ceremony. The Dron and Stum ceremonies are performed before meals. A fire should be continually burning near the place where the flowers, fruits and water are kept, and fragrance should be offered to it. Cf. the Nirangestan and Persian Rivayats.

The geti-kharid ("world purchased") ceremony is performed in the hope of "purchasing" salvation in the world to come. Erachji will discuss this later in the catechism.

Q. What ceremonies (kriyas) should be performed during the Gatha days?

A. Each Gatha day the Yasna of Gatha, Gahambar and Ardafrawash [all holy fravashis], and the Dron and Afrinagan ceremonies in honor of them should be performed. In the Ushahin gah of the last Gatha day, a Dron and Afrinagan ceremony in honor of the Gatha days should be performed. Cf. the Persian Rivayats of Darab Hormazdiyar and the Pahlavi Rivayat.

Q. What is the reason for performing ceremonies in the Ushahin gah of the last Gatha day?

A. At dawn of that day the holy farohars return to the other world and therefore are remembered at that time.

Q. What advantage is received from this remembrance of the holy farohars?

A. The holy farohars give great benefit to the creatures of this world. Therefore it is necessary to remember them. Cf. Vendidad 19[.37]: "I remember the strong, holy farohars who benefit all creatures."

Q. How should we live during the All-Souls (Frawardigan) days?

A. During those days people should not be engaged in worldly business and every day they must keep their body, mind and dress clean. They must also do bandagi five times a day and say other Avestan prayers. For the first five days of Frawardigan they must say the prayer Fra Mraot or 1200 ashem vohus. During the next five days they must say the appropriate chapters of the Gathas, or 1200 yatha ahu vairyos and do patet. Cf. the Persian Rivayat of Barzo Kamdin.

The words fra mraot are the beginning words of chapter 20 of the Yasna, which praises the prayer ashem vohu (righteousness is good). During the holy All-Souls days righteousness should be extolled. If one is unable to read the Yasna, then he can recite 1200 ashem vohus. On each of the Gatha days the relevant scriptural Gatha should be recited from memory or read. Yatha ahu vairyo is an ancient, powerful and efficacious manthra. Finally, patet is essential. The year is coming to a close with the five Gatha days and one should say penitentiary prayers for sins done knowingly or unknowingly.

Q. How should we remember the souls of the departed?

A. The souls of our parents and ancestors visit our dwellings on the day of their demise. In order to make them joyful on these days we must perform the Yasna, Dron and Afrinagan ceremonies on their behalf so that they, being pleased, will bless us. If we forget to do ceremonies on these days, they become displeased and curse us. Cf. Saddar Nazm.

This is rather strongly stated by Erachji. When he says "curse" he is stressing that one should not forget to perform the ceremonies on these days. But even though they are not remembered by the relatives, there are so many ceremonies performed every day for the whole multitude of souls, though not by individual name, that there is always a certain amount of offering sent to the departed souls. The reason the religion stresses these observances as duties of the faithful is that in the ceremonies you are inviting spiritual beings into this world and supplying them with spiritual food. Through their blessings prosperity increases in this and the other world.

CHAPTER TWENTY-THREE

The Gathas

The word Gatha refers to the holy songs of Zoroaster in chapters 28-34, 43-51, and 53 of the Yasna; to the last five days of the year when these songs are especially remembered; and to the five fireshtes who preside over these Gatha days. Unfortunately, the Gathas of the Yasna that we possess today are incomplete. We know this from internal evidence. The fourth and fifth Gathas have only one chapter each, yet at the conclusion of each the term handata is used which means 'group' or 'collection'. This indicates that some chapters have been lost. The last compilation of the Avesta was in Sasanian times when all that could be retrieved of the Avesta was collected and codified.

Q. Give the names of the five Gatha [days].

A. The days are named after five fireshtes:

Ahunawad ['possessing Ahunwar']
Ushtawad ['possessing happiness']
Spentomad ['Holy Spirit']
Wohukhshathra ['good dominion']
Wahishtoisht ['best riches']

Q. Over what things do the Gathas [fireshtes] preside?

A. They preside over our souls, protect them and provide spiritual food and clothing for them in the other world. Cf. Yasna 55[.2]: "The Gathas are the lords of our souls, protectors and providers of spiritual food and clothing."

Because they are the lords over our souls, we must recite as many Gatha prayers as possible during the three days after death.

Q. Should we remember the Gathas?

A. Yes. Every year during Frawardigan we must offer homage to the Gathas. If we do not, we become sinners. It is so stated in the Nirangestan: "If the Gathas are not remembered once a year then a person becomes a tanapuhr sinner."

CHAPTER TWENTY-FOUR

Festivals of celebration and the co-workers of the *fireshtes*

Q. What is the meaning of *jashan* and how many are there?

A. *Jashan* means 'rejoicing' or 'an assembly of rejoicing' or 'fulfillment of desire.' It is an ancient rule, from the times of Pishdadian kings, that when the day name and month name are the same, that day should be understood as a day of celebration (*jashan*). Besides these there are many other *jashans*. Our ancient kings used to consider the *Jashan of Jamshedi Nawruz* very great. It is so stated in the *Farhang-e Jahangiri*.

Q. What is *Jamshedi Nawruz*?

A. During the course of the year the sun passes through the 12 signs of the zodiac. On the day *Ohrmazd* of the month *Frawardin* (i.e. the first day of the new year) the sun enters Aries. Our King Jamshed of Pishdadian times considered this day very auspicious, so he ordered all to rejoice and be festive on new year's day (*Nawruz*). He did a *jashan* with great pomp in his royal court and showered gifts on the people. He gave them food and clothing, and released captives from jail. The rejoicing continued for many days. King Jamshed's original name was Jam. But one day when he sat on the throne in the early morning with the crown on his head studded with diamonds and pearls, the light of the sun fell on the crown so that it began to shine like the sun. The people saw the light of the two suns, rejoiced and appended the word *shed* to Jam. *Shed* means 'light.' That day was considered a great one and was called *Jamshedi Nawruz*. On that day the people began to do *jashan*. After *Jamshed*, the kings of Iran continued to perform that *jashan*. This custom lasted until the last king, King Yazdegird. Cf. the *Persian Vajarkard Dini* and *Burhan-e Qate*.

Assigning the date of March 21 to Nawruz, as some Parsis do, is an anachronism. There was no such date at the tim of Jamshed. Nawruz simply refers to the new year's day that occurred at the time of spring. Many Zoroastrians are concerned today about this whole matter of proper calendars and calendar dates. There are three calendars used among Zoroastrians today: Shahanshahi, Qadimi, and Fasli. Of the three, the Fasli or 'seasonal' calendar is most unacceptable from a religious point of view because it intercalates one day every four years instead of the traditional way of one month every 120 years. By followi this method of intercalation, the Fasli calendar breaks with our centuries-old tradition on several counts: 1) there is no mention of 366 days in any of the Avestan or Pahlavi scriptures; 2) since each day of the traditional calendar bears the name and presence of a fireshte the Fasli day of intercalation, which they call ruz-e wahizag ('intercalary day"), has no fireshte, and 3) ritually speaking, if important events fall on this intercalary day, how are they to be properly observed in the following months and years?

But I do not want to be misunderstood. If the Faslis wis to call this innovation what it is, namely a secular day borrowed from the Gregorian calendar, and they wish to hold a secular jashan (festival) on that day, I will pray and enjoy it with them. Preservation of our sense of com munity should be of primary importance for all Zoroastrians. The Qadimis--those who adhere to the 'ancient' calendar--follow the same calendrical method of reckoning as do the Shahanshahis ('monarchical'). Thus if the whol group of Qadimis wish to merge with the Shahanshahis, aft intercalating one month as the Shahanshahis once did in India (possibly in the 12th century A.C.), then let us do it. Let us be brought together, for the basic point about the calendar is the religious one, that we remember with devotion all seasons and all watches of the day. The seasons are not uniform across the world, nor are the days and nights the same everywhere in the world.

What is important is not that we are all observing the same ceremony at the same time anywhere in the world. What is important is that as a community, no matter where we live in the world, we share the same religious conviction and practice that appropriately commemorates the spiritual significance of each season, month, day and hour.

Q. Why do we name the day Khordad of the month Frawardin Khordad-sal-khoday?

A. Khordad is a fireshte who presides over the year, month, day and time. We call him Khordad-sal-Khoday, meaning "Khordad, lord of the year". The first day of the new year, Khordad, we call Khordad-sal. We offer homage to the great Khordad so that during the whole year he will give us happiness and delight. For this reason we rejoice greatly on that day and perform a jashan.

Q. What should we do on Khordad-sal?

A. After cleansing our body and putting on clean clothes, and keeping our thoughts pure, we must pray to God. In the Hawan gah we must say the litany to Khorshed [the sun] nine times and the litany to Mihr [yazad associated with the sun] three times. In the Rapithwin gah and the Uzerin gah [we must say] the Khorshed litany three times and the Mihr litany once. We should also have Dron and Afrinagan ceremonies performed on that day. Cf. the Persian Rivayat of Shapur Bharuchi.

Q. What events have occurred on the day Khordad-sal?

A. On that day Gayomard, Hooshang and Kay Khosraw were born. King Jamshed stopped [premature] death from occurring. King Faridoon divided his kingdom among his three sons. King Minocheher killed Selam and Tur to avenge the death of his maternal grandfather Erach. Kay Khosraw killed Afrasiyab on that day. He also ascended into the heavens. King Lohrasp was set on the throne and King Vishtasp accepted the religion. King Vishtasp promulgated the Zoroastrian religion and Zoroaster accepted the religion from God. Cf. the Persian Vajarkard Dini and the Rivayat-e Dini.

There is another Pahlavi text, the Ruz i Hordad Mah i Frawardin which lists the many events that occurred on this day.

Q. Why is the jashan of the day Frawardin of the month Frawardin considered greater than others?

A. On the day Frawardin of every month the holy farohars come to this world and the fireshte Frawardin presides over our souls. When the names of the month and day are the same it is even more appropriate to remember the holy farohars. We should go to the dakhma and praise the farohars in remembrance. For these reasons it is considered a great jashan. Cf. the Pahlavi Commentary on Chapter 8 of the Vendidad and the Persian Vajarkard Dini.

Zoroastrians go to the dakhma on this day because this is the last station of the deceased in this world. From there the souls depart. Therefore we perform a ceremony (the Frawardin Yasht) near the dakhma in honor of the farohars.

Q. Why is the jashan of the day Tir of the month Tir considered important?

A. On this day, besides the jashan of Tir, there is also a jashan of [the maidyoshahem] gahambar and so it is considered very important. Also, the jashan celebration is an event from the days of Minocheher. Afrasiyab had attacked Iran but had not succeeded completely in conquering her, so he made a treaty with Minocheher. The condition of the treaty was that the boundaries of King Minocheher's kingdom would be determined by the distance an arrow [Pers. tir] could be shot. The wise people made an arrow with great craftsmanship. That tir (arrow) was shot by Aresh from atop a mountain in Tabiristan. He shot the tir eastward and it sailed in the air for half a day. After 12 hours it fell near the Jehun Sea. Afrasiyab then retreated to that place. That event occurred on the day Tir of the month Tir. Everyone rejoiced and a great jashan was held on that day. It is so stated in the Persian Vajarkard Dini.

In today's history books the story goes that Aresh shot the arrow from Mount Damawand and the arrow pierced an eagle or big bird which then flew to the sea. This version was probably written so that the story could be believed! The best reason for jashan on the day Tir is that a gahambar falls on this day. Such an incident as related above may have occurred but it has been colored and elaborated upon by commentators.

Q. Why do we consider the jashan of the day Mihr in the month Mihr a great one?

A. This jashan is called Mihragan and is a time for love and gratitude for life. [In ancient times] King Zohak was very cruel to the people. So a blacksmith named Kaveh, with the help of others, sought out Faridoon who then caught Zohak and killed him on Mount Damawand. Faridoon then became king and the peoples' lives were saved. For these reasons, King Faridoon and all the people had a great jashan on that day. It is so stated in the Persian Vajarkard Dini.

Erachji gives the popular etymology of the word mihragan (mihr, 'love' and gyan or jan, 'life'). With the death of Zohak many lives were saved, hence the festival.

Q. Our people think that Zohak is still alive. Is that correct?

A. In the Afrin i Ardafravash it is stated that King Faridoon bound Zohak on Mound Damawand. The same story is written in some other books. However, in Yasna 9[.7-8] it is stated that Zohak was killed by King Faridoon. This is the Avestan passage: "From the seed of Athwiyan a son was born named Faridoon the brave who killed Zohak."

The Afrin is in Pazand, the Yasna is in Avestan. In later times Pahlavi writers found the Zohak episode very attractive and so the story was elaborated upon and linked with the resurrection, as in the Pahlavi Bahman

Yasht. The author of the Afrin story may have derived his version from some source other than the Avesta. His lively rendition has value as an interesting story. Some even interpret the story metaphorically. But we must believe the Avesta when it comes to such discrepancies.

Q. Why do our people call the day Frawardin of the month Adar a jashan day?

A. Just as the holy farohars come to this world on the Frawardigan days [days dedicated to All-Souls], so also they come on the day Frawardin of the month Adar. Thus the day Frawardin of the month Adar is given great importance. If a Zoroastrian dies and the day, month or year is not known, we must commemorate his demise on the day Frawardin of the month Adar. This is the injunction of the religion. Also, if a Zoroastrian dies during the Gatha days the day Frawardin of every month should commemorate his demise. These are the reasons why our people do jashan and Yasna on behalf of the holy farohars in the month of Adar. It is so stated in the Pahlavi commentary on chapter eight of the Vendidad. *The reason why the month of Adar is so important and is associated with the farohars relates back to the calendar at the time of the Pahlavi commentators. Iranians used to intercalate one full month every 120 years. The last five epigomena days, i.e. the Gatha days, must have followed different months each year. The calendar, in other words, was different in former times from what it is now. In the time of the Pahlavi commentators the five Gatha days must have followed the month Aban. The next month, the first month of the new year would then have been Adar, which was therefore a month considered holy for farohars.*

Q. On what day should we do jashan in the month of Day?

A. According to our religion there are three Day fireshtes: Day-pa-Adar, Day-pa-Mihr, and Day-pa-Den. Since we must do jashan on those days when the name of the day and month are similar, we should do it on these three days plus on the day Ohrmazd during this month. Cf. Farhang-e Jahangiri.

Q. Is there any other jashan in the month of Day?

A. Yes. On the day Khorshed of the month Day the prophet Zoroaster passed away. So on that day, in order to remember the fravashi of our prophet, it is necessary to do the ceremony of jashan.

Q. Our people call one jashan, Jashan-e Sada. On what day is it performed and what is this jashan?

A. 'Sada' means 'leaping flames of fire' (light). It is the jashan of the day Aban of the month Bahman. On this day King Hooshang was out hunting. He saw a snake and threw a stone at it but missed. The stone dashed against another stone, a fire was ignited and the grass nearby began to burn. Seeing this, Hooshang said: "This fire is the nur [glow] of God. It has killed and burned my enemy the snake." He stayed there at night, kept the fire burning, rejoiced, and did jashan. On that day many fires are lit. Cf. the Persian Vajarkard Dini and the Shahnama.

There were many jashans of the name sada performed on various days at different times and locations. The one mentioned by Erachji is the best known social festival. The word sada means '100', and jashan-e sada means 'the festival of the 100th day' before New Year's day. In India among the Parsis, the jashan-e sada is no longer celebrated, though years ago it was celebrated in Navsari on the day Ashtad of the month Adar. This festival is still performed among the Zoroastrians of Iran, however, for it is a time when they look hopefully to the coming of spring after the winter months.

Q. What is meant by myazd and afrinagan?

A. Myazd means an 'assembly of gladness.' Our people do the myazd of jashan; it is also just called myazd. Afrinagan means "blessings," i.e., the ceremonies of blessings.

There are five days in a month allotted for doing myazd: Mihr, Rashn, Bahram, Ashtad and Anagran. The term myazd in fact means 'fruits'; it is a kind of jashan where the participants make paywand [maintain 'contact' with each other by holding handkerchiefs] and recite benedictory prayers (afrinagan).

Q. How many persons should there be for myazd and jashan?

A. There should be at least three persons because an assembly is formed by a minimum of three persons according to our religion. When the kriya of jashan is performed in such a place, 10,000 holy fravashis attend it. Cf. the Dadestan i Denig.

The fravashis come to the ceremony in large numbers. Thus much joy and delight results for both the living and the spirits of the departed.

Q. What type of person should attend myazd and jashan?

A. Those who are very pious, for then God approves of such a kriya. If bad persons attend a jashan and myazd, then the kriya is considered null and void. Cf. the Dadestan i Denig.

The Dadestan i Denig was written by an orthodox, pious and straightforward-thinking priest named Manushchihr who felt responsible for upholding the tenets of the religion in post-Sasanian times. He guided the destiny of the people while the Zoroastrian community was being suppressed by the Muslims. The best thing to do at that time, therefore, was to remain steadfast in the religion, uphold the tenets, and be energetic in doing good deeds. The priest firmly believed that good character and good thoughts had power to make the jashan effective, and bad thoughts and character had a nullifying effect on any ceremony.

Q. What are hamkar?

A. Hamkar means 'co-workers,' i.e., those who work in connection with others. The following is a list of the seven Bountiful Immortals (amahraspands) with their hamkar totalling 33 in all:

Days	Hamkar
1) Ohrmazd	Day-pa-Adar, Day-pa-Mihr, Day-pa-Den
2) Bahman	Mah, Gosh, Ram
3) Ardwahisht	Adar, Srosh, Bahram
4) Shahrewar	Khorshed, Mihr, Asman, Anagran
5) Spandarmad	Aban, Den, Ard, Mahraspand
6) Hordad	Tir, Frawardin, Wad
7) Amurdad	Rashn, Ashtad, Zam

These 30 fireshtes also designate the day names of the Zoroastrian calendar. The three additional fireshtes that make the total 33 are: Burz, Hom, and Dahm. Ceremonies dedicated to them are performed on the day Shahrewar, following that of Anagran.

CHAPTER TWENTY-FIVE

The 'world-purchased' liturgy, ceremonies for living souls, and the twelve fireshtes

Q. In our religion we say geti-kharid. What does it mean?

A. Geti-kharid means "to buy this world." That is, on behalf of the other world we must perform good deeds in this world today. According to our religious practice, two priests perform the Yasna ceremony with great piety and care; we call this ceremony geti-kharid. The Yasna ceremony is performed for nine days in the geti-kharid ceremony.

This ceremony is exactly the same as that of nawar, the ceremony of initiation into the first level of the priesthood. A person should have this service performed at least once in his lifetime, for it brings blessings to the person through ritual and abolishes the effect of any bad thought, word or deed he may have committed. Thus it is purchasing good deeds in this world for the sake of one's ultimate destiny. The modern mind is averse to accepting the fact that ceremonies (kriyas) can "purchase" good deeds for you. Some Zoroastrians say: 'How can a ceremony bring you heaven if you are not good and just?' But consider this: If the priest is holy and pious the ceremony has great efficacy and can counterbalance through its blessings any bad deeds one has committed.

Q. What advantage is gained by the one who ordered geti-kharid performed, and by those who perform it?

A. When the person who ordered geti-kharid passes from this world and his soul approaches the Chinwad bridge on the dawn of the third day, many souls will come to receive him and take him with pleasure to his place in the other world. Cf. Saddar Bundahesh.

That is, the souls will come to direct him to his place. The ceremony of geti-kharid can be performed for the living or the dead. It is a ceremony of the highest merit and strongly emphasizes that the deeds you perform in this world have value for the next world.

Q. What is zinda-rawan and how is it performed?

A. Zinda-rawan means "remembering the souls of the living." When a person dies we perform ceremonies for him for four days and throughout the year. In the same way all the ceremonies can be done for the living soul, either for four days or the whole year. It is our duty to perform zinda-rawan. A man of means can do it every year. One who is not as fortunate should do it at least once in his lifetime. The reason is that if a man passes away while traveling and nobody knows about it and the ceremonies for the first three days are not performed, the ceremonies performed for him while he was living will help him. There is great merit in having the zinda-rawan performed. Cf. the Persian Rivayat of Shapur Bharuchi.

The religious injunction is to have the zinda-rawan ceremony performed for oneself at least once in a lifetime, for the reasons stated by Erachji. Many Parsis, however, do not do so, and shirk this religious obligation. To offset this, people have begun to have their own zinda-rawan ceremony of four days performed at the time of their husband's or wife's demise. In other words, the ceremonies for the living soul are performed side by side with the ceremonies for the departed soul (anosha-rawan). In addition, when the death of the widow or widower occurs, ceremonies for the previously departed one (anosha-rawan) are again performed simultaneously with those four day ceremonies for the recently deceased. These are called ceremonies for the pair and are frequently requested by Parsis of India today. However, the first of the pair to die has not had a zinda-rawan performed in his or her name, though he has had the ceremonies for the deceased performed twice. The real point is that the souls of the living and of the departed are in need of and greatly benefit from ceremonies performed in their name.

One could ask the question: What about the souls of those who are not Zoroastrians and thus do not have the benefit of these ceremonies for their souls. A Zoroastrian reply to this is: Certainly such people must have some ceremonies of their own instituted by their prophets which will elevate the soul. In addition, our ceremonies bring blessings to all: goodness is universal. One should always respect other religions, but one can only worship within his own.

Q. What is duwazdah-homast and who should perform it?

A. Duwazdah-homast means "to adore the 12 fireshtes." This ceremony can be performed in two different ways. One, called the small duwazdah-homast, involves the performance of 144 Yasnas and 12 Vendidad ceremonies. The other, called the large duwazdah-homast involves 144 Yasnas and 144 Vendidad ceremonies. Women, especially, should have it performed. Cf. the Persian Rivayat of Shapur Bharuchi.

To perform this, one could employ 12 pairs of priests and it would not take too long to complete.

Q. Who are these 12 fireshtes and why should the ceremony be performed for women?

A. The 12 fireshtes are Ohrmazd, Tir, Khorshed, Mah, Aban, Adar, Hordad, Amurdad, Spandarmad, Wad, Srosh, and Ardafravash. This ceremony is prescribed for women in order to atone for the sins of not being able to observe the rules of menses, and, either wittingly or unwittingly, touching those things under the custody of these 12 fireshtes.

This ritual serves as patet (confession) for women to expiate these sins. Our old ritual books in manuscript form, however, list 18 fireshtes, not 12. Formerly, it was probably 33 in number. It is possible that the number was reduced from 33 to 18 to 12 on the grounds that only the most essential yazads whose things were defiled during a woman's period need to be mentioned.

CHAPTER TWENTY-SIX

The consecrated white bull and the holiest liturgy of our religion

Q. In our religion we speak of warasyo. What is it?

A. The Avestan word varesa means 'hair'. After performing ceremonies, we cut three to five hairs from the tail of a totally white bull and tie them ceremonially to a gold or silver ring. This is used in the Yasna, Vendidad and other ceremonies. If there is no white bull available, we cannot perform any high ritual. The bull who gives this waras is called warasyo.

Consecrated white bull's hair is called waras by Parsi priests. The bull selected for consecration is carefully inspected by experienced priests. There can be no black spot anywhere on the bull's body; his hoofs and horns should be light white; he must be uncastrated and fit to give urine. If kept in a field with cows, the consecrated bull (the warasyo) should be tended by a servant to see that he does not engage in fights with other bulls and come to harm.

Q. Is this warasyo used in any other way?

A. Yes. In order to purify a person who has become defiled

and unclean (riman) we give him consecrated bull's urine (nirang) to drink. In the ceremonial preparation of the bull's urine (nirang) it is necessary to take the nirang from the bull (warasyo) in the same way that the priests who take ritual ablution (barashnom) take the nirang. Vendidad 19[.21] states: "O Zarathushtra, take the nirang of an uncastrated young bull which is consecrated."

The urine is taken from the bull in a carefully prescribed ritualistic way, and when it is consecrated in the Nirangdin ceremony, it becomes nirang. The barashnom is a nine-night ritual of purification administered either in a desolate place or in a specific ritual precinct which is a walled-in enclosure open to the sky. Involved in this nine stage purifying process are recitations of prayers five times a day, washing of the body with gomez, sand and water, and the ritual drinking of nirang.

Q. Is there a religious injunction about taking the hair only of a bull?

A. In the Nirangestan it is written that one can take the hair of a bull or a horse.

The Rivayats state that if you take the hair of a horse you should take it from the mane, whereas if from a bull it should be from the tail. But an example of consecrating a horse is not known in Parsi history.

Q. What is Nirangdin?

A. Nirangdin means the "liturgy (kriya) of the religion (den)." First two priests take the barashnom of nine nights in the name of the person in whose honor the liturgy is performed. They perform the Yasna for six days in honor of the same person. Then on the sixth day they consecrate a vessel (a pot), dry it, and after collecting the nirang from the warasyo in another pot, pour it into this vessel. Some 30 or 40 bulls are brought in and their nirang is taken and added to the pot.

These additional bulls are not necessarily white, but

the warasyo must be white, including his hoofs and horns. Also, the number of bulls used varies. At present in Bombay only eight are used. This ceremony is usually said in honor of the soul of someone deceased. If it is performed for a living soul the likelihood is that that person is doubtful about his offspring ever ordering the ceremony done for his sake.

Another pot is then consecrated and filled with water. That night, in the Ushahin gah, both priests perform the Vendidad ceremony in honor of Srosh yazad. The two pots are covered with metal lids. At certain points in the ceremony one of the priests lifts the lids of both pots and looks into them while continuing the ceremony. Following that they finish the whole liturgy of the Vendidad. This completes the Nirangdin. This consecrated nirang is used as a [purifying] drink by Zoroastrians. Much piety and care is taken in the performance of this ceremony and (often) at night while the liturgy is being performed many high priests (dasturs) and priests (mobeds) witness the ceremony, as the priests do it with great care and seriousness. Cf. the Persian Rivayats of Kamdin Shapur and Kama Vohra.

When the priest stares into the first pot he utters ashem ('holiness') followed by vohu ('is good') while looking into the second pot. In this manner ritual power ('amal) is effected and penetrates the nirang. The Nirangdin is a costly ceremony; it costs about 5000 rupees [ca. $600.00], compared to a geti-kharid which is about 1000 rupees and a simple Afrinagan which might be only ten rupees. The person who pays for the ceremony is called jajman in Gujarati (Skt. yajman) which literally means 'host.' He is a 'host' in the sense that he pays the priests for the ceremonies performed for the spiritual powers who are the invited guests.

CHAPTER TWENTY-SEVEN

Impurity and demons of pollution*

Q. How many types of demons of pollution (druj i nasush) are enumerated in our religion?

A. There are five types. The greatest is that which attacks the person who dies.

When a person dies, pollution comes to his body, and that pollution can be detrimental to the living if no precaution is taken. The body decays and polluted things come out of it.

Somewhat less is the pollution which comes to a woman who has given birth. Third, and less polluting than the second, is the pollution of a woman in menses. Fourth, and less polluting than the third, is when a man approaches a woman.

That is, when a man has intercourse with his wife. Afterwards it is necessary for both to take a bath. This is not to say that intercourse itself is polluting, for procreation brings increase to the world.

Fifth, and less polluting than the fourth, is answering the call of nature. There is an express injunction for one to do padyab-kusti immediately. If he does so he is considered clean.

Q. How can we purify a leather garment which has become impure (riman)?

A. If there is any putrid secretion from the thing which is riman stuck on the garment, it is impure.

That is, it should be disposed of.

If there is no blot on the leather, then it should be purified three times with gomez, dust and water. After that it should be exposed to the sun for three months. Then it is pure. Cf. Vendidad 7.

---

*In this chapter Erachji only offers general references to chapters in the sources and does not quote the Avestan passages with translation. This may be due to his use of Pahlavi glosses.

Q. How can a cotton or wool cloth which has become riman be purified?

A. If there is any putrid secretion from the thing which is riman on the cloth or marking it, it cannot be purified. But if there is no marking, then it should be washed with gomez, dust and water six times, and kept in the sun for six months. Then it is purified.

All these procedures should be followed if something is riman. One can approach a riman thing by first equipping oneself with the baj of Srosh (invoking the protection of Srosh yazad) and keeping "contact" (paywand) with someone else.

Q. Who should put on riman clothes after they are purified?

A. Our people do not purify riman clothes according to the above injunctions. But if they do, then a woman in menses should use them [for padding] in the area of menses when they need cloth. Other than this, we should not make use of such clothes. Cf. Vendidad 5.

A woman's clothing worn during the time of menses is not considered riman, unless some marking or pus is there.

Q. If dead matter (nasa) has fallen on wood, can the wood be made pure?

A. The log should be cut all around the place where the dead matter has fallen. The remaining wood should be washed with water and kept for one year in the open, exposed to the sun and cold weather. Then it can be used for anything except fuel for a fire or any other matters requiring purity.

After being exposed for a year it can be used, for example, for building material, but not for anything attendant to temple practices.

Q. If dead matter has fallen on grain or on a heap of grass, how can it be made pure?

A. We do not purify grain or grass, but if we wish to, then we must stake out an area at a distance of two bazay [2 arm lengths] all around the place where the dead matter had fallen. That area should be washed and kept separate for one year. But the devout should not eat such grain. They may give it to some other person, but that grass should not be given as food to any animal used in religious ceremonies. Cf. Vendidad 7.

To eat something polluted is much worse than to touch it. To purify something internal requires the whole barashnom process. It is a more serious thing.

Q. If metal of any kind becomes riman, how can it be purified?

A. Gold, if it has become riman, should be washed once with gomez, once with dust, and once with water. Then it is pure. Likewise silver, if it is washed two times in the same way. For iron, lead, copper and bronze, three times in the same way; for steel, four times; stones, six times. If a vessel of pearls and crystal, or jade and diamonds, becomes riman, it should be washed three times in the same way. If a vessel of clay becomes riman it cannot be made pure. Cf. Vendidad 7 and its Pahlavi commentary.

Q. Why are we enjoined to wash all these things which have become riman in so many different ways?

A. It must be kept in mind that anything which water, or something similar, can penetrate becomes riman more easily. Hence the injunction is to wash them many times. Something which is dense and less porous and which water and similar substances cannot penetrate can be purified by washing a fewer number of times. This is what accounts for the differences.

Q. How can a person who has touched dead matter become pure?

A. He can become pure by taking the barashnom ceremony which is appropriate to one who has become riman.

There are different types of barashnom ceremonies, some longer and more detailed than others. For example, corpse bearers are not required to take the nine-night barashnom, but rather a simple (sada) barashnom, using gomez. However, supposing a corpse bearer wished to marry and therefore wished to go to the temple. Then he must purify himself in the nine-night ceremony.

Q. If a man has eaten dead matter (nasa) how can he be purified?

A. He is impure forever. It is so stated in Vendidad 7.
Our religion prohibits the eating of dead matter, for by doing so, a man becomes impure forever. One can, however, partake of the cooked flesh of healthy, properly nourished animals which provide us meat and are described as good sacrificial animals in the Pahlavi texts.

Q. If a domestic animal has eaten nasa, how is it purified?

A. For one year you should not use her milk or prepare things from her milk, nor use it is religious acts. She becomes pure after one year and her milk, etc., can then be used. Cf. Vendidad 7.

Q. Can we cultivate earth on which nasa has fallen?

A. We should not cultivate it for one year, but after that we can cultivate it. However, we should not do anything to earth in which nasa has been interred. If we cultivate that, it is a sin. Cf. Vendidad 6.
Fertilizer is not nasa. It is not polluting but regenerating to the earth. The rays of the sun act upon manure spread over the soil to make the earth fertile. Manure is dirty but not riman.

Q. How can we purify a pond of water in which nasa has fallen?

A. If nasa has fallen into a pond the water around the area for a distance of six steps is impure. We must first take the nasa out of the water of the pond and then take out half to a third or a fourth or a fifth part of that water The remainder is then considered pure. Cf. Vendidad 6.
The impurity is considered floating on the top.

Q. If nasa has fallen into a well, how can that water be purified?

A. The nasa should be taken out of the well first. Then a half to a third, fourth, or fifth part of the water should be taken out. The remaining water is pure. Cf. Vendidad 6.

Q. If a man dies in a well after falling into it, we do not use that water for 13 months. What is the reason for this?

A. The likelihood is that in a well in which a man has fallen and died, pus and blood and such things mingled with the well water. Therefore we must take out all that water from the well and the well must dry under the light of the sun. But it is not possible to take out all that water from a well or throw the riman water into some distant secluded place. For this reason we do not use the water in the well for 13 months. Also, in many places the interior of the well is constructed with wood, so we do not use it for 13 months. There is some explanation of this in Vendidad 6 and its Pahlavi commentary.

Q. If nasa has fallen into running water, how can the water be purified?

A. The running water in which nasa has fallen is impure in the area three paces below and six paces all around it, as well as nine paces in the direction in which the nasa is slowly moving. After the nasa is taken out, the running water which flows up and down and back and forth purifies itself. Cf. Vendidad 6.

Q. Should we bury the dead in the earth?

A. No. It is a sin. By doing so the master of the earth (Spandarmad amahraspand) becomes greatly displeased. If anyone has buried nasa in the ground we must dig it out. It is a great act of merit (sawab). Cf. Vendidad 3.

Q. What places and things please the earth or the master of the earth?

A. First, those places on which the abodes of fires are erected and holy persons do pious deeds and utter the words of the Avesta. Second, those places on which the houses of holy persons are constructed and cattle walk to and fro. Third, those places where agriculture is pursued and water is sprinkled in the gardens. Fourth, those places where cattle lodge and give birth to their young. Fifth, those enclosed places where cattle graze. Such places are always pleasing and good to look at and please the master of the earth, Spandarmad amahraspand. It is so stated in Vendidad 3.

CHAPTER TWENTY-EIGHT

The jurisdictions of the thirty fireshtes and the naming of the twelve months

Q. What things do the 30 fireshtes of the 30 days preside over?

A. 1) Ohrmazd, the name of God himself, is the creator of both worlds.

2) Vohuman [Good Mind] is the promoter of the mind and keeps anger away. He presides over animals.

The term gospand, translated 'animals,' refers to all beneficent docile and harmless domestic animals, similar in nature to the quiet, calm mind which avoids anger.

3) Ardwahisht [the Best Righteousness] is the promoter of merit [sawab] and presides over heaven [behesht] and fire.

4) Shahrewar [Desirable Dominion] fulfills the ambition of kings, promotes treasures, nourishes the poor, and presides over all metals.

The sky was thought of as metallic by Zoroaster, hence the natural association of Dominion with the 'all-encompassing' crystal sky which dominates earth.

5) Spandarmad [Holy Devotion] presides over perfect-mindedness, charity, and the earth.

The earth gives in abundance and does so with equanimity and bears all hardship with perfect-mindedness. It is intimately related to charity and devotion.

6) Hordad [Perfection or Health] presides over the year, month, day, time and water.

7) Amurdad [Immortality or Life] promotes all types of humanity and presides over trees [vegetation].

The waters and the vegetation of earth sustain our existence and effect the Health and Life of all living creatures.

8) Day-pa-Adar [the day of the Creator (Day) before the day Adar] presides over deeds of justice.

Day-pa-Adar is a co-worker (hamkar) of Ohrmazd.

9) Adar [yazad of fire] bestows nur [glow] on people and presides over fire.

10) Aban [yazad of the water] increases milk in women, gives strength to men and presides over water.

Hordad also presides over water.

11) Khorshed [yazad of the shining sun] presides over the sun, light and heat.

12) Mah [yazad of the moon] presides over the moon and seed of cattle.

13) Tir [yazad of Tishtar, i.e. the Dog Star] presides over rain and the clouds.

14) Gosh [yazad of cattle and earth] presides over the soul (rawan) and body (tan) of cattle.

15) Day-pa-Mihr [the day of the Creator (Day) before the day Mihr] repels tyranny, sorrow, disease and pain.

16) Mihr [yazad of light, contract, friendship] takes an account of all souls, presides over love and is the guardian of the forest.

Mihr is light, and real love is light. One of Mihr's epithets is 'having wide pastures', i.e., his light spreads far and wide even through the dense forest, and his light is associated with true love as it penetrates and shows the way.

17) Srosh [yazad of obedience] protects this world, cares for the soul for three days after a man dies and gives inspiration to man through God.

It was Srosh who first chanted the Gathas, and after him, Zoroaster.

18) Rashn [yazad of truth, justice] presides over truthfulness and reigns in the other world.

19) Frawardin [yazad of guardian spirits] looks after souls and is the treasurer of heaven.

The blessings of Frawardin are the treasure referred to, and they are bestowed upon the house which pleases him.

20) Bahram [yazad of victory] presides over victory, repels enemies, keeps watch over travelers, and guides those who are lost in the wilderness.

There is also the Panth yazad, the yazad of the 'path.' Before one embarks on a journey, he should have a Dron service performed in honor of this yazad so that his journey may be safe. The khshnuman (dedicatory formula) in this service is to Bahram.

21) Ram [yazad of joy] presides over joy and happiness.

At the time of marriage, for example, the performance of a Dron service in honor of Ram yazad is appropriate.

22) Gowad [yazad of the wind and atmosphere] presides over the wind and bestows manhood.

Manhood refers to virility, manliness, courage, prowess; it is always a dynamic quality. Also Way i weh, the good fragrant wind, is a divinity opposed to the demon Way i wattar, the stench of hell.

23) Day-pa-Den [the day of the Creator [Day] before the day Den] directs one on the true path of the religion with sincerity.

24) Den [yazad of religion] presides over the Mazda-worshipping religion and wisdom.

25) Ard [female yazad of good blessings] presides over wealth, treasure, and daily bread.

That is, the bread you earn from your own labor.

26) Ashtad [female yazad of rectitude] presides over the increase of the world, gives freshness and greenness, and presides over the construction of new houses in this world.

27) Asman [yazad of the sky] presides over the sky and gives light and comfort in heaven.

28) Zam [yazad of the earth] presides over the fairies of paradise, fruit-bearing trees and agriculture.

Erachji reveals late Persian influence in this statement. He treats 'fairies' (Guj., pari) as a lesser type of good spirits who inhabit the sky, trees, the mountains and agricultural areas. The Avestan word pairika in fact refers to female evil spirits unrelated to Zam, the yazad of the earth.

29) Mahraspand [yazad of beneficent manthra] presides over the divine words of the Avesta, over their preservation, and over the justness of religion, the intellect and all endeavors.

30) Anagran [yazad of endless light] presides over the bestowal of light and over marriages and betrothals. Cf. the Siruza and Sifat-e Fireshtegan.

Q. What are the sources for the names of the 12 months?

A. The names are those of fireshtes, but the names are derived from the seasons and periods of the year in the country of Iran.

The following meanings given by Erachji are far-fetched if examined in the light of philology (see Appendix II). Erachji is relying on the book Khweshtab, a book now seen as highly inaccurate.

1) Frawardin means 'observer of the religion'. Spring awakens in this month with the blossoming of trees and an abundance of waters. The pleasant air blows, the whole world blossoms, and the hearts of men are refreshed and nourished. That is why this month is called Frawardin. Cf. Khweshtab and the Persian Vajarkard Dini.

2) Ardwahisht has a meaning similar to 'heaven' (behesht). In this month spring is in full bloom and the world blossoms like heaven. Secondly, Ard means 'to sing'; in this month all flying creatures sing songs perched in trees and people also sing songs with gladness because of the fullness of spring. That is why it is so named. Cf. Khweshtab and the Persian Vajarkard Dini.

3) Hordad means the 'provider of meals'. It is the time when wheat, barley and fruits ripen. Hence people have sufficient food. That is why it is so named. Cf. Khweshtab.

4) Tir means 'share' or 'portion'. During this month people share wheat and other kinds of grains. Summertime begins and that portion of hot weather is separate from cold weather. That is why it is so named. Cf. Khweshtab.

5) Amurdad means the 'giver of sweet fruits'. In this month all kinds of fruits ripen and people have an abundance of fruits to eat. That is why it is so named. Cf. Khweshtab.

6) Shahrewar means the 'increase of royal treasure'. The people pay revenue to the king in this month, hence there is an increase in the treasure of the king. That is why it is so named. Cf. Khweshtab.

7) Mihr means 'friendship and love.' In this month everyone sends grains and fruits as gifts to relatives and the poor. That is why it is so named. Cf. Khweshtab.

8) Aban means 'water'. The rains begin in this month, and because snow falls on the mountains the levels of the streams rise. Everyone begins to use the water for cultivating the land. That is why it is so named. Cf. Khweshtab.

9) Adar means 'fire'. The cold winds begin in this month and everyone sits near the burning fire to ward off the cold. Because everyone has the need for a fire, the month is so named. Cf. Khweshtab.

10) Day means 'the earth remaining very far from pleasure'. That is, in this month the earth is not full of blossoms, nor is it prosperous or of good appearance. That is why it is so named. Cf. Khweshtab.

11) Bahman is the name of a tree on which many flowers grow in this month, and the flower is called gul-e Bahman. The flower has white and red colors.

Everyone eats these flowers by mixing them with milk on the day Bahman of the month Bahman. That is why it is so named. Cf. Khweshtab.

12) Spandarmad is the name of a fruit, i.e. 'aspand', which grows in excess (spand) in this month. That is why the month is so named. Cf. Khweshtab.

CHAPTER TWENTY-NINE

High priest, judge, ritual priest, priest and preaching

Q. Whom should we call a dastur?

A. A person who understands all matters of religion, who speaks the truth and promotes piety should be called dastur. Cf. Yasna 19[.17]: "A dastur is he who is well versed in religion and whose acts are (those of) increasing piety in the world."

Dasturship in India is usually hereditary; a son becomes a dastur at the death of his father who is a dastur. However, as Erachji points out, it is the qualities of piety, learning and truth-speaking that are the true indicators of one who is worthy of being called a dastur.

Q. What is the Avestan word for dastur and what is the reason for having a dastur?

The following answers by Erachji are not philologically sound, but the spirit is clear. The Persian word dastur means 'a person of authority, a minister.' The Pahlavi form is dastwar, 'a high priest,' one who has the religious authority to enforce injunctions of the scriptures.

A. The Avestan words for dastur are de or deng. This is a very significant position because it is the dastur who succeeds Zoroaster and shows [the way of] the religion. The guiding role of the prophet should not be absent; thus there is need for dasturs.

Among the Parsis there are high priests (dasturs), but there is no one priest above all other priests (a dastur-e dasturan, the Iranian counterpart being dastir mas). However, the Navsari priests who are descendants of the first dastur, Dastur Meherjirana, are given ceremonial precedence over other high priests. In 1579 A.D., after Meherjirana arrived in Navsari from the court of the Moghal Emperor Akbar the Great, the whole anjoman (assembly) of Navsari recognized his dastурship. Erachji is a lineal descendant of Dastur Meherjirana.

Q. Who is called dawar in our religion?

This is the Persian form of the word; Pahlavi is dadwar, meaning judge.

A. A dawar is one who inquires and renders just decisions about matters of religion.

Q. What kind of person should a dawar be?

A. He who acts justly in truthfulness should be considered a dawar. One who deceives persons should be regarded as worthy of hell. Cf. Yasna 49[.2]: "A dawar who conceals truthfulness and is deceitful is worthy of hell."

Q. Who should be considered the head of the priests (athornans)?

A. One who is well-versed in the Mazda-worshipping religion and is mature should be considered as such. Cf. Yasna 13[.3]: "He who knows a great deal [who holds much information] about the Masdayasnian religion should be considered chief of the athornans."

Q. Is there an injunction regarding preaching?

A. It is a required duty to give information about the religion to everyone and to explain it. Cf. Yasna 53[.5]: "It is necessary to teach religious knowledge through good mindedness (Bahman) for the benefit of both worlds."

To offer religious knowledge through good thoughts means that whatever you say is truthful, honest and a benefit to the listener; it is an innocent, sinless, saintly virtue. If it happens that you say or do something in good conscience but in fact it turns out wrong, you must honestly admit the bad judgment and reward the wronged person doubly. In this way one teaches religious knowledge through good mindedness.

Q. What benefit does a person who propagates the religion receive?

A. A person who gives strength to our religion and propagates it is much loved by God. Cf. Yasna 45[.11]: "Ohrmazd becomes a friend, a brother and a father to the dastur or leader who is beneficent and promotes the religion."

To propagate means to teach those who seek knowledge of the religion. In the Avesta there is evidence that Zoroastrians of old used to do 'missionary' work in India and even China. Now it is more a matter of tending to our co-religionists. It is not necessary that our ceremonies (kriyas) be universally practiced. The truths we speak of are universal, but the ceremonies are part of our identity as a community. It is expressly stated in Pazand: "May this good Mazdayasnian religion spread over the seven regions of the earth"; that is, may God and his blessings bring progress to the entire world. But other religions may have their own ceremonies. Our ceremonies give us our identity. We are the continuation of an ancient culture which exists nowhere else in the world; we are the sum and substance of ancient Iran. We are preserving a nation, and like every nation, we have the right to exist.

Q. What does one gain by inquiring about the religion?

A. By making inquiries about the religion one maintains good thoughts and comes to know much more about things. Cf. Yasna 44 [.8]: "He who inquires into the religion with good words and thoughts receives all knowledge about it in this world owing to his piety."

Scholarship, learning, is important to us. But it must always be remembered that scholarship is largely of the mind, and the heart is more important. We must first be pious, i.e., know righteousness (Asha) and be a pahrezgar, one who is disciplined, whose conduct is exact, polite, attentive, extremely devout and pious, and who recites manthra every day and devotes much time to remembering God. Such a man has lustre on his face, for ours is a cheerful, optimistic religion, full of innocent laughter. Scholarship can be an attractive embellishment to these more essential qualities of the heart.

Q. Should we enter into religious discussions?

A. Yes. If we discuss religion honestly and truthfully, we will discover many new things from which many advantages will accrue. Cf. Yasna 43[.12]: "Those who discuss religion in truthfulness are the best possessors of benefits."

Q. Should we listen to false preaching?

A. No. We should not listen to or learn things from those devious persons who translate falsely because they can make us lose our way. Cf. Yasna 31[.18]: "Do not listen or learn the manthras from bad people."

Q. Should we respect the directives of a dastur?

A. Yes, we must listen to his order, respect it, and accept it. Cf. Yasna 45[.5]: "Accept the order of a dastur."

Q. What is the meaning of mobed?

Again, Erachji does not give us a philologically sound answer, but the general meaning is there.

A. 'Mobed' means 'he who understands much'. A mobed is a wise man and sage, who always says Avesta and performs the Yasna ceremonies. Cf. the Persian Rivayat of Nariman Hooshang and Burhan-e Qate.

The titles mobed, dastur, and ervad are used somewhat loosely nowadays, but the traditional differences between them are as follows: An ervad is one who has undergone a nawar ceremony (the first initiation ceremony for a priest) and can perform common ceremonies, i.e., Afrinagan (Blessings), Stum (praise), and Farokhshi (praise of the fravashis). Such a person could make his living by being a priest or doing some other business. A mobed is at a stage beyond the ervad. He has undergone the maratab (second initiation) ceremony and is a full-fledged priest. He can perform high liturgical (paw-mahal) ceremonies. He must lead a life of self-control to retain his ritual power ('amal). The priesthood is his vocation.

A dastur is in a sense a chief mobed. The previous stages are preconditions for becoming a dastur. He is a seasoned priest, well-versed and experienced in the intricacies of ritual, and can supervise others with competence. Such a position was highly respected in ancient times. The titles are derived from Avestan words.

Q. Who is an ervad?

A. Ervad means one who becomes ervad by learning Avesta. A person who has become an ervad is also spoken of as one who has done navjote, and in every work has become worthy of becoming a zot [chief officiator; priest], which is also called nawar and maratab. The meaning [of the term] ervad is "one who serves fire, who keeps purity and piety." It also means one who gives his undivided attention to God and says prayers (bandagi). Cf. the Persian Rivayat of Nariman Hooshang and Burhan-e Qate.

Philologically the term ervad means the 'master of scriptures', i.e., one who has learned the scriptures by heart. Erachji is describing qualities that make a good ervad rather than giving an exact meaning of the term itself. Erachji also seems to make the terms nawar and maratab synonomous with ervad, when in fact they refer to two different ceremonies which qualify priests to perform various types of liturgies. Navjote, in India, is used to mean the 'new initiate' (lit. 'new priest'), and is the ceremony which qualifies a person to enter the religious life of the community, wear the sudre-kusti and say prayers (bandagi).

Q. Who is a yozdathregar?

A. A yozdathregar is one who makes purity. He is a priest (athravan) who speaks the truth and always piously performs high liturgies such as the Yasna and Vendidad in the Dar-e Mihr [ritual precinct of fire temples]. Cf. Vendidad 9.

Q. How should we use the titles of younger and older persons in our religious ceremonies?

A. In religious ceremonies for a nameless infant from a priestly or lay family we must use the word wahman as a title. If he has been given a name but has not yet been invested with sudre-kusti, the title khud or khurd should be used.

Regarding the two words khud and khurd, the correct word is khurd; it means "small". Khud means 'self' and is not applicable.

After he has put on sudre-kusti the son of a priest is termed osta and that of a layman behdin for the remainder of their lives. Once the son of a priest earns the title of ervad he retains it throughout his life.

If a priest is appointed dastur, then, of course all ceremonies in his honor would use the title of dastur when mentioning his name.

Q. What do wahman, khud or khurd, and osta mean?

A. Wahman means 'without name'. Khud means 'self'; khurd means 'small' or 'worthy'. Osta means 'good' or one who is 'worthy of doing bandagi.'

There are different options for the meaning of osta. The term may be related to the Pahlavi hawisht which means 'disciple'. A priest's son, before undergoing the first initiation ceremony (nawar), is a student or disciple of an experienced priest. The title osta is used in religious ceremonies for the living or the dead, but not as a title like dastur or ervad prefixed to a person's name. Erachji's rendition 'good' refers to the person whose navjote is performed and is supposed to be a good member of the religious community. The term khud means 'self, himself, herself' and is prefixed to the name of a deceased person when penitentiary prayers are said on behalf of his or her soul (patet rawani).

Q. Who is a yozdathregar?

A. He is one who is pure of nature, manifests innate wisdom, is steadfast in the religion and always remembers God. He has the spiritual world in mind, is pure in thought, and is a truth-seeker. He acts with prudence, has a pure body, and speaks with a sweet tongue. He can recite the Avesta accurately and completely, and is pahrezgar, i.e., one who knows the ceremonies well and lives his life observing the rules of purity (khub). Such a person should be called a yozdathregar. Cf. the Persian Rivayat of Shapur Bharuchi.

Q. What merit (sawab) does a dastur or mobed receive by doing ceremonies well?

A. If someone has entrusted him with the work of doing Yasna or Vendidad and he does it according to the injunctions of the religion, he receives merit (sawab) equivalent to that which the person who orders the ceremony receives. He gains honor in the other world. If he does the contrary, he is full of shame in both worlds and his soul receives just punishment in the other world. Cf. the Persian Rivayat of Bahman Punjia. *It is a heavy responsibility to perform the kriyas; you either have glory on your face, or a curse. There are not only material merits (sawab) but also spiritual blessings, and the priest who understands that is honored.*

CHAPTER THIRTY

Miscellaneous questions

Q. What is den (religion)?

A. The word is Pahlavi, Pazand and Arabic. It means 'to praise, to obey, path, practice, dignity, to reward, piety, to offer prayers (bandagi). Cf. Shamsu-'l Lughat and Burhan-e Qate.

Erachji is defining a religious person more than he is the term itself.

Q. What is the Avestan word for den?

A. The Avestan word is daena.

Q. How is our religion (den) referred to in the Avesta?

A. In the Avesta our religion is called daena mazdayasni zarathushtri.

Q. What is the meaning?

A. [It means] the Zoroastrian religion, believing in Ohrmazd; i.e., the monotheistic religion according to the teachings of Zoroaster.

Ours is a special, distinct type of religion according to the teachings of Zoroaster. There may not be any close parallels to other religions.

Q. We are worshippers of God in the same way those of other religions must be. By what name, then, are we known?

A. Zoroaster has shown us the religion meant for worshipping God. Hence in the Avesta we are called mazdayasno zarathushtrish, i.e., Zoroastrians worshipping Mazda, and our religion is also called the Zoroastrian religion (den).

Q. Why are we called Zoroastrians?

A. The name of our prophet was Zoroaster and we honor and love his religion and commandments. Cf. Yasna 16[.2]: "We honor the Zoroastrian religion; we love the wish and commandment of Zoroaster.

Q. Who are the paoiryo-tkaesha?

A. The paoiryo-tkaesha are the people who lived from the time of Gayomard up to the time of Vishtasp. Their religion was called paoiryo-tkaeshi, which means, those belonging to the primeval faith. Cf. the Persian Rivayat of Shapur Bharuchi.

Zoroaster incorporated in his religion the four fundamentals of the primitive faith called the paoiryo-tkaeshi din: the ceremonial use of barsom, of hom, the preservation of fire attended to ritually, and the wearing of sudre-kusti. Zoroastrianism is a reformed religion accepting many of the basics of the former faith.

Q. What does khwetodas mean?

A. Marriage with a near relative is called khwetodas. It is a merit (sawab) to do so, and according to our religion everyone praises such a couple. Cf. Visperad 3[.3]: "We praise khwetodas".

The Avesta word khvaetvadatha literally means 'giving of oneself', i.e., self-dedication. Therefore we cannot be sure what the word means in the Visperad. It is generally taken to mean marriage within the family group. It has a narrower meaning than the term endogamy, which refers to marriage within a clan or tribe. It is not commonly practiced today. Its purpose was to safeguard family virtues and qualities. Up to two generations ago it was practiced in the context of the joint-family system, where 60 or 70 persons were in a house, closely knit, and one could make good marriage matches within one's family. But times have changed, and today considerable numbers of Parsis marry outside the family.

Q. What is jadangoi?

A. Suppose there is a person who in his heart has not the slightest desire to do the good deeds of the religion. And suppose that some other person persuades him into doing good deeds. That instigator is called jadangoi and he is granted heaven by God. Cf. the Dadestan i Denig.

Erachji is again giving the traditional meaning of the term, i.e., someone who persuades another, in some way or other, to do good and thereby multiply as many good deeds as is possible. The Pahlavi term jadag-gowih means 'intercession', i.e. speaking on behalf of another, an arbitrator, mediator.

Q. How many types of wisdom are there in our religion?

A. There are two types. One is called asn khrad [natural, innate wisdom], and the other is goshosrud khrad [wisdom heard with the ears], i.e. knowledge from a teacher which increases wisdom.

Q. Should we draw water from a well at nighttime?

A. When there is need we can take out water after saying yatha ahu vairyo. In the litany to Khorshed it is stated that the well water is purified through the sun's rays, hence it is forbidden to draw water at night. It is also forbidden to waste much water at night. Cf. Pahlavi Rivayat.

Q. Should we walk barefoot?

A. According to our religion it is forbidden to walk barefoot. By walking barefoot we harm our feet and become guilty for knowingly damaging our body. So states the Saddar Nazm.

Q. According to our religion, what kind [of man] should a ruler be?

A. If a ruler commits sinful acts and gives bad commands the state will suffer much hardship and damage. So states the Denkard.

Q. Should we beat a dog?

A. According to our religion we should not beat a dog. There are many kinds of dogs with many characteristics and virtues. They are faithful and useful, so we must nourish them. If anyone beats them, his soul will be punished in the next world. In Vendidad 13[.8] God says: "Those who kill the dog of a shepherd, of the street, or of a traveler will subject their souls to much pain and lament and will not enter paradise (garothman)."

Q. What does our religion require regarding the taking of barashnom?

A. A man or woman after reaching the age of eight must take barashnom at least once in [his/her] lifetime so that their bodies may always be full of cleanliness. Cf. the Saddar Nazm.

Everyone is enjoined to take barashnom, but most persons pay for a barashnom (a fee of about 400 rupees) to be undergone by a priest who does it in their name. Priests themselves require barashnom often so that they can continue to conduct high liturgies. If a priest leaves his locality, for example, say he lives in Navsari and goes to Bombay, he needs to take barashnom before proceeding with the ceremonies. Taking barashnom requires that the priest remain in the ritual precinct of the temple (Dar-e Mihr) for nine nights, prays five times a day, and dedicates whatever he prays to the soul of the one in whose honor the ceremony is being performed.

Q. What is the merit (sawab) for enabling a son of a priest to become a priest (ervad)?

That is, what merit does a layman receive who pays for the initiation ceremonies of a poor priest's son. A moderate cost today is about 1000 rupees for the maratab (second initiation) ceremony, and 4000 rupees for the nawar (first initiation) ceremony.

A. The son of a priest learns by heart the holy words of the Avesta and then becomes a priest (ervad) and initiate (maratab). The person who gives money in his own name to make someone a priest or initiate earns great merit because it is as if, by giving money, he has taught that priest's (mobed's) son all the Avesta he has learned. To teach knowledge is a charitable act. Also, this son of a priest (mobed) will say the Avesta throughout his life, will perform good and righteous acts, and earn his living with simplicity, and all the merit so acquired will go to the one who has made him priest (ervad). So states the Saddar Nazm.

Q. What should we do before going to bed at night?

A. First, say one yatha ahu vairyo and one ashem vohu. Then make a confession of sin (patet). If we are not able to make a confession (say patet), then we must say these words three times: az hama gunah patet pashemanom pa patet hom [I repent of all sins through patet]. By so doing one earns merit. Also, while turning to one side or the other at night, one must say an ashem vohu. That is also meritorious. Cf. the Saddar Nazm.

Another translation of the Pazand phrase cited above is: 'I repent of and desist from all sins.' It is the sincere desire to avoid sin that is of importance here, and to make such vows every night before going to bed is very effective in avoiding sin.

Q. Are we enjoined to say ashem vohu or yatha ahu vairyo in every action?

A. The summary meaning of ashem vohu is: merit and truth are very great gifts and the speaker of truth is very righteous and good. The meaning of yatha ahu vairyo is: by doing good deeds in this world in accordance with the will of God and by nourishing the poor, God grants us good thoughts and heaven. From this it appears that we should always remember good thoughts and adhere to truthfulness and do everything according to the will of God. For this reason, it seems, we are enjoined to say the yatha ahu vairyo and ashem vohu prayers.

Erachji is explaining the religious consequences of uttering these manthras; he is not defining the meanings of the words.

CHAPTER THIRTY-ONE

A brief history of Iran

Q. Before Gayomard how did the world prosper?

A. It has been said that from its beginning the world has prospered. In former times [prior to Gayomard] there were many long aeons of thousands of years. The first person of the millenium that preceded Gayomard's millenium was Mehabad. He was a great prophet of God. A book called the Dasatir was given to him. A small portion of that book has survived.

As we have already noted, Erachji, like many of his contemporaries, believed that the Dasatir was an ancient text. Zoroastrian scholars today, however, consider it a product of the 17th century A.C. It is an eclectic work, and extols the life of the recluse, encourages celibacy and self-mortification and expounds other such philosophies which are diametrically opposed to the optimism, cheerfulness and dynamism of the Zoroastrian faith.

Q. What are the names of the prophets who lived after Mehabad?

A. The first was Mehabad; the second, Jia Afram; third, Shai Kaliv; fourth, Yasan.

These so-called prophets who flourished before Gayomard are not mentioned in any Zoroastrian text considered authentic.

Q. What are the names of Gayomard's ancestors?

A. Gayomard, Yasan Ajam, Yasan, Shai Mahbul, Shai Kaliv, Jai Alad, Jai Afram, Abad Azad, Mehabad.

Q. How many royal dynasties were there?

A. Four: 1) Peshdadian 3) Ashkanian [Parthian]
2) Kayanian 4) Sasanian

Zoroastrians usually date Zoroaster as having lived about 8000 years ago, i.e., about 6000 B.C. Also note that in the above list of four dynasties, the Achaemenians are left out. The Pahlavi tradition had forgotten the Achaemenians. There were no parchments or book records of them. Greek records, however, were better informed than the Persian memory on this matter.

Q. What do these names mean?

A. Peshdadian means 'the first administrators of justice.' Kayanian means 'king of kings', 'those having great status, pomp and justice'; it also means 'organizers, distributors of punishment, the powerful.' Ashkanian refers to the first king of this dynasty named 'Ashk.' Sasanian comes from the word 'Sasan', which means 'those who walk on the path of God.'

The meanings Erachji ascribes to these terms are for the most part fabrications. His rendering of Peshdadian comes closest to the literal meaning of the term; it is based on the word peshdad which means 'ancient law-giver', from pesh, 'before', and dad 'law'. The meanings of the other terms, like the historical narratives he deals with in the remainder of this chapter, seem to have been taken from the Sharestan. It would have been better had Erachji relied on the indigenous sources of the Avesta, or the Shahnama, for the history of ancient Iranian kings. Even some of the Pahlavi texts like the Denkard could have provided him with useful material.

Q. How many years did Gayomard rule?

A. Gayomard means 'mortal life'. His habitation was on mount Sarandip and he founded a city called Uruse. The name of his son was Syamak who died during the lifetime of Gayomard. Gayomard ruled for 30 years. Thereafter Hooshang became king.

Q. How many years did Hooshang rule?

A. Hooshang means 'one having intelligence.' His father's name was Syamak, his mother's Faranak. He founded three cities: Babul, Shus and Kufe. He ruled for 40 years. During his lifetime he discovered fire by striking stones together. After him Tahmurasp became king.

Q. Who was Tahmurasp?

A. Tahmurasp means 'a soul speaking about the sky.' His father's name was Hooshang and his mother's Shaheriyar.

He founded six cities: Amel, Tabaristan, Sarue, Isfahan, Madain, and Saba-e erak-e Arab. He destroyed many evil persons and was called Tahmurasp-e Diwband, 'one who takes daevas captive.' He ruled for 30 years. After him Jamshed became king.

Q. Who was Jamshed?

A. Jam means 'pure', also 'intelligent'; shed means 'light'. Hence the name means 'pure light', or the 'light of intelligence.' His father's name was Vivanghan, his mother's Gulnar. During his time no premature deaths occurred, nor difficulty or pain, and the world increased [in size] three times. Mankind was divided into four groups in his time. He began the construction of buildings and introduced other skills. He ruled for 700 years. Zohak killed him and usurped his throne.

The deluge occurred during Jamshed's time. Jamshed was warned beforehand, having been inspired by God. He selected the best and most able-bodied pair of each species so that life on earth would be saved. He constructed a war (a Pahlavi term meaning an 'enclosure or cave', perhaps a reference to an ark) to keep them safe. This war was a place shielded from the impact of the deluge. In the Avesta Jamshed is spoken of as full of glory, so it may be that it was a descendant of his who lost the khwarrah [glory] and was usurped by Zohak.

Q. Who was Zohak?

A. Zohak is also called deh-hak, meaning 'having ten defects'. He was 1) ugly, 2) a pigmy type, 3) tyrannical, 4) shameless, 5) a glutton, 6) abusive, 7) a liar, 8) hasty, 9) a coward, and 10) foolish. He was also called biwarasp, 'having 10,000 horses'. His father's name was Mardas, who was very pious. By treachery Zohak killed him by throwing him into a pit. There were two diseased deformities on both of Zohak's shoulders shaped like serpents. As a cure he used to kill men with cruelty and place their brains upon his diseased shoulders. He ruled for 1000 years. But one day, because of his tyranny, the people brought forth Faridoon. He took Zohak to the mountain Damawand and killed him there. Faridoon took the throne on the day Mihr of the month Mihr.

Q. Who was Faridoon?

A. The name means 'wisdom of the eighth sky'. His father's name was Athwiyan, his mother's Franak. He had three sons: Selam, Tur, and Erach. During his lifetime he divided his whole kingdom among his sons. The region to the West he gave to Selam. He gave China and Turkestan to Tur, and Iran to Erach. Selam and Tur were displeased with this division. They grew angry with their father and wrote him hateful letters. In order to seek some compromise Erach went to see his brothers. They killed him. From that time to the time of the last kingship in Iran there was enmity between Turan and Iran. Faridoon ruled for 500 years. Thereafter, Minocheher sat on the throne.

It is difficult to know just how to understand these historical stories. What are we to make of a 500 year reign? Perhaps they calculated time differently in those times or there may have been several kings of the same name whose ruling period might have been collectively recounted.

Q. Who was Minocheher?

A. Minocheher means 'face of paradise' (behesht). He was the son of the daughter of Erach. His father's name was Pashang, his mother's Gordafrid. He revenged the death of his maternal grandfather and killed Selam and Tur. The administration of his kingship was run by Sam Nariman. He ruled for 120 years. His son Nozar sat on the throne after him.

Q. Who was Nozar?

A. Nozar means 'precious', or 'approved.' His father's name was Minocheher, his mother's Ferangis. He had two sons, Tush and Gastaham. Afrasiyab, the son of the Turanian Pashang, killed Nozar in revenge for the death of his grandfather Tur. Afrasiyab held the throne of Iran for some time after that. Nozar ruled for seven years.

Q. Who was Zub Tehmasp?

A. When Nozar was killed and his sons were not able to sit on the throne, Zal searched out Zub Tehmasp, the grandson of Selam and great grandson of Faridoon, who was living in Iran, having resolved to seat him on the throne. Zub fought with Afrasiyab, banished him from Iran and acceded to the throne. He died after five years. After him, his son Kersasp came to the throne. *Zal was the son of Sam and the father of Rustam, the most prominent hero of the Shahnama.*

Q. Who was Kersasp?

A. Kersasp sat on his father Zub's throne for nine years before he died. At the time [of his death] there was no other person who could act as king; the throne remained empty. Afrasiyab learned of this and prepared to attack Iran. Zal came to know about it and called upon Kay Kobad to take the throne. Kay Kobad was a descendant of King Faridoon and was living at the time on Mount Alborz.

These names which Erachji is discussing all appear in our benedictory prayers (afrins), in Pahlavi and post Sasanian literature, and in the Avesta. Firdausi, the author of the Shahnama, made use of such Pahlavi books to prepare his famous epic. He may also have had access to the Avesta. Certain couplets are quite mystical in nature. Firdausi must have been a pure Iranian, otherwise he could not have described Zoroaster and his religion as he did.

Q. Who was Kay Kobad?

A. Kay Kobad means a 'proper worker'. His father's name was Zab and his mother's name Roshnak. His throne was in Isfahan. The title Kayanian began with Kay Kobad, he being the first king of the second dynasty. It was in his time that Afrasiyab attacked Iran and Rustam fought him. Being defeated Afrasiyab had to make a treaty with Kay Kobad. After Kay Kobad's death, his son Kaus came to the throne. Kay Kobad ruled for 100 years.

Q. Who was Kay Kaus?

A. Kaus means 'pure'. It also means 'light'. His father's name was Kay Kobad and his mother's Gordafrid. Kaus was a very wrathful and rash king. He went to fight the King of Mazandaran and Hamavaran. He was capture there and Rustam freed him. He tried to ascend to the sky to take the kingship of the sky. While doing so he fell to the ground.

According to Firdausi, Kaus attempted to fly by tying live eagles to a wing-like attachment which had a place for him to sit. He hung two pieces of meat in front of the eagles. Up he went, only to land in the forest. The father of Rustam scolded him for such rash adventures.

His son Syawakhsh was very righteous. Because of strained relationships, Syawakhsh went to Turan and married Ferangis, the daughter of Afrasiyab. Karshevaj [Afraziyab's brother] instigated Afrasiyab against him and consequently Syawakhsh was killed. At that time Ferangis was pregnant and gave birth to a son named Kay Khosraw. He sat on the throne of Kaus. Kaus ruled for 150 years.

Q. Who was Kay Khosraw?

A. Kay Khosraw means 'just'. His father was Syawakhsh, his mother Ferangis. In order to avenge the death of his father he had to fight Afrasiyab for a long time, but ultimately killed him. He ruled for 60 years, after which time he gave the reign of the kingdom to Lorasp and renounced the world in order to offer prayers to God. That is, he went to an unknown place and left no trace of his whereabouts.

He had fulfilled his task--that of killing Afrasiyab and his brother Karshevaj. Then he left the throne to do bandagi to God. He was a saintly king, and is thought to be living today, preserving the Zoroastrian religion.

In Pahlavi literature, saintly kings of ancient times are called the Immortals. Their deeds and works are still alive in the tradition, which is continuous. Kay Khosraw is mentioned everyday in the recitation of the Avesta and in our prayers and formal benedictions (afrins). It seems strange that despite all the internal evidence from Avestan and Pahlavi books which attest to the historicity of these figures, and despite the fact that these histor-ical personages have always been a part of Iranian history, still some scholars doubt their existence. Why? Because they were not mentioned by Greek historians centuries later! Zoroastrian ritual has kept the names of these kings since time immemorial, but the skepticism of the 20th century dismisses it as mythical. But we are conservative and remain tenacious. The immortals are preserving our religion in its pristine purity. Peshotan is immortal, and he, together with 150 disciples, is looking after and preserving the religion, with all 21 Nasks, and the time will come when they will appear and show us.

Q. Who was Lohrasp?

A. Lohrasp means 'proper'. His father was Arvand, his mother Tanaz. His throne was in Balkh [in Bactria]. During his reign the prophet Zoroaster was born. Lohrasp reigned for 120 years and in his lifetime gave his kingdom to his son Vishtasp and then remained engrossed in offering prayers (bandagi) to God in his own city of Balkh.

Q. Who was Vishtasp?

A. Vishtasp means 'one benefitting the world through God.' His father was Lohrasp, his mother Azadeh. In the 13th year of his reign, Zoroaster proclaimed the religion and Vishtasp with his people accepted it. His son Aspandyar took the lead in propagating the religion. His other son Peshotan renounced the world and sought a place to be engrossed in bandagi to God. At this opportune time Arjasp attacked Iran and tried to destroy the religion. The result was Zoroaster's death, [inflicted] by the warrior Turbaratur. Vishtasp ruled for 120 years. Asfandyar was killed by the hand of Rustam, and after Vishtasp, Bahman, son of Aspandyar, came to the throne. *After Asfandyar, the historical details are uncertain, as the Achaemenid times had been completely forgotten and later history was thought to be connected to the Kayanian dynasty. The following kings, from Bahman up to Dara, ought to be Achaemenid, not Kayanian.*

Q. Who was Bahman?

A. Bahman means 'one having good thoughts.' His original name was Ardashir, but because of his good acts he was called Bahman-e daraz-dast meaning 'he who attained success over many countries.' His father was Asfandyar and his mother Farhang. He killed Framarz, the son of Rustam, in revenge for his father. He took revenge on the Jews and devastated the place of the Kaaba.
All these references are anachronisms.
He commanded that all believe in one God only and constructed Atash Bahrams in Turan, Rum and Seistan. He constructed bridges and inns in Iran. He ruled for 110 years and died of a snake bite. His daughter Humai succeeded him to the throne.

Q. Who was Humai?

A. She was the daughter of King Bahman. She was very generous and holy. She made Isfahan prosper and in the city of Istakhr-Pars built a palace having 1000 pillars. This palace was devastated by Alexander. Humai had a son. She believed, because of a vision, that if her son remained in Iran, great ruin would come to the country. Consequently Humai put him in a wooden box, with jewels, and set it off to sea. The box [drifted] to another city where a washerman saw it. He opened the box, took out the boy and nourished him, giving him the name Darab which means 'one who is kept by water'. Humai fought with the King of Rum and ruled for 32 years. Her son Darab reigned after her.

Q. Who was Darab?

A. Darab means 'one who is kept by water'. His father's name was Bahman. He fought Philkush and ruled for 12 years. His son Dara succeeded him.

Philkush is the Muslim spelling of Philip; this may be a reference to the father of Alexander. Erachji, unwittingly, understands these events which occurred in the Achaemenian period as belonging to the Kayanian period. The name Bahman for Darab's father is also puzzling, since Bahman is the maternal grandfather of Darab. Perhaps the explanation is rather simple, however. If Bahman had had no male issue, his daughter may have been married on the condition that her first male issue would become the adopted son of Bahman.

Q. Who was Dara?

A. His father's name was Darab. Dara conquered the emperor of China and founded ten cities. He installed the Atash Bahram of Goshnasp-Burzin and set apart treasures for its maintenance. He ruled for 14 years. He fought in a great battle with Alexander who invaded Iran. Dara's two generals killed him through treachery, and Alexander was able to sit on the throne of Iran.

Q. Who was Alexander?

A. In some books Alexander is called the son of Darab, and in others he is called the son of Philkush. Alexander ruled Iran for 14 years. In this period he conquered many countries and introduced many arts to the world. He had the religious books of Zoroaster copied and translated into his own language and sent to Rum. He then had the religious books of Zoroaster burned. He travelled much by sea and land. He travelled further in order to seek 'the ever-living water' the ab-e hayyat, but returned despondent. He died a natural death. After him a man named Ashk came to the throne of Iran.

Q. Who was Ashk?

A. Ashk means 'one who treads on the path of God.' He was the son of Dara and was the first king of the third dynasty, the Ashkanian, which is named after him. After the demise of Alexander Iran was without a king. Ashk, at the time, was the governor of a province. The Iranians helped him secure the throne of Iran. Ashk ruled for 12 years. After him his son Shapur came to the throne.

Dara (Darius III) was in fact the last of the Achaemenian kings. Parthian is another name for the Ashkanian dynasty. It is interesting to see how much our knowledge of history has progressed over the past century of scholarship. Through modern archaeological and numismatic research we now know of many kings of the Parthian dynasty who were unknown to Erachji.

Q. Who was Shapur?

A. Shapur means 'the son of a king'. His father's name was Ashk. Shapur ruled for 20 years and 8 months. In his time, Christ was born. After Shapur, his son Bahram came to the throne.

Finally, Erachji has given us a correct rendition of a name. Shapur does mean 'the son of a king.'

Q. Who was Bahram?

A. Bahram's father's name was Shapur. He was surnamed Gudarz. He had many inscriptions carved on mountains and built a new city called Anbar. He built a big building for the Atash Bahram. In his time, the Romans attacked Iran but they were driven out. He ruled for 11 years. His son Palash succeeded him to the throne.

The Greek name for Gudarz is Gotarzes.

Q. Who was Palash?

A. Palash means 'one who has knowledge of God'. He ruled for 11 years. After him his son Hormazd came to the throne.

The Denkard's name for Palash is Walakhsh, called Vologeses by the Greeks. According to the Denkard Walakhsh ordered the restoration of scattered Avestan scriptures.

Q. Who was Hormazd?

A. Hormazd means 'nourisher'. His father's name was Palash.

He ruled for 19 years. In his time a man named Yunas claimed to be a prophet.

Yunas is the Persian form of Jonah, one of the 12 minor prophets mentioned in the Old Testament.

Q. Who became king after Hormazd?

A. A man named Khosraw became the king. His father's name was Palash. He built seven-storied palaces in Iran. He built a city called Sirgan. He ruled for 30 years. His brother Palash succeeded him to the throne.

Q. Who was Palash?

A. His father's name was Hormazd. He dreamt one night that a spiritual being (fireshte) informed him that his death would be at his own hand. So he always felt unhappy. One day he was reclining against a pole of his tent when another post fell on his head and he died. He ruled for 12 years.

Q. Who ruled after Palash?

A. Ardawan was the son of Palash. During his reign there was a three-year drought. Idol worship spread over many regions at this time. He lived in Isfahan during the summer, and in Ahwaz in the winter. He ruled for 13 years.

Here ends the history of the Parthian kings. Erachji now goes on to describe the kings of the Sasanian dynasty. He does not always cite accurately the number of years each king ruled.

Q. Who ruled after Ardawan?

A. Ardashir [226-240 A.C.]. He was called Babagan since he was the maternal grandson of Babag. He was the son of Sasan. His mother's name was Gohrafrid. He was the first king of the fourth dynasty [the Sasanian]. He conquered many countries. He built a fortress in the city of Pars and had many inscriptions carved in the city of Istakhr-Pars. People were happy in his time. He revived Zoroastrianism; he built many Atash Bahrams. Ardag Wiraz performed many miracles in his time. He ruled for 14 years. He conferred kingship on his son Shapur during his lifetime.

Q. Who was Shapur? [Shapur I, 240-270 A.C.].

A. Shapur was the son of Ardashir Babagan. He conquered Rum. In his time a painter named Mani claimed himself as prophet in the city of Pars. Shapur summoned him, but Mani being afraid, fled. Shapur ruled for 30 years. Hormazd succeeded him to the throne.

Q. Who was Hormazd? [Hormazd I, 270-273 A.C.].

A. Hormazd was the son of Shapur. He was living in Khorasan. He ruled for one year and five months. His son Bahram succeeded him to the throne.

Q. Who was Bahram? [Bahram I, 273-276 A.C.].

A. Bahram was the son of Hormazd. The painter Mani who claimed to be a prophet in the time of Shapur and who fled at the time was caught by Bahram and hanged at the gate of the city. He ruled for one year and three months. His son Bahram II succeeded him to the throne.

Q. Who was Bahram II? [Bahram II, 276-293 A.C.].

A. Bahram II was the son of Bahram. He was living in Seistan. He ruled for three years and three months. His son Bahramyan succeeded him to the throne.

Q. Who was Bahramyan? [Bahram III, 293 A.C.].

A. Bahramyan was the son of Bahram II and he ruled for four months.

Q. Who ruled after Bahramyan?

A. Narsi [293-302 A.C.] was the son of Bahramyan. He ruled for nine years. His son Hormazd succeeded him to the throne.

Erachji makes Narsi the son of Bahramyan, but he was the third son of Shapur I.

Q. Who was Hormazd? [Hormazd II, 302-309 A.C.].

A. Hormazd was the son of Narsi. He ruled for nine years. His son Shapur succeeded him to the throne.

Q. Who was Shapur [Shapur II, 309-379 A.C.].

A. Shapur was the son of Hormazd. He was called zul aqtaf [breaker of shoulders]. He used to strike out at the

Arabs severely since he had a vision that the Iranian sovereignty would fall into the hands of the Arabs. He ruled for 70 years. His brother Ardashir succeeded him to the throne.

Q. Who was Ardashir? [Ardashir II, 379-383 A.C.].

A. Ardashir was the son of Hormazd. People called him nekokar [doer of good deeds]. He ruled for ten years.

Q. Who was Shapur? [Shapur III, 383-388 A.C.].

A. Shapur was the son of Shapur zul aqtaf. He ruled for five years. He died when the post of a tent fell on his head.

Q. Who was Bahram? [Bahram IV, son of Shapur II, 388-399 A.C.].

A. Bahram was the son of Shapur. He was ruling in Kerman during his father's reign and so was also called Kermanshah. He ruled for 11 years. He was killed by one of his relatives. His son Yazdegird succeeded him to the throne.

Q. Who was Yazdegird? [Yazdegird I, son of Shapur III, 399-421 A.C.].

A. Yazdegird was the son of Bahram. He was called bazakgar [a sinner]. He ruled for 22 years and 5 months. His son Bahram succeeded him to the throne.

Q. Who was Bahram? [Bahram V, 421-439 A.C.].

A. Bahram was the son of Yazdegird. He was also called Bahramgur. He married the daughter of the king of Hindustan. He ruled for 63 years. One day he went hunting. There he pursued a wild boar which fled into a steep ravine. Bahram disappeared there. His son Yazdegird succeeded him to the throne.

The name Bahramgur comes from his fondness for boar-hunting; the Persian gur means 'a boar.'

Q. Who was Yazdegird? [Yazdegird II, 439-457 A.C.].

A. Yazdegird was the son of Bahramgur. He was also called Khosraw. He installed Atash Bahrams and built places of worship. He ruled for 18 years. His son Hormazd succeeded him to the throne.

Q. Who was Hormazd? [Hormazd III, 457-459 A.C.].

A. Hormazd was the son of Yazdegird. He ruled for one year. His brother Firuz succeeded him to the throne.

Q. Who was Firuz? [Firuz, son of Yazdegird II, 459-484 A.C.].

A. Firuz was the son of Yazdegird. After one year of his rule there was a severe famine for seven years in Iran, as it did not rain. Firuz spent enormous sums from the state treasury and did not allow any man or animal to die. He assembled people and prayed to God and asked for rains, and it rained. He ruled for 11 years. His son Palash succeeded him to the throne.

Q. Who was Palash? [Palash, son of Yazdegird II, 484-488 A.C.].

A. Palash was the son of Firuz. He ruled for five years. His brother Kobad succeeded him to the throne.

Q. Who was Kobad? [Kobad I, son of Firuz, 488-531 A.C.].

A. He was the son of Firuz. After ten years of his rule, a man called Mazdak came to the city of Istakhr-Pars claiming to be a prophet. With his father's permission, Kobad's son Noshirwan punished Mazdak and his followers. Kobad ruled for 43 years. His son Noshirwan succeeded him to the throne.

Mazdak was the first communist of the world. He taught equal distribution of wealth and women. The Zoroastrian clergy opposed such sinister doctrines (as the former discouraged individual freedom and marred creative instinct in man and the latter perpetrated immortality) and asked Noshirwan to put him to death. Kobad was temporarily forced to leave the throne from 496-498 for his encouragement of Mazdak. Zamasp, the son of Firuz, ruled for that brief period.

Q. Who was Noshirwan? [Khosraw I, 531-579 A.C.].

A. Noshirwan was the son of Kobad. He was also called Kesra [i.e. Khosraw, Av. husravah 'well-known, celebrated; a king']. He ruled with justice and hence was called Noshirwan Adil [Noshirwan the Just]. He built a famous palace in Madain. The prophet Muhammad was born in his time. He ruled for 48 years. His son Hormazd succeeded him to the throne.

Q. Who was Hormazd? [Hormazd IV, 579-590 A.C.].

A. He was the son of Noshirwan. He lived in the city of Armin. He went blind. He ruled for 12 years. His son Khosraw succeeded him to the throne.

Iran was ruled from 590-591 by the usurper Bahram Chobin, who was defeated by Khosraw II with the help of Maurice, the Byzantine emperor.

Q. Who was Khosraw? [Khosraw II, 591-628 A.C.].

A. Khosraw was the son of Hormazd. He was also called Parviz. In his time Muhammad claimed to be prophet. Muhammad wrote a letter to Khosraw asking him to accept his religion. Khosraw tore up that letter in his public court. He was killed by his son Sheroy. He ruled 38 years. His son Sheroy succeeded him to the throne.

Q. Who was Sheroy? [Kobad II, 628 A.C.].

A. Sheroy was the son of Khosraw Parviz. He was also called Kobad. He ruled for seven months. His son Ardashir succeeded him to the throne.

Q. Who was Ardashir? [Ardashir III, 628-629 A.C.].

A. Ardashir was the son of Sheroy. He came to the throne when he was only seven years old. He ruled for one year and six months.

Q. Who ruled after Ardashir?

A. A man called Guraz came to the throne. He was called Framin. He ruled for 50 days.

Q. Who ruled after Guraz?

A. Purandokht, the daughter of Khosraw Parviz, came to the throne. She ruled for four months. The prophet Muhammad died in her time.

Q. Who ruled after Purandokht?

A. Azarmidokht, another daughter of Khosraw Parviz, came to the throne and ruled for one month.

Q. Who ruled after Azarmidokht?

A. Farrokhzad, the son of Khosraw Parviz, ruled for one month.

Q. Who came after Farrokhzad?

A. Yazdegird, the last king of the Sasanian Dynasty. [Yazdegird III, 632-651 A.C.]. He lived in the city of Pars and ruled for 20 years. In his time Caliph Omar, the father-in-law of Muhammad, attacked Iran. Yazdegird fled but was killed in the city of Marv. The Parsis have been without a king from that day on. The year Yazdegirdi, which we use today, dates from his accession to the throne. I have written this history from the Shahnama, the Sharestan and the Persian Vajarkard Dini.

Anno Yazdegirdi is 632 A.C. The present date is 1350 A.Y (1980-81 A.C.) Yazdegird III was the grandson of Khosraw II. When he ascended to the throne the Sasanian empire was much weakened through court intrigues and eventually fell to invaders. The Parsis have been without a king since 651 A.C.

This chapter of Erachji's is important from an historical point of view. It shows how Zoroastrians understood history a century ago and through what sources.

CHAPTER THIRTY-TWO

A history of the coming of the Parsis to India

Q. Why did the Zoroastrians come to India?

A. When the reign of Yazdegird weakened, the people knew that the end had come. Some Zoroastrians, therefore, in order to preserve the religion, took all the religious books they had, left all of their belongings, and went into the mountains in the vicinity and lived there for 100 years.

The number of years Erachji cites is an approximate number and is given in the Qissa-e Sanjan.

Q. Did they leave their mountain homes?

A. As the power of the Muslims slowly began to dominate those places as well, they left the mountains and went to the city called Hormazd. There they stayed for 15 years.

Q. Why did they leave the city of Hormazd?

A. There also the power of wicked persons increased, and the sages feared their religion would not be well-preserved. They thought then of leaving for India. They set out in ships from the city of Hormazd and came to India. They landed at a city called Div and stayed there for 19 years. There are a few Zoroastrians still living in Div who are their descendants.

Div is possibly a port city or island on the coast of Gujarat.

Q. Where did they go from Div?

A. They stayed in Div for 19 years. A high priest named Neryosang Dhaval and other sages learned Sanskrit and Gujarati. There was no oppression from anyone of an alien faith, but the climate there was not suitable to all. Hence they resolved to go to the city of Sanjan and set out in ships. During the voyage a great tempest struck them and they were all about to drown, when, becoming one in heart they pleaded to God and vowed that if they reached Sanjan safely they would install an Atash Bahram there. Their pleas were answered. All arrived safely in Sanjan in 772 Samvat, the month of Shravan, on the day Vad 9.

Here Erachji gives dates according to the Hindu calendar, Samvat being the name of the Hindu year, followed by Hindu month and day names. These dates occur in old mss., and no doubt have been handed down for generations. But scholars debate the accuracy of these dates. S.H. Hodivala, in a book titled Studies in Parsi History (Bombay, 1920) established that 772 was a misreading for 992, which would be the Christian year 936 A.C. The date is two centuries later than Parsis have usually thought. Traditions die hard, however, and many still hold to the earlier date. There is no mention of such a move, however, in the Pahlavi books of that period, a face which supports Hodivala's contention that the later date is most accurate.

Q. What did they do after landing in Sanjan?

A. Neryosang and a few sages disembarked and went before King Jadirana and placed some presents before him. They blessed him and said, "We have heard that you are a very kind king. In order to preserve our religion, we have left our country and have come to your city. Give us shelter."

Q. What did the King reply?

A. When the king heard them speak such words, he was happy. But upon seeing their height and majesty he was afraid lest they would take his kingdom. So thinking, he replied: 'First you must agree to my conditions. Give me your reply: 1) explain to me what is your religion; 2) give up your Iranian tongue and adopt the language of Hindustan [i.e., Gujarati, the language of the region]; 3) ask your women to dress just like our women do; 4) henceforth do not retain any of your weapons; 5) and in your marriage ceremony, tie knots with thread in the manner we follow. If you agree to these conditions, I will give you any place of your choice.'

This story is given in the Qissa-e Sanjan written in 1599 A.C. Hodivala has shed considerable light on this subject in his superb Studies. He has proven, in the light of historical evidence, that the Hindu Rajah ruling then was Vajjadevrai. Regarding the statement that Dastur Neryosang led the Parsi founding fathers, one cannot be sure. There is no unanimity among scholars as to whether a Neryosang really existed at that time. There may be confusion here with the celebrated Sanskrit scholar Neryosang of the 12th century A.C. It is noteworthy that the Qissa-e Sanjan does not mention him either as the leader of the devout immigrants or as the priest who led the consecration of the famous Atash Bahram named the Iranshah, which Erachji discusses below.

Q. Did they accept everything the king said?

A. Yes. All assembled and resolved that they should explain their religion to the king, speak the tongue of Hindustan ask the women to wear the sari and bangles, give up their weapons, and tie the thread in the marriage ceremony. By so doing, no damage was done to the religion. Thereupon they went to the king and accepted his conditions. A learned high priest (dastur) explained to the king in Sanskrit all matters relating to the religion. Hearing this the king was very pleased. He ordered them to go and stay at the place of their choice.

Q. What did they do in Sanjan?

A. All the Zoroastrians resolved to install an Atash Bahram. Several went to the king and requested that he kindly issue orders to the effect that no Hindu be allowed inside their ceremonial places. The king so ordered and with much delight helped them in a number of ways.

Q. Who directed the ceremonies for [the installation of] the Atash Bahram?

A. Dastur Neryosang Dhaval directed all ceremonies and the Atash Bahram was installed in Samvat 777, day nine, month nine, and was given the name Iranshah, meaning the King of Iran.

Q. How many years did they live in Sanjan after installing the Atash Bahram?

A. All the Zoroastrians stayed there for about 300 years.

Q. Where did they go after that?

A. Wherever their occupations took them, they settled. Some went to Navsari, Ankleshwar, Broach, Khambat, etc. Those remaining in Sanjan stayed for about another 324 years. In all, then, the Zoroastrians lived in Sanjan for 624 years.

Q. What did the Zoroastrians do after leaving Sanjan?

A. Those who were in Sanjan resolved that all priests (mobeds) should be divided into five groups and through mutual understanding, should perform their duties for the layman (behdin). All were pleased with the proposal of the Sanjanas, and documents were drawn up.

The process which led to five different groupings of priests must have been a gradual one.

Q. How did they distribute the five panthaks?

A panthak is an ecclesiastical jurisdiction within which a group of priests is entitled to perform ceremonies (kriyas). Such priests make up a panth or group of their own. There are in all five original groups of priests among the Parsis. Their names and the areas of jurisdiction demarcated by rivers are given by Erachji in the following answer.

A. The boundary for the Sanjana priests runs from the river Dantora to the river Par, near Bulsar. The boundary of the Bhagarias is from the Par river to the river Variav [i.e. Tapi]. The boundary of the Godavaras is from Variav to Ankleshwar. The boundary of the Bharuchas is from Ankleshwar to Khambat. For the Khumbata priests it is in and around Khambat. In this way the five panthaks were distributed.

The panthaks are demarcated in the following way:

1. *Sanjana priests: from the river Dantora to the river Par.*
2. *Bhagaria priests: from the river Par to the river Tapi.*
3. *Godavara priests: from the river Tapi to the river Narmada.*
4. *Bharucha priests: from the river Narmada to the river Mahi.*
5. *Khambata priests: from the river Mahi to the river Sabarmati.*

Q. What did they do afterwards?

A. Those who lived in Sanjan lived there in happiness for 324 years. In 700 A.Y. Sultan Mahmud, called Mahmud Begdo attacked Sanjan with an army led by Alafkhan.

Q. What was the result?

A. When Alafkhan attacked Sanjan with 30,000 soldiers, the Hindu king, a descendant of Jadirana, summoned the Parsis and said: "My ancestors gave you asylum. Now i is your turn to help me." The Parsis said: "We have a treaty with your ancestors not to bear weapons. If you cancel that treaty then we shall certainly bear weapons." The king agreed. Among the Parsis, 1,400 men came to fight for the king. The king gave them all they required and sent them with his army to fight.

Q. How did they fight?

A. The general of the Muslim army was Alafkhan. The general of the King's army was a Parsi named Ardashir. Ardashir fought for three days and repulsed the Muslim army. During the second advance Ardashir killed one of the leaders in Alafkhan's army. Alafkhan then came face to face with Ardashir and in that fight Ardashir was killed, as were many Parsis. The king's army was defeated and Sanjan fell into the hands of the Muslims.

Q. When Sanjan fell into the hands of the Muslims, where did the Parsis live?

A. At that time when preparations for battle were being made in Sanjan, a few Parsis, with the Atash Bahram, went to the mountain called Bahrot. There they stayed for 12 years. When Sanjan fell into the hands of the Muslims, all the Parsis settled there in the mountains.

Q. Where did they go after leaving the mountain of Bahrot?

A. From Bahrot they went to Bansda with the Atash Bahram. They stayed there for 14 years. Zoroastrians from all over then came to Bansda to the Atash Bahram.

Q. Where did they take the Atash Bahram from Bansda?

A. There was a famous layman (behdin) named Changa Asa in Navsari. He used to go to Bansda every year from Navsari. He persuaded the Zoroastrians of Bansda to bring the Atash Bahram to Navsari in Samvat 1475 of the month Akhad, on Sud 5.

The date Samvat 1475 does not tally well with the historicity of other contemporary events and personalities. Hodivala convincingly argues that the Iranshah Atash Bahram was brought to Navsari about 50 years later than Samvat 1475 (about 1469 A.C.).

Q. How many years did the *Atash Bahram* remain in Navsari?

A. They brought the *Atash Bahram* in Samvat 1475 and it remained in Navsari for 314 years.

Q. Where did they take the *Atash Bahram* after that?

A. At that time there was oppression by robbers in Navsari. So from Samvat 1790 to Samvat 1792 the *Atash Bahram* was shifted to Surat.

Q. Where was the *Atash Bahram* taken after Surat?

A. It was brought back to Navsari where it remained for three years, Samvat 1793-1796.

Q. Where was it taken after Navsari?

A. There was a quarrel between the Sanjana and the Bhagaria priests of Navsari about matters relating to their *panthaks*. Consequently the Sanjanas took the *Atash Bahram* from Navsari and brought it to Bulsar in 1796. The *Atas Bahram* stayed there for two years, up to Samvat 1798.

Q. From Bulsar where did they take the *Atash Bahram*?

A. Bulsar was also within the *panthak* of Navsari, so they could not stay there. Therefore, they shifted the *Atash Bahram* to Udwada, which is within their own boundaries, in Samvat 1798. It remains burning there till this very day.

Q. Who then consecrated the *Atash Bahram* in Navsari?

A. The leader of the Bhagarias of Navsari was Desai Khurshedji Tehmulji. With his own money he constructed the *Atash Bahram* in Samvat 1822 on the day *Srosh* of the mont *Ardibehesht*. All the ceremonies were directed by Wada Dasturji Sorabji Rustomji Meherjirana. The above histor was gathered from *Qissa-e Sanjan* and other stories and written documents.

It was not Desai Khurshedji who arranged for the Atash Bahram. Rather, it was the local assembly of all adult Zoroastrian men, i.e., the anjoman, that arranged it. The wealthy Parsis of Surat, Broach and other centers offered material and moral support in the undertaking. Khurshedji was a benevolent and influential Parsi of that time, and he gave money required for the consecration of the Atash Bahram *to the* anjoman. *The* anjoman *paid it back over the years. For decades his descendants administered the affairs of the* Atash Bahram, *and so people thought it was the* Atash Bahram *of Desai Khurshedji, and so it is written by Erachji. But Desai Khurshedji himself wrote in his records that the* Atash Bahram *belonged to the* anjoman. *Nowadays it is called the* Anjoman Atash Bahram.

GLOSSARY, APPENDICES I & II

GLOSSARY

ABBREVIATIONS:

Av.	Avestan	Pers.	Persian
Ar.	Arabic	Phl.	Pahlavi
Guj.	Gujarati	Skt.	Sanskrit
Paz.	Pazand		

A

Aban (Phl., Pers.) : lit. 'waters'; name of a female spirit being presiding over waters and virtuous women; also the name of a Zoroastrian month and day.

Achaemenian : name of a royal dynasty of Iran (550 B.C.-330 B.C.), founded by Cyrus. The name is derived from Cyrus's ancestor Hakhamanish.

Adar Burzin (Phl.) : 'exalted fire'; the miraculous fire Zoroaster brought from God.

Adarbad Mahraspandan (Phl.) : Adarbad, the son of Mahraspand, was an orthodox Zoroastrian High Priest and prime minister of Shapur II (309-379 A.C.).

Afrasiyab (Pers.) : a Turanian king opposed to Kay Kaus and Kay Khosraw, an arch-enemy of the Iranians.

afrin (Phl.) : as a general term it means 'blessing, benediction'; also applied to specific Pazand prayers of blessing.

afrinagan (Phl.) : a common ceremony of blessing which can be performed in any clean place.

Afrin i Ardafrawash (Phl.) : benedictory prayer in Pazand said by the priest at the conclusion of most common ceremonies.

Afrin i Gahambar (Paz.)	: benedictory prayer in Pazand commemorating the creations of Ohrmazd, said during the six seasonal festivals (*gahambars*).
Ahunwar (Phl.)	: one of the most efficacious prayers of the Zoroastrians; it begins with the Av. phrase *yatha ahu vairyo* and has 21 words corresponding to the 21 books of the Avesta.
Ahura Mazda (Av.)	: omnipotent, omniscient and omnipresent God of the Zoroastrians; the Pahlavi word is Ohrmazd.
Akoman (Phl., Paz.)	: lit. 'one having an evil mind'; the name of a demon opposed to the spirit being Vohuman.
Alexander	: the Macedonian king who overthrew the Achaemenian dynasty in 330 B.C.
amahraspandan (Phl.)	: the Holy Immortals, called *Amesha Spenta* in Avestan, who are the highest spirit beings created by Ohrmazd.
'amal (Ar.)	: the ritual power which makes a priest qualified to perform high lituriges.
Ameretat (Av.)	: see Amurdad.
Amurdad (Phl.)	: the Holy Immortal presiding over vegetation; Av. *Ameretat*, 'Immortality.'
anjoman (Pers.)	: an assembly of the faithful.
ardafrawash (Phl.)	: the holy spirits of the departed.
Ardashir (Pers.)	: Ardashir (226-240 A.C.), the son of Babag, was the founder of the Sasanian dynasty.
Arda Viraf (Pers.)	: the name of a saintly priest of the early Sasanian period who saw visions of heaven and hell; Phl. form is Ardag Wiraz.

Ardibehesht (Pers.) : see Ardwahisht.

Ardwahisht (Phl.) : the Holy Immortal presiding over fire; Av. Asha Vahishta, 'Best Righteousness'.

Aresh (Phl., Pers.) : the famous archer of ancient Iran, mentioned in the Av. Yashts, the Phl. Bundahishn and the Shahnama.

Asha (Av.) : 'righteousness, righteous order'; a foundational concept of Zoroastrianism and refers to Asha Vahishta the Bountiful Immortal 'Best Righteousness'.

Asha Vahishta (Av.) : see Ardwahisht.

ashem vohu (Av.) : one of the holiest prayers of the Zoroastrians which praises righteousness.

Ashk (Phl.) : Arsaces I, founder of the Parthian (Ashkanian) dynasty (250 B.C.-226 A.C.); cf. Av. arshan, 'hero'.

Ashkanian : another name for the Parthian dynasty (250 B.C.-226 A.C.).

Ashtad (Phl.) : name of an angel presiding over the 26th day of the Zoroastrian calendar.

asn khrad (Phl.) : inborn or natural wisdom.

Astwihad (Phl.) : a demon of death opposed to the spirit being Spandarmad.

Aspandyar (Parsi Pers.) : a son of Kay Vishtasp who fought for the Zoroastrian religion against the Turanian king Arjasp; Pers. Ispandiyar.

atash (Phl., Pers.) : a general term for 'fire'.

Atash Bahram (Pers.) : a consecrated fire of the highest degree.

athornan (Paz.) : a term designating the hereditary priestly class; also applied to an individual belonging to that class.

Avesta (Pers.) : the name applied to the whole of the Zoroastrian scriptures or to individual sections of it. The Phl. form is abistag.

Az (Phl., Pers.) : a demon of lust opposed to the spirit being Khordad.

B

Bahman[1] (Pers.) : see Vohuman.

Bahman[2] (Pers.) : name of a king of the Achaemenian dynasty whom Erachji misplaced in the Kayanian period.

Bahram[1] (Pers.) : name of a spirit being of victory.

Bahram[2] (Pers.) : many kings in Iranian history bear this name.

baj (Pers.) : the name of any spoken Avestan formula (manthra) which precedes, accompanies or follows an action for the purpose of encircling that act with the power of holy speech; also the name of a high liturgical service (Dron service); finally, the monthly or anniversary day of the deceased.

bakhtar (Phl.) : one who apportions, a distributor; used as an attribute of the moon (mah).

bandagi (Pers.) : prayer

barashnom (Phl.) : nine-day purificatory ritual bath.

barsom (Phl.) : a bundle of twigs (present practice substitutes metal wires) held by the priest in his left hand while performing high liturgies; also the name of the grass strewn on the earth for the spirit beings (yazads) to sit on.

bazay (Phl.) : a measure, the length of an arm; Av. bazu.

behdin (Pers.) : a follower of the good religion, a Zoroastrian; now restricted to the lay members among the Parsis of India.

behesht (Pers.) : paradise.

Bhagaria (Guj.) : a group of priests with headquarters in Navsari.

Bharucha (Guj.) : a group of priests with headquarters in Bharuch (Broach).

boy (Phl.) : a ceremony of offering fragrance (boy) such as sandalwood and frankincense to the consecrated fire in each of the five watches of the day.

boywara (hybrid) : a priest whose turn it is to tend the consecrated fire and perform its boy; Phl., boy, Guj., wara (waro, wari), 'turn'.

Bushasp (Phl.) : a demon of slothfulness opposed to the spirit being Shahrewar.

C

chaptan (Parsi Guj.) : a fried sweet dish prepared by Parsi women on baj days of the deceased.

Chinwad (Phl.) : bridge of the separator where the departed souls are judged for their deeds in the material world.

D

daena (Av.) : the good religion; see den/din.

daeva (Av.) : demon

Dahm (Phl.) : the name of a spirit being in whose honor an afrinagan is performed on the dawn of the fourth day after death; also a cognate term, when used in the plural (dahman) for hamkar.

dakhma (Av.) : originally a tomb; later, a tower of silence where a corpse is exposed to birds of prey.

Damawand (Phl., Pers.): name of a famous mountain in Iran closely associated with the religion and history of ancient Iran.

Dara (Pers.) : name of the last Achaemenian king (Darius III Codomanus) defeated by Alexander; mistaken by Erachji as belonging to the Kayanian dynasty.

Darab (Pers.) : name of a king of the Achaemenian dynasty whom Erachji misplaced in the Kayanian period.

Dar-e Mihr (Pers.) : the ritual area of a fire temple where high liturgies are performed. The phrase means 'Court of Mihr'. Most ceremonies are performed in the morning hours, a time when Mihr is the presiding spirit being.

dashtan (Phl., Pers.,) : menstruation.

dastur (Pers.) : a man of authority, a Zoroastrian priest; in present usage applied to a High Priest; from the Phl. dastwar.

dawar (Pers.) : a judge, from Phl. dadwar.

den/din (Phl., Pers.): lit. 'religion'; also the name of a spirit being presiding over the 24th day of the Zoroastrian calendar.

dervish (Pers.) : a poor person, a mendicant.

dew (Phl.) : a demon; from Av. daeva.

dharma-putra (Skt.) : an adopted son.

dharma-shala (Guj.) : charitable institution.

dozakh (Pers.) : hell.

dron (Phl.) : sacred bread; a service in which sacred bread is consecrated.

druj (Av.) : lie, falsehood; demoness of falsehood.

druj i nasush (Phl.) : the demon of putrefaction.

duwazdah homast (Phl.) : the name of a high liturgy comprised of a number of rituals in honor of 12 specific spirit beings.

E

Erach (Pers.) : one of the three sons of Faridoon, killed by his two brothers Selam and Tur according to the _Shahnama_.

ervad (Parsi Guj.) : a title for a member of a priestly class who has undergone the _nawar_ ceremony; Phl. form is _erbad_.

F

Faridoon (Pers.) : an illustrious king of ancient Iran who flourished centuries before Zoroaster.

farohar (Pers.) : guardian spirits of the souls of the living and the dead; the term is a Middle Iranian dialect form of Av. _fravashi_.

farokhshi (Guj.) : Parsi name for a ceremony dedicated to All-Souls (_fravashi_) involving the recitation of Yasht 13.

farziyat (Ar.) : a group of obligatory prayers for every Zoroastrian, to be said in each of the five watches of the day.

Fasli (Pers., Ar.) : lit. 'seasonal'; those Zoroastrians who follow a seasonal calendar which intercalates one day every four years on the pattern of a Gregorian calendar.

Firdausi (Pers.) : the author of the Persian epic *Shahnama* (*Book of Kings*).

fireshte (Pers.) : a spirit being worthy of worship; a term interchangeable with *yazad*.

fravashi (Av.) : guardian spirits of the souls of the living and the dead.

Frawardigan (Phl.) : All-Souls days.

G

gah (Phl., Pers.) : a watch or period of the day. There are five watches for every 24 hour period (see Appendix II).

gahambar (Phl., Pers.) : six seasonal festivals commemorating the six creations: 1) *maidyozarem* (mid-spring), 2) *maidyoshahem* (mid-summer), 3) *paitishahem* (bringing in the corn), 4) *ayathrem* (homecoming of cattle), 5) *maidyarem* (mid-winter), 6) *hamaspathmaidyem* (coming of the whole group [of *farohars*])

garothman (Parsi Guj.): the name of the highest heaven; Phl. form is *garodman*.

Gatha (Av.) : holy songs of Zoroaster (*Yasna* chapters 28-34, 43-51, 53); also the name of the five supplementary days at the end of the year and the *fireshtes* presiding over them.

gaw (Phl., Pers.) : an ox, bull or cow.

Gayomard (Phl.) : according to some Phl. texts, Gayomard was the first man created by God; Av. *gayo-maretan*, 'mortal life'.

geh-sarnu (Parsi Guj.) : chanting of the *gathas* (*Yasna* chapters 28-34) during a funeral service; cf. Phl. *gahan-srayishn*.

getig (Phl.) : material world, distinguished from *menog*.

geti-kharid (Pers.) : lit. 'world-purchased'; the name of a ceremony corresponding to nawar, involving the consecration of the Yasna service for nine days, thereby purchasing good deeds in this world for the sake of the other world.

giriban (Pers.) : a small bag on the collar of the sudre (sacred shirt); also called kissa-e kerfa (the bag of good deeds) in Persian.

Godavara (Guj.) : a group of priests with headquarters in Ankleshwar.

gomez (Phl.) : bull's urine not consecrated.

goshosrud khrad (Phl.) : acquired wisdom; lit. 'ears-heard wisdom'.

gospand (Phl.) : beneficent animal; in recent usage, sheep.

gumbad (Phl.) : a consecrated room, with dome, in which the holy fire is installed; the sanctum sanctorum.

H

hamistagan (Phl.) : a 'place of equal mixture'; a neutral place between heaven and hell.

hamkar (Phl.) : co-workers or associates of the seven amahraspands; the term dahman is also used by priests.

haoma (Av.) : name of a spirit being; also the name of a plant from which juice is extracted in high liturgies; Phl. hom.

Haurvatat (Av.) : see Hordad.

hom (Phl.) : see haoma.

Hooshang (Pers.) : the son of Syamak and the founder of the Peshdadian dynasty; he is the discoverer of fire according to tradition.

Hordad (Phl.) : the Holy Immortal presiding over water; Av. Haurvatat, 'Perfection' or 'Health'.

Hormazd (Pers.) : name of kings of the Parthian and Sasanian dynasties mentioned by Erachji.

I

Iranshah (Pers.) : the name of the most ancient Atash Bahram in India, at present located in Udvada.

J

jadangoi (Paz.) : speaking on behalf of another; arbitration, intercession.

Jamasp (Phl.) : prime minister of King Vishtasp and the son-in-law of the prophet Zoroaster.

Jamshed (Pers.) : name of an illustrious king of ancient Iran who received the divine glory (Av. Yima).

jashan (Phl. Pers.) : an act of worship in which an afrinagan ceremony is performed by two or more priests on behalf of the anjoman (assembly of the faithful) and a living or deceased Zoroastrian.

K

Kaveh (Pers.) : the famous blacksmith who revolted against the usurper Zohak and defeated him with the help of Faridoon.

Kayanian : the royal dynasty that followed the Peshdadian, founded by Kay Kobad; Av. kavaya, 'royal'.

Kay Kaus (Phl.) : the name of a king of the Kayanian dynasty who worked hard to destroy evil-doers of his time.

Kay Khosraw (Pers.) : grandson of Kay Kaus and an illustrious king of ancient Iran.

Kay Kobad (Pers.) : founder of the royal Kayanian dynasty; Av. Kavi Kavata.

Kay Vishtasp (Phl.) : the son of Lorasp and patron king of Zoroaster; Av. Vishtaspa, Pers. Gushtasp.

kem na mazda (Av.) : an Avestan prayer protecting the reciter from all evils, visible and invisible.

Kersasp (Phl.) : the name of a king of the Peshdadian dynasty who ruled for nine years according to the Shahnama.

Khambata (Guj.) : a group of priests with headquarters in Khambat (Cambay).

kheshm (Phl., Pers.) : a demon of wrath.

Khorda Avesta (Pers.): the 'Small Avesta' (see Appendix I).

Khordad-sal (Pers.) : the name of the sixth day of the first month of the new year (day six, month one) reckoned by Zoroastrians to be the birthday of Zoroaster.

Khorshed (Parsi Pers.) : 'sun'; the name of a spirit being presiding over the eleventh day of the Zoroastrian calendar; Pers. Khurshid.

khrad (Phl.) : wisdom, either innate or acquired.

Khshathra Vairya (Av.) : see Shahrewar.

khshnuman (Phl.) : an Avestan dedicatory formula to the yazad in whose honor a ceremony is being performed.

khub (Phl.) : ritual power received through the performance of a Dron service in honor of the hamkars of the day, or by the performance of a Yasna service in honor of mino nawar (the spirit of nawar).

khuda (Pers.) : a term derived from Av. khvadhata 'self-created', applied to God; later the word came to mean 'lord, king'.

khwarrah (Phl.) : divine glory, an emanation of the virtuous life (through the observance of Zoroastrian ethics and practices).

khwetodas (Phl.) : marriages between relatives in order to safeguard family virtues; derived from Av. khvaetvadatha, 'self-dedication'.

kriya (Skt.) : ritual activity accompanying the recitation of holy texts.

kusti (Pers.) : name of the sacred cord; also refers to the ritual of untying and retying the sacred cord.

L

Lohrasp (Phl.) : the father of Kay Vishtasp according to the Av. Aban Yasht and the Phl. Bundahishn; Pers. Lohrasp, Av. aurvat-aspa.

M

mah (Phl., Pers.) : 'moon, month'; name of the 12th day of the Zoroastrian calendar.

Mani (Phl., Pers.) : founder of Manichaeism; lived from 216 A.C.-275 A.C. and was imprisoned by Bahram I.

manthra (Av.) : holy and efficacious recitation of Avestan and Pazand scriptures.

maratab (Ar.) : a ceremony, a degree higher than nawar, which qualifies a priest to perform rituals of all types.

margarzan (Phl.) : mortal sin.

Mashye-Mashyane (Phl.) : mankind's first parents according to the Phl. Bundahishn, brought forth from the seed of Gayomard, the first man.

Meherjirana : Meherji, the son of Rana, the first 'priest-of-priests' of the Navsari anjoman: appointed in 1579 A.C. after fulfilling his religious mission at the court of the Mogul emperor Akbar; Dastur Erachji is his descendant.

menog (Phl.) : spiritual world, distinguished from getig.

Mihr (Phl., Pers.) : a spirit being presiding over the 16th day of the Zoroastrian calendar; also an associate of the fireshte Hawan, presiding over the first watch of the day when high liturgies are performed.

Mihragan (Phl.) : a festival in honor of Mihr, falling on the 16th day of the seventh month.

Minocheher (Pers.) : the son of Erach who avenged his father's death. He was a king of the Peshdadian dynasty.

mobed (Pers.) : a Parsi priest well-versed in rituals.

myazd (Phl.) : a jashan ceremony in which the whole assembly takes part, followed by tasting of fruits and other food offerings.

N

namaskar (Guj.)	: a short Av. prayer recited four times, once in each major direction, extolling the creations of God; a form of greeting, 'obeisance, bowing'.
Nam Stayishn (Phl.)	: the name of a beautiful Pazand prayer in praise of Ohrmazd.
nasa (Pers.)	: dead matter, corpse.
nask (Phl.)	: 'book' or 'volume'; in Sasanian times the Avesta was gathered and compiled in 21 'nasks' or books to correspond to the 21 words of the Ahunwar prayer.
nasush (Phl.)	: demon of corruption or putrefaction.
navjote (Parsi Guj.)	: a ceremony of investiture with sacred shirt and cord; the original meaning of the Phl. word nawzud is 'a new initiate into priesthood, a nawar.'
Navsari (Pers., Guj.)	: a town in Gujarat which has been a stronghold of Zoroastrianism in India for centuries.
nawar (Phl.)	: a ceremony which qualifies a member of the priestly class to be an ervad.
Nawruz (Pers.)	: the New Year Day.
Neryosang (Phl., Pers.)	: Erachji refers to Neryosang as the leader of the Parsi emigrants to Sanjan; probably confused with the learned Phl. and Skt. scholar Neryosang Dhaval.
nirang (Phl.)	: consecrated bull's urine; also an efficacious Avestan or Pazand piece.

nirangdin (Phl.) : the most exalted and elaborate of Zoroastrian high liturgies, culminating in the consecration of bull's urine (nirang).

niyayesh (Pers.) : a Zoroastrian litany, five in number.

Nozar (Pers.) : a Peshdadian king who ruled for seven years according to Firdausi; Av. naotar, Phl., Pers. nodar.

nur (Ar.) : light, lustre, shining glory, equivalent to the Phl. khwarrah.

O

Ohrmazd (Phl.) : the Almighty God of the Zoroastrians; the Av. name is Ahura Mazda.

P

padyab-kusti (Pers.) : washing of hands, face, feet before doing kusti, followed by the ritual untying and retying of the sacred cord.

pahrezgar (Parsi Guj.) : a pious Zoroastrian.

Paoiryo-tkaesha (Av.) : ancient sage, upholder of orthodoxy.

palaka (Skt.) : adopted son.

Palash (Parsi Pers.) : Vologeses I (51-80 A.C.), a Parthian king mentioned in the Denkard as one of the restorers of the Zoroastrian religion; Phl. walakhsh.

panj tay (Pers.) : name of a foundational Dron service in honor of the hamkars of the day; completion of the service qualifies the priest to perform any high liturgy for the day. It is performed with five

	barsom wires (or twigs), i.e. panj tay.
panthak (Guj.)	: priestly jurisdiction, a 'diocese'.
Parthian	: name of the royal dynasty originally from the region called Parthia (250 B.C.-226 A.C.); also called the Ashkanian dynasty from its founder Ashk.
patet (Phl.)	: prayer of penance.
paywand (Phl.)	: a connection; a ritual contact between two persons serving as a shield against pollution caused by dead matter.
Pazand (Phl.)	: Pahlavi texts in which the Aramaic components of the language are replaced by their Iranian equivalents, transcribed in the Avestan or Persian or any other script.
Peshdadian	: name of the first Iranian dynasty; Phl., Pers. peshdad, Av. paradhata, 'ancient law-giver'.
Peshotan (Pers.)	: Peshotan, son of Vishtasp, one of the immortals.
Pourushasp (Phl.)	: the name of Zoroaster's father; Av. Paorushaspa.

Q

Qadimi (Pers., Ar.)	: lit. 'ancient'; those Parsi Zoroastrians who follow the 'ancient' calendar of the Irani Zoroastrians which began in 632 A.C. with the coronation of the last Sasanian monarch, Yazdegird III.

qibla (Ar.) : anything opposite; that toward which people direct their prayers, which, for Zoroastrians, is any luminous object, like fire.

R

Rapithwin (Av.) : name of the noonday watch of the day and its spirit guardian; the watch lasts for the first seven months of the Zoroastrian calendar, the remaining five months it is replaced by the Second Hawan (see Appendix II).

Rashn (Phl.) : the spirit being presiding over the 18th day of the Zoroastrian calendar.

rawan (Phl.) : soul; Av. urvan.

riman (Phl., Pers.) : something impure due to contact with dead matter.

rimani (Pers.) impurity arising out of contact with dead matter.

Rivayat (Ar.) : lit. 'tradition'; a collection of replies written by dasturs of Iran to questions by their Indian counterparts on a variety of matters relating to the Zoroastrian tradition, written from the 15th through the 18th centuries.

Rustam (Pers.) : the name of a celebrated hero who rendered invaluable services to the kings of the Kayanian dynasty according to the Shahnama.

S

sagdid (Phl.)	: 'seen by a dog', a dog's gaze.
sagri (Guj.)	: a technical term for a room at the site of the dakhma where a fire is burning.
Sanjana (Guj.)	: a group of priests with headquarters formerly in Sanjan, now in Udvada.
Sasanian	: name of a royal dynasty of Iran (226 A.C.-652 A.C.).
sawab (Ar.)	: an act of merit as distinguished from gunah, 'sin'.
Selam (Pers.)	: one of the three sons of Faridoon mentioned in the Phl. Bundahishn and the Shahnama.
Shahanshahi (Pers.)	: lit. 'monarchical'; those Parsi Zoroastrians who follow the ancient Iranian calendar but with a difference of one month from the Qadimi calendar due to an intercalation done most probably in the 12th century A.C.
Shahrewar (Phl.)	: the Holy Immortal presiding over metals; Av. Khshathra Vairya, 'Desirable Dominion'.
siroza, siruza (Pers.)	: lit. '30 days'; a prayer containing an eulogy to the 30 spirit beings presiding over the Zoroastrian calendar, plus three others: Burz, Hom and Dahm (see Appendix II).
Spandarmad (Phl.)	: the Holy Immortal presiding over the earth; Av. Spenta Armaiti, 'Bountiful' or 'Holy Devotion'.
Spenta Armaiti (Av.)	: see Spandarmad.

Spozgar (Paz.)	: a demon of thunderstorms, opposed to Righteousness and to Tishtar, the spirit being presiding over the rains.
Srosh (Phl.)	: a spirit being acting as the guardian of one's soul for three days after death; also presides over the 17th day of the Zoroastrian calendar; Ohrmazd's vice-regent on earth.
stum (Parsi Guj.)	: a common ceremony in which cooked food is offered to the spirit beings; coined from the Av. staomi, 'I praise'.
stur (Phl.)	: variously translated 'trustee, guardian, curator'; the term refers to an adopted son who can fulfill the prayer duties of the departed.
sudre-kusti (Pers.)	: sacred shirt and girdle.
Syamak (Phl.)	: the son of Gayomard, the first king of Iran, according to the Shahnama; he was killed in a fight with demons.
syaw (Parsi Guj.)	: a set of white garments with kusti, given as alms in a Dron service; derived from the Ar. thiyab, 'clothes'.
Syawakhsh (Phl)	: a pious and truthful son of Kay Kaus killed by Afrasiyab.

T

Tahmurasp (Pers.)	: the son of Hooshang; he controlled the demons for 30 years.
tanapuhr (Phl.)	: name of a mortal sin; in the context of good deeds, this term refers to an extremely good deed.

tan-dorosti (Paz., Pers.) : a prayer said to bring blessings to oneself or others.

Tir (Phl.) : the spirit being presiding over the 13th day of the Zoroastrian calendar.

Tishn (Phl.) : a demon of thirst opposed to the spirit being Amurdad.

Tur (Pers.) : one of the three sons of Faridoon mentioned in the Phl. Bundahishn and the Shahnama.

U

uthamnu (Guj.) : a common ceremony performed in the third and fifth watches of the day (3 p.m. to sunset and midnight to daybreak) on the third day after a person's demise. Relatives and friends take part and recite the patet for the departed soul. If the deceased was childless an adopted son (palaka) is proclaimed in the presence of all in the afternoon uthamnu.

V

Vendidad (Pers.) : name of a high liturgical service in which the 19th nask of the Avesta, the Vendidad (Phl. jud-dew-dad) is recited. The ceremony starts at midnight and lasts about seven hours.

Vishtasp (Phl.) : see Kay Vishtasp.

Vispa Humata (Av.) : a short Av. prayer recited three times in the morning in order to start the day with good thoughts, words and deeds.

Visperad (Phl., Pers.) : a high liturgical service, dedicated to Ohrmazd; it augments the Yasna service with additional invocations and offerings to the lords (ratus) of both the physical and spiritual worlds.

Vohuman (Phl.) : the Holy Immortal presiding over the second day of the Zoroastrian calendar; Av. Vohu Manah, 'Good Mind'.

Vohu Manah (Av.) : see Vohuman.

W

wahisht (Phl.) : paradise

wahman (Phl.) : lit. 'such and such', a title for a nameless child to be remembered in ceremonies.

warasyo (Parsi Guj.) : consecrated white bull, named from the hair (Phl. wars) which the bull provides for ritual use in all high liturgies; Av. varesa.

way i wattar (Phl.) : lit. 'the evil atmosphere'; name of a demon who drags the wicked soul to hell.

way i weh (Phl.) : lit. 'the good atmosphere'; name of a spirit being who assists the departed soul on its journey to heaven.

Y

yasht (Phl.) : a hymn of praise in honor of spirit beings.

yasna (Av.) : a section of the Avestan texts; the name of a high liturgical service in which the text of the Yasna is recited, accompanied by rituals.

yatha ahu vairyo (Av.) : the opening phrase of one of the most efficacious prayers of the Zoroastrians, the *Ahunwar*.

yazad (Phl.) : a created spirit being worthy of worship, a term used interchangeably with the modern Pers. term *fireshte*.

Yazdegird (Phl.) : the last king of the Sasanian dynasty, popularly known as Yazdegird III (632-651 A.C.).

yenghe hatam (Av.) : the beginning words of one of the three most ancient and efficacious prayers of the Zoroastrians.

yozdathregar (Av.) : the 'purifier', i.e. the priest who administers the *barashnom*; also the proper term applied to any priest who is performing high liturgies; Av. *yaozdathragar*.

Z

Zarthosht (Parsi Guj.) : Zoroaster, the prophet of ancient Iran; Av. *Zarathushtra*, Phl. *Zartosht*, *Zardusht*.

Zinda-rawan (Pers.) : the soul of a living person as distinguished from an *anosharawan*, the soul of a deceased person.

Zohak (Pers.) : a non-Iranian tyrant king of ancient Iran.

zot (Phl.) : the chief officiating priest in all major ceremonies.

Zub Tahmasp (Phl.) : Zub, of the family of Tahmasp, ruled Iran for five years according to the Phl. *Bundahishn* and the *Shahnama*. The former states that Zub discovered the child Kobad on a river bank and adopted him.

APPENDIX I

The following list of books describes briefly most of the texts Erachji refers to in the catechism:

Ardag Wiraz Namag 'A Book on Holy Wiraz': a visionary Pahlavi text, composed in the ninth century A.C., attributed to the ancient sage Wiraz whose spirit traveled in the other world to learn the fate of the soul after death. Its Persian and old Gujarati versions were translated by Zardusht Bahram and Rustam Peshotan Hamjiar, respectively.

Avesta-o-Zand: the term used by some dasturs to refer to the traditional writings of the Parsis (written in India) as distinguished from the Persian Rivayats written by the dasturs of Iran.

Bundahishn 'The Original Creation': a Pahlavi work on cosmogony. It survives in two recensions, the Great or Iranian Bundahishn and the abridged Indian Bundahishn. As with many Pahlavi works, its final recension belongs to the ninth century A.C.

Burhan-e Qate: a celebrated Persian dictionary compiled by Mohammad Hussein Burhan-e Tabrizi in 1651-52 A.C.

Dabestan 'A Place of Learning': an anonymous writing from the 17th century describing mystic sects and their abstemious habits. Until the last century it was looked upon by some with great respect as an indispensable guide to the Zoroastrian religion. It is now known to be an artificial product.

Dadestan i Denig 'Religious Decisions': a Pahlavi work of the ninth century A.C. which contains answers given by Dastur Manushchichihr i Goshnajaman of Pars and Kerman, Iran, to 92 queries put to him by his co-religionists.

Dasatir 'Ordinances': A book of mediocre worth considered

valuable in the last century but which is now scientifically proved to be a mixture of Hindu, Buddhist and Platonic philsophies. It cannot be classified among authentic Zoroastrian writings.

Denkard 'Acts of the Religion': an encyclopaedic work on Zoroastrianism complied by the High Priests Adurfarnbag i Farrokhzadan and Adurbad i Emedan in the ninth and tenth centuries A.C. Only seven volumes (Books 3-9) out of nine are extant today.

Farhang-e Jahangiri: a Persian dictionary begun 1596 A.C. in the time of Akbar, and finished during the reign of Jahangir, by Mir Jamaluddin in 1609 A.C. Akbar summoned Ardashir of Kerman to India in 1592 A.C. to assist the compiler, and he introduced many Zoroastrian religious terms in the Farhang.

Farziyat Nama of Darab Pahlan: a treatise in Persian verse made in the 17th century by Dastur Darab Pahlan of Navsari. It contains a memorandum on religious duties to be observed by Zoroastrians in daily life.

Gulshan-e Farhang 'A Bouquet of Knowledge', the full title being Gulshan-e Farhang dar A-'yin-e Zardusht' Bouquet of Knowledge in the Zoroastrian Religion', 1858 A.C.; said to have been written by Kay Khosraw, son of Kay Kaus.

Hadokht Nask: the name of a division (nask) of the Avesta corresponding to the 20th word of the Ahunwar prayer. Only three chapters now survive. It was formerly recited with ceremonial rites like the Vendidad.

Jamaspi: a prophetic text in Persian derived from a Pahlavi text Jamasp Namag in which Jamasp the seer speaks of miseries and misfortunes that will befall King Vishtasp of the Kayanian dynasty.

Khorda Avesta 'Small Avesta': a collection of short prayers (such as prayers for each watch of the day), litanies (niyayeshes) and hymns (yashts) to various spirit powers. There is no standard collection of prayers designated by the term. It is to be distinguished from the 'complete Avesta' (Taman Avesta) which contains the whole of the extant Avesta.

Khweshtab: it cannot be considered an authentic book on Zoroastrian theology. It contains a Persian translation by Mobed Sarosh, a disciple of Azar Kaiwan, of the original text written by one Hakim Khweshtab. It is a 17th century writing.

Makhzanu-'l Akhbar: this book has not been identified, but judging from Erachji's use of it, the book describes among other things, the propagation of the Zoroastrian religion by King Vishtasp.

Menog i Khrad 'The Spirit of Wisdom': a book of precepts written in comparatively simple Pahlavi. It expounds Zoroastrian doctrines and exhorts the people to follow the Zoroastrian way of life. It was composed in Sasanian times.

Mojezat-e Zartoshti 'Miracles of Zoroaster': a Gujarati book on the Zoroastrian religion describing the miracles of Zoroaster and his teachings. It was written and published in 1840 A.C. by Dastur Edalji Darabji Sanjana, the first Dastur of the Wadiaji Atash Bahram, Bombay.

Nirangestan 'Code of Rituals'; an Avestan text on ritual with Pahlavi rendering and detailed explanatory glosses. Essentially it is an encyclopaedia of various types of Zoroastrian rituals with detailed directions for their proper performance.

Pahlavi Rivayat: treats of miscellaneous subjects of Zoroastrian religion, customs and practices. In its final redaction it is a post-Sasanian work.

Pand Namag i Adurbad 'A Book of Precepts by Adurbad': a collection of the wise sayings of Adurbad i Mahraspandan, a High Priest of Iran who flourished in the third century A

Pand Namag i Buzorg-Mihr 'A Book of Precepts by Burzorg-Mihr': a work attributed to Buzorg-Mihr, the prime minister of Khosraw I (531-579 A.C.).

Persian Bahram Firuz Nama: this book has not been identified, but judging from Erachji's use of it the book seems to contain guidance regarding proper Zoroastrian observances during and following ceremonies for the deceased. The book is referred to in the Persian Rivayat of Dastur Darab Hormazdyar.

Persian Rivayats: a collection of answers by Iranian priests to queries on religious laws and traditions by the knowledge-seeking Parsi priests of India. The Rivayats cover a period of about 300 years dating from 1478 to 1773 A.C. They bear the names of the emissary who brought them from Iran, such as the Rivayat of Nariman Hooshang, of Kaus Kamdin, of Shapur Bharuchi, etc.

Persian Vajarkard Dini 'Exposition of the Religion': a Persian Rivayat containing various discussions of Zoroastrian religion, customs and morals. It is also called the Persian Denkard due to the variety of subjects treate therein. The name of the author is not known.

Qissa-e Sanjan 'The Story of Sanjan': a history text written in Navsari in 1599 A.C. by Bahman Kekobad Sanjana. It describes the events which took place when the first Iranian immigrants landed in Sanjan, India. It also describes the consecration of the Atash Bahram in Sanjan.

Qissa-e Zartoshtian-e Hindustan 'The Story of the Zoroastrians of India': written in 1765 A.C. by Shapurji Maneckji Sanjana on the occasion of the installation of the Atash Bahram of Navsari. It contains a vivid description of the events that occurred at the time of consecration.

Rivayat-e Dini 'Religious Traditions': this text cited by Erachji is properly titled Mutaffariqat-e Dini 'Miscellaneous Subjects of Religion'. It is a collection of questions and answers on the Zoroastrian religion culled from the Persian Rivayats.

Saddar Bundahesh 'One Hundred Chapters of Bundahesh': a treatise in Persian dealing with Zoroastrian customs, traditions and liturgies. It is written on the model of Saddar Nasr, having 100 chapters, and begins with a section on cosmogony (Bundahesh) and ends with a chapter on eschatology. Another name for this book is Shayast Na-Shayast (the opening phrase). The author is not known; it was written before 1528 A.C., as the oldest manuscript bears this date.

Saddar Nasr 'One Hundred Chapters in Prose': an old Persian Rivayat dealing with the religious laws, customs legends and traditions of the Zoroastrians. There is no unanimity among scholars as to the age and author of the prose Saddar. It can be said tentatively that it was composed before 1496 A.C., since the metrical Saddar is derived from it.

Saddar Nazm 'One Hundred Chapters in Verse': this text, written in metrical verse, presents a hundred sections bearing on Zoroastrian religion and morals. It was composed from the prose Saddar Nasr by Iranshah Malekshah of Kerman in 1496 A.C.

Shahnama 'The Book of Kings': a Persian verse epic composed by Firdausi and presented to Sultan Mahmud of Ghazni in the year 1010 A.C. It contains the history of the ancient Iranian kings down to Islamic times. It is largely based on the lost Pahlavi *Khwaday Namag*, and is part legendary, part historical.

Shamsu-'l Lughat 'The Sun of Languages': Persian dictionary written in India in the 19th century by an Englishma

Sharestan, an abridged title for *Sharestan-e Chahar Chaman* 'A City of Four Gardens'; written by Bahram Farhad who belonged to the mystic school of Azar Kaiwan. It treats of creation and the legendary history of the ancient Iranians.

Shkand Gumanig Wizar 'Doubt-dispelling Explanation': a text written by Mardanfarrokh i Ohrmazddadan in the ninth century. It contains an appraisal of Zoroastrian beliefs and criticises the doctrines of alien faiths. It survives partly in Pahlavi and Pazand with Sanskrit translation.

Sifat-e Fireshtegan 'A Description of Angels': this is the Persian title given to the Pahlavi text *Stayishn i Sirozag* 'Praise of 30 days' which treats of the qualities and functions of the 30 spirit beings (*fireshtes*) presiding over the 30 days of the Zoroastrian calendar.

Siruza 'thirty days': the name of two collections of spoken formulas (*khshnumans*) dedicated to the spirit beings (*yazads*) presiding over the 30 days of the Zoroastrian month, and to three additional *yazads*: *Hom* (spirit guardian of the *haoma* plant), *Burz* (representati of the source of waters), and *Dahm* (guardian over the prayers of the faithful). One collection, called the (*nana*) *siruza*, contains brief dedicatory formulas; the other collection is the larger (vada) siruza containing longer dedications.

Vaetha Nask: the name given to a composition of Avestan-Pahlavi quotations, partly genuine and partly forged, that has vaetha as its opening Avestan word. The Avestan and Pahlavi scriptures know no nask by the name Vaetha.

Vendidad: a liturgical text of 22 chapters (fragards) recited by priests between midnight and early morning accompanied at intervals by the texts of the Yasna and Visperad. According to the Sasanian classification of the Avesta into 21 divisions (nasks) the Vendidad corresponds to the 19th word. There also exists a Pahlavi translation of the Avestan Vendidad with a commentary (zand) and an independent commentary in Pahlavi summarizing most of the chapters of the Vendidad.

Vishtasp Yasht: generally known as Yasht 24, this hymn (yasht) contains eight chapters and was formerly used in the ritual called Vishtasp Sast Nask performed by priests on the pattern of the Vendidad.

Visperad: the Parsi priests in India perform the Visperad ceremony during the six seasonal festivals (gahambars). It is also performed in the 'world-purchased (geti-kharid) ritual and in the initiation ritual (nawar) for priesthood. The Pahlavi texts do not restrict its performance to these occasions, however. The Visperad text has 23 sections (kardags) and when recited by priests together with the 72 chapters of the Yasna, comprises the Visperad ceremony. Its celebration requires great skill and thorough knowledge of the ritual. Its Pahlavi rendering survives.

Yasna: an Avestan ritual text of 72 chapters (Phl., hats) recited by priests as a distinct service by itself, or as part of the Visperad or Vendidad ceremonies. As a distinct service it is always performed in the morning hours (the hawan gah). Its Pahlavi translation survives.

Zardusht Nama: 'The Book of Zoroaster': a Persian text in verse-form written by Zardusht Bahram Pazdu in 1278 A.C.. Zardusht seems to have derived his material about the life of Zoroaster from the Pahlavi Zardusht Namag as given in Book 7 of the Denkard. The Persian was translated into old Gujarati (Prakrit) verse by Mobed Rustam Peshotan Hamjiar, a poet-priest of Surat, in the 17th century A.C.

APPENDIX II

The Zoroastrian calendar and the five watches of the day

Names of the five watches (gahs) of each day

1. Hawan (sunrise to midday, i.e., 12 noon).
2. Rapithwin or Second Hawan (noonday to 3 p.m.).
3. Uzerin (from 3 p.m. to sunset).
4. Aiwisruthrem (from sunset to midnight, i.e. 12 p.m.).
5. Ushahin (from midnight to daybreak).

Names of the days

Each Zoroastrian month has 30 days, divided into four weeks. The first day of each week is dedicated to the Creator Ohrmazd. That is, the first day of each week bears the name Ohrmazd or the Pahlavi term day meaning 'Creator'. In order to avoid confusion, each of the three day (Creator) references is named in conjunction with the name of the day it precedes. The first two weeks have seven days, the last two have eight. Variant spellings and meanings associated with the names of the days are also given below.

1. Ohrmazd, 'the Lord Omniscient'.
2. Vohuman, Bahman, 'the Good Mind'.
3. Ardwahisht, Ardibehesht, 'the Best Righteousness'.
4. Shahrewar, 'Desirable Dominion' or 'Kingdom'.
5. Spandarmad, Asfandarmad, 'Holy or Bountiful Devotion'.
6. Hordad, Khordad, 'Perfection or Health'.
7. Amurdad, 'Immortality or Life'.

8. Day-pa-Adar, 'the day of the Creator (day) before Adar'.
9. Adar, 'fire'.
10. Aban, 'waters'.

11. Khwarshed, Khorshed, 'the shining sun' (khwar, 'sun).
12. Mah, 'the moon'.
13. Tishtar, Tir, 'shooting star'.
14. Goshorun (Av. geush urvan, 'the soul of the earth'), Gosh, 'earth'.

15. Day-pa-Mihr, 'day before Mihr'.
16. Mihr, 'light, friendship, contract'.
17. Srosh, 'obedience'.
18. Rashn, 'truth, justice'.
19. Frawardin, 'the protecting one, guardian spirit'.
20. Warharan, Bahram, 'victory'.
21. Ram, 'joy'.
22. Wad, Gowad, 'wind, atmosphere'.

23. Day-pa-Den, 'day before Den'.
24. Den, 'revelation, religion'.
25. Ard, Ashishwangh, 'good blessings'.
26. Ashtad, 'rectitude'.
27. Asman, 'sky'.
28. Zam, 'earth', Zam Yazad, 'Yazad of the earth'.
29. Mahraspand, 'holy word'.
30. Anagran, Aneran, 'endless lights'.

The Five Gatha days

These five days do not belong to any particular month and are fixed to the end of the year. Prayers and ceremonies performed during the five Gatha days, therefore, do not include any mention of a month name.

1. Ahunawad, 'possessing Ahunwar'.
2. Ushtawad, 'possessing happiness'.
3. Spentomad, 'holy spirit'.
4. Wohukhshathra, 'good dominion'.
5. Wahishtoisht, 'best riches'.

Names of months

All the month names are included in the list of day names above. The order of the months is as follows.

1. Frawardin
2. Ardwahisht, Ardibehesht
3. Hordad, Khordad
4. Tir
5. Amurdad
6. Shahrewar
7. Mihr
8. Aban
9. Adar
10. Day
11. Vohuman, Bahman
12. Spandarmad, Asfandarmad

INDEX

Note: this index covers the translation and commentary, not the Introduction, Glossary or Appendices. For ease of scanning, terms underlined in the text are listed without underlining in the Glossary and Index.